Praise for *HOLLYWOOD STORIES*

"A wild, fun ride through tinsel town, past and present!"
—Jan Wahl, *KCBS AM/FM & KRON-TV*

"*Hollywood Stories* is a piece of history. It needs to go up in the Smithsonian because nowhere on earth is there a book like this one. I thoroughly enjoyed it."

—Dorothy Thompson, *Literally Speaking*

"…a treasure trove for the casual reader looking for a few quick reads as well as the serious fan looking for information."

—*Blog Critics*

"The book is great fun to read on many levels."

—Alan Caruba, *Book Views*

"…a thoroughly entertaining read. With many humorous parts, you find yourself laughing out loud, feeling connected with the individual being presented."

—*Book Pleasures*

"Packed from cover to cover with fascinating tales."

—*The Midwest Book Review*

"Whether you're looking for a fees quick smiles from the other side of the camera or researching violence in the movies this book will become a welcome addition to your library."

—*Blog Critics*

"Fun, fun, fun!"

—*Feathered Quill Book Reviews*

Winner of the 2012 Global Ebook Award for Entertainment and Performing Arts (Music/Dance/Film), Non-Fiction

Short, Entertaining Anecdotes About the Stars and Legends of the Movies!

by
STEPHEN SCHOCHET

HOLLYWOO

Short, Entertaining Anecdotes Abou

STEPHEN S

Hollywood Sto
Los Ang
www.hollywo

D STORIES
the Stars and Legends of the Movies!

CHOCHET

ies Publishing
eles, CA
dstories.com

Inquiries should be directed to:
Permissions
Hollywood Stories Publishing
3767 Clarington Street
Suite 336
Los Angeles, CA 90034

Groups interested in special sales, promotions, or customized tours may contact us at the above address, or via email to htales@ca.rr.com.

Second Edition
Schochet, Stephen 1962-
Hollywood Stories: Short, Entertaining Anecdotes About the Stars and Legends of the Movies!
(Film/Entertainment)
Includes index and bibliography
ISBN 978-0-9638972-5-1 (hc.)
ISBN 978-0-9638972-6-8 (pbk.)
LCCO 2009913690

Cover illustration and layout by Adam McDaniel.

CONTENTS

**The short tales in this book are the scripts from the
Hollywood Stories one minute radio feature, plus
extra stories that relate to the originals.**

GREAT HOLLYWOOD COMEDIANS

"We never see ourselves as others see us."
– Oliver Hardy

"And awaaay we go!"
– Jackie Gleason

The Universal Maniac

In 1999, an Australian gentleman told me about an interesting experience he and his family had at Universal Studios. They were on the backlot tour passing one of the theme park's main attractions, the Bates Motel used in the 1960 horror classic *Psycho,* about a murderous young man named Norman Bates who loved his mother a little too much. As the guide gave out information about how director Alfred Hitchcock shot the picture, a tall man, dressed in drag and carrying a large knife, emerged from behind the old set and charged toward the tram. The narrator seemed to know nothing about the Norman Bates look-alike and clammed up completely. The make-believe killer wore such a convincing maniacal expression that some of the paying customers were frightened and screamed when he raised his weapon. Then the "fiend" pulled off his wig and he turned out to be comic Jim Carrey; the thirty-seven-year-old star was clowning around during a work break. After his laughing "victims" calmed down, Jim was happy to pose for pictures and sign autographs.

Extra: Jim Carrey's second wife, actress Lauren Holley, once complained that her husband freaked her out because he couldn't pass a mirror in their mansion without stopping, staring into it, and making funny expressions for at least fifteen minutes. The same face-changing habit helped the Canadian-born comedian earn the praise of directors, adoration from his fans and millions of dollars.

Extra: Jim Carrey's big break came in 1982 when fifty-two-year-old Mitzi Shore, the owner of the famed Comedy Store on the Sunset Strip, took a mother-like interest in his career. Three years earlier, Shore's world was rocked when her unpaid performers went on strike. After all, if the waiters and the bartenders got wages, why not the talent? Why should Shore get rich while they made nothing? In Mitzi's eyes, she gave comics a showcase to hone their acts and move on to bigger venues. She even provided some of them with free food and housing. How could they do this to her? It had been especially galling that thirty-two-year-old David Letterman, one of her favorites, had joined the work stoppers. When a car struck a disgruntled picketer who ended up in the hospital, Mitzi decided to settle up before someone got seriously hurt. (It turned out the "victim," David Letterman's three-years-younger friend and future late-night TV rival Jay Leno, faked his injuries in a successful attempt to end the conflict.) The whole ugly incident left a bitter taste in Shore's mouth; she banned several of the labor dispute instigators from the club.

When Carrey arrived on the scene, Mitzi thought the newcomer was someone special. He had an elastic body that seemed to be made of Silly Putty, was respectful and (unlike many of the other comics who the proprietor saw) looked good and always wore suits. Out of hundreds of comedians who auditioned at the Comedy Store each week, Shore gave Jim prime opportunities to perform nights at her club, publicly gushed over him and important people in Hollywood took notice.

Extra: A knife-wielding "Norman Bates" charging the tram later became a feature on some of the Universal Studios' Tours.

The Lunch Prank

George Burns loved playing tricks on his best friend and fellow comedian Jack Benny. Once, they were getting lunch at the famed Brown Derby restaurant in Hollywood. George ordered Jack's favorite dish, bacon and eggs, and wondered why his friend settled for cereal. Benny explained his wife Mary had been giving him a hard time at home about his diet and would kill him if he had bacon and eggs. The exasperated Burns shook his head. How pathetic! What was the point of working hard to become rich, famous and powerful if you were going to be henpecked? And Mary wasn't even present. The inspired Benny nodded and changed his order. When they finished their hearty meals, George declared to the waiter that Jack would pick up the tab. The famous cheapskate turned red. "Why the hell should I pay it?"

"Well, if you don't I'll tell Mary you ate bacon and eggs."

The Three Stooges' Pain

In the early 1930s, when Moe Howard of The Three Stooges decided childlike violence would be their trademark, it caused decades of repercussions for both the comics and their followers. After appearing in some two hundred films, middle Stooge Larry Fine lost all feeling on one side of his face. Curly Howard, the junior member of the team, wore a disguise in public to avoid being kicked in the shins by fans. Shemp Howard, who left the act and came back after younger brother Curly suffered a stroke in 1946, almost got knocked out by a young actress that he criticized after several takes for being too ladylike with her punches. Moe led his partners through orchestrated mayhem aimed at adult movie audiences for twenty-five years. He never imagined that beginning in the late fifties, the Stooges shorts would constantly replay on TV in front of impressionable kids. A sentimental family man in real life, Moe traveled throughout the country to teach youngsters the techniques of harmless, two-fingers-to-the-forehead eye poking.

Extra: One evening in the late 1920s, Shemp Howard (1895-1955) accused Larry Fine (1902-1975) of cheating at cards and poked him in the eyes. As Larry rolled on the floor writhing in pain, and Shemp apologized, Moe Howard (1897-1975) held onto his sides laughing. The eventual leader of The Three Stooges thought the incident was the funniest thing he'd ever seen, and incorporated similar violence into their act.

Extra: By the late 1930s, Jerome "Curly" Howard (1903-1952) had become the most popular Stooge. A skilled basketball player and ballroom dancer, Jerry's athleticism came in handy for his energetic antics on the big screen. Unlike Moe, who learned his scripts to the letter, the childlike Curly was a spontaneous performer. One time during filming, the youngest Howard brother suddenly got down on the floor and spun like a top for a few minutes until he remembered his lines.

Young Frankenstein Follies

Director Mel Brooks and the cast of the 1974 parody *Young Frankenstein* almost went overboard with their ad-libbing. British comic Marty Feldman, who played the dim-witted lab assistant Igor, came up with a running bit where his hunchback kept moving. Several days passed before Marty's co-workers noticed; the displaced hump gag was added into the script so the other characters could react to it.

Gene Hackman shone as a kindly blind man who abused Peter Boyle's creature by spilling scalding hot soup on his lap, breaking his wine glass during a toast and accidentally lighting the cigar-smoking demon's thumb on fire. As the screaming monster ran off in pain, Hackman topped off the scene by making up the line, "Wait! I was gonna make espresso."

Brooks himself provided a yowling cat sound when Gene Wilder's Frederick Frankenstein threw an errant dart off camera. The players had so much fun creating extra material they ended up with a ponderous three-hour picture.

Some hasty editing by Brooks removed the flat jokes, which cut *Young Frankenstein's* length in half thus resulting in a comedy classic.

Larry David's Job Security

When comedian Larry David joined the writing team of the weekly TV comedy program *Saturday Night Live* in 1984, he lamented it was the first time in his life that he couldn't make a friend. No one seemed to notice him or even wanted to go have coffee with him. Even worse, very few of Larry's sketches were used. The volatile performer, who sometimes screamed at unresponsive audiences during his stand-up routine, finally reached a breaking point. One Saturday night right before show time, Larry told producer Dick Ebersol that *SNL* stunk and he quit! But when David got home, he realized that he would miss his fifty-thousand-dollar-a-year salary. On Monday morning, Larry returned to work pretending nothing had happened. The incident later inspired David to create a similar episode for his alter ego, George Costanza, on the hit TV show *Seinfeld*.

Extra: When forty-three-year-old Larry David co-created the *Seinfeld* TV show (1990-1998), the comedian stated that he was a nice guy, but if he did all the rotten things he'd really like to do, he would be George Costanza. Thirty-one-year-old Jason Alexander who played the neurotic, selfish and self-loathing George on the small screen, sometimes questioned the credulity of David's writing. Like the time George bought a cashmere sweater for a female friend as a thank-you gift and then she accidentally found out it was a hand-me-down. Or what about when Costanza quit his real estate job because he was forbidden to use his boss's private bathroom? What happened to George could not possibly take place in real life. And even if it did, no one would react like he did. David told Alexander that the wild things in the *Seinfeld* scripts really did happen to him and that George's reactions to them were exactly like Larry's.

Stop Complaining About Being a Virgin

Comedian Steve Carell had an idea about a nerdy guy who plays poker with three buddies and is unable to keep up with their sex talk. The premise grew into the 2005 summer comedy *The 40-Year-Old Virgin*. Screenwriter and star Carell subscribed to the theory that men will laugh at other men in pain. Steve insisted that an excruciating scene, where some body waxers ripped off his ample chest hair, be real. During the one and only take, the other guys on the set tried to stop from snickering while the women offered him Advil. But one lady had no sympathy. When Steve complained about how hard the shoot was, his wife reminded Carell that he wrote the scenes that required him to spend hours kissing beautiful women, while she stayed at home with their kids and she didn't want to hear it.

Laurel after Hardy

After Oliver Hardy's death in 1957 at the age of sixty-five, his long-time partner Stan Laurel refused to perform publicly again. The British-born Laurel was far from reclusive. He lived in a small apartment in Santa Monica and was listed in the phonebook. Well-wishers would call up and ask to visit. Stan would welcome them with great stories and belly laughs that made him seem very different from the quiet, sad sack people saw onscreen. But why didn't he live in some big mansion in Bel Air? The comic explained that his divorces plus bad business investments had not left him well off. Ownership of the Laurel and Hardy screen characters belonged to producer Hal Roach who teamed the two of them together in the late 1920s. With a smile, Stan told the sad tale of the time he and his partner wanted to buy Laurel and Hardy dolls as gifts for their families; they received no royalties and had to pay full price.

Extra: In his later years, the very friendly Stan Laurel (1890-1965) was better off financially then he let on. After his comedy partner Oliver Hardy (1892-1957) died, Stan and his wife bought a large seven-room house in Santa Monica. It was too big for two retirees; they soon moved into a one-bedroom beach apartment. Stan was happy to welcome guests into his home whether they were famous or not. The smaller living space helped to discourage younger, lesser-known comics from hitting Laurel up for money.

Extra: Stan and Ollie were not always close off the screen. Laurel would spend his after-hours in the editing room where he had a reputation for drinking and carousing. The Harlem, Georgia-born Hardy, who was more actor than funny man, would usually leave to play golf as soon as the workday was done. Then in 1932, the two men hit on the idea of a joint vacation in England. Stan planned to see his family and Babe Hardy looked forward to checking out the British golf courses. The journey was meant to be private, but Hal Roach and some MGM Studios public relations men let the cat out of the bag. Both members of the comedy team, used to working in the relative isolation of the studio, were amazed at the crowds of people that greeted them abroad. Nine fans were injured in a mob scene when the two movie clowns disembarked at a train station. When Stan tried to return to his childhood home, the small market town of Ulverston, throngs of admirers prevented him from getting to the front door. The shocking realization of their worldwide stardom drew Laurel and Hardy much closer together as friends, especially after their bosses, who benefitted greatly from the international publicity of Stan and Ollie's trip, docked their salaries for the time they missed work.

Extra: In the early 1920s, Oliver Hardy's Italian barber patted his face with talcum powder and said, "Nice a baby."
Ollie's friends heard about it and the actor became known as Babe.

Milton Berle, Picture Snatcher

Director Stanley Kramer was surprised how well his all-star cast of comedians got along while making *It's a Mad, Mad, Mad, Mad World* in 1964. The funny actors, who played a bunch of greedy motorists in search of stolen treasure, enjoyed the challenge of making each other laugh. Only the scene-stealing antics of Milton Berle threatened to disrupt the company's harmonious relations. The renowned joke thief found irritating ways to be the last one left in the camera shot. Berle's upstaging trickery included dropping his hat and staring at what everyone looked at just a few seconds longer. Uncle Miltie's subterfuge did not go unnoticed. In one sequence, his obnoxious mother-in-law, played by Ethel Merman, belted him several times with her purse. Afterward, Berle angrily complained to director Kramer that Merman really hurt him. The famous singer of show tunes opened her handbag and pulled out some heavy costumed jewelry. "Oh, I must have forgotten these were in here," she remarked, without any apparent remorse.

Extra: Ethel Merman (1908-1984) and Milton Berle (1908-2004) spent so much time together on *It's a Mad, Mad, Mad, Mad World* that the two show-business legends reminded their co-stars of a bickering married couple. After Berle found out the name of Merman's new dentist, he hinted that the same hygienist recently made a painful mess of his teeth. Merman was apprehensive for a week before discovering that she'd been tricked and plotted revenge. Ethel casually let it slip to Berle that she was getting higher billing than her *Mad World* co-stars. Not realizing he'd been lied to, the angry ex-television clown immediately called his agent and demanded equal treatment.

Extra: Uncle Miltie, one of TV's earliest stars, used to drive his fellow comedians crazy with his joke stealing. Famed gossip columnist Walter Winchell (1897-1972) once dubbed Berle "The Thief of Bad Gags." Milton once bragged to Groucho Marx, "Groucho I took some of my best material from your act."

"Then you weren't listening!" Marx angrily snapped back.

Extra: Milton Berle once testified in a courtroom trial after being instructed by his lawyer only to answer yes or no. While in the dock, the old vaudevillian stated that he was the greatest comedian in the world. Later, the legal expert admonished him for not following instructions. Milton shrugged, "Hey, I was under oath."

Chico's Sure Thing

Chico Marx's lifelong gambling addiction kept getting him in and out of trouble. After the Marx Brother's 1933 comedy *Duck Soup* crashed and burned at the box office, Chico, along with younger brothers Harpo and Groucho, were fired by Paramount Studios and spent two years lost in the Hollywood wilderness. Chico scored a bridge game with MGM bigwig Irving Thalberg and charmed the producer into giving the famous comedy team a new contract. The savvy Thalberg cast the Marxes in the 1935 classic *A Night at the Opera*; it became the biggest hit of their careers. Two years later, the piano-playing comic once again got into financial hot water on the set of the newest Marx offering, *A Day at the Races*. Right before shooting the movie's climactic steeplechase scene, Chico made a large bet on a horse that lost in the script. When asked for an explanation, the once-again broke fifty-year-old shrugged, "The crew gave me twenty-to-one odds."

Extra: Leonard Chico Marx (1887-1961) was a compulsive gambler from the age of nine. His father, who was a tailor, learned never to trust his son with a delivery. Leo hocked the clothes and blew the money in pool halls. No amount of beatings or admonishments from his old man could deter the boy from his risky hobbies. As he reached adulthood, Chico became a skilled card player but often took needless chances, which caused him to lose. Friends recalled him giving them expensive presents, then asking for them back within hours to use as bets. As his fellow movie-star brothers became rich, the old piano man performed in seedy dives to get by. Even after his frustrated siblings put him on an allowance, Chico continued to blow his meager funds till the end of his life. But once, the skirt-chasing comic scored big on an unlikely life-and-death long shot. After losing to mobster Benjamin "Bugsy" Siegel (1901-1947) in a high-stakes poker game, Chico paid him off with a bad check. The hot-tempered thug was gunned down in a probable gangland hit before he tried to cash it.

Extra: In 1929, Paramount Studios head Adolph Zukor (1873-1976) reneged on a deal one of his underlings made to pay the Marx Brothers seventy-five thousand dollars. Sure, the comedy team's play *The Coconuts* was a hit on Broadway, but they were unproven in pictures. The mogul scheduled a meeting with Chico Marx, and ordered his wayward executive to attend so he could learn how a talent negotiation should be done. The oldest Marx Brother praised Zukor to high heaven. It was such an honor for Chico to meet the man who practically invented the motion-picture industry. It would be the thrill of a lifetime for the brothers to make a film at Paramount for a mere one hundred thousand dollars. Smiling, Zukor turned to his assistant and said, "Well, that sounds reasonable."

Extra: In 1934, the Marx Brothers felt insulted by MGM bigwig Irving Thalberg (1899-1936). How dare he say that their movies needed fewer laughs and more romance? And why did this young man keep them waiting when they scheduled meetings? The Marxes were from vaudeville where promptness was demanded. The comics plotted their revenge. One day they barricaded Irving's office door with filing cabinets, and then escaped through the window. Another time, the once again tardy producer entered his workplace to find the comics completely naked and roasting potatoes in his fireplace. The good-humored Thalberg told the brothers to wait; he then called the MGM commissary and asked them to send up some butter.

Bob Couldn't Always Trust Bing

Bing Crosby would stick up for his friend and sometimes-rival Bob Hope, but loved playing jokes on him in private. One time during a morning round of golf, the screen partners discussed a hurtful magazine article that called the very rich Hope a cheapskate. Bing promptly went home to write an angry letter to the editor. People didn't realize that when Bob did free benefits for the US armed forces, he also gave up tons of money he could earn in other venues. After Hope thanked him, the crooner wanted a favor. There were a group of sailors on leave in New York who could use entertaining. Bing's schedule was full; could Bob do it? The patriotic comedian agreed and quickly left Hollywood for the East Coast. Bob was stunned when the military audience sat stone-faced, not laughing at any of his jokes. Crosby hadn't mentioned to Hope that the servicemen were members of the Royal Dutch Navy, who didn't speak a word of English.

Extra: Crooner Bing Crosby (1903-1977) and comedian Bob Hope (1903-2003) met while they were each performing at New York's Capitol Theater in 1932. They became drinking buddies and planned out a routine to enhance each other's act. Bob would come out on stage and say he had to do the show alone tonight. His partner had unfortunately locked himself in his dressing room. Bing then appeared in the wings, holding a plank of wood with an attached doorknob. "I'll be going solo tonight," Crosby told the crowd. "My partner has a stomach ache."

"But I don't have one," Hope protested.

"You will after I make you swallow this!"

Audiences were delighted and Hollywood studio executives took notice.

Extra: Crosby and Hope sometimes had a tense relationship and did not always appreciate being the butt of each other's jokes. A particular sore spot for Crosby was when Hope made fun of his toupee. During a scene in *Road to Singapore* (1940), the two men were about to settle down and get some shuteye when the director noticed something wrong. "Bing, why don't you take your hat off?"

"What are you talking about?" the singer replied. "This is how I sleep."

No amount of arguing or front-office pressure could change the leading man's mind; Crosby's head and hairpiece stayed covered throughout the shot.

Extra: Bob Hope was one of the Masters of Ceremonies when Bing Crosby won the Oscar for playing a priest in the sentimental comedy *Going My Way* (1944). The comedian later said that smiling as Crosby received his statue was the greatest acting job of his life.

A Christmas Story

William Claude Dukenfield, better known as W. C. Fields, who once claimed he would only play the role of Ebenezer Scrooge if he didn't have to repent at the end, one time displayed a sentimental side during Christmas. In the winter of 1895, the fifteen-year-old vaudevillian was robbed by his manager, and found himself stranded and broke at the Kent, Ohio, train station. The man behind the counter noticed him sitting quietly. "Are you an actor?"

W. C. nodded. "People don't trust your kind," the worker noted.

The young Fields, who had committed acts of larceny since he had run away from his father back in Philadelphia, said nothing. The clerk pulled a bill out of his wallet. "Listen, son, here's ten dollars. Pay me back when things are better for you."

Shocked by such kindness in a cruel world, William burst into tears. Two years later, on Christmas Day, the ticket seller received a note thanking him for his gesture with the original loan, plus another ten dollars in interest. It was all the money Fields had, so he spent the holiday in a soup kitchen.

Extra: Movie star W. C. Fields (1880-1946) often performed great acts of kindness and charity, but kept that side of his personality to himself. One December in the 1930s, the rich curmudgeon was shooting the breeze in the halls of Paramount Studios with Bob Hope, when they were approached by two charity workers. "Gentlemen, there are so many who suffer during the holiday season. Could you see your way to help them out?"

The normally tight-fisted Hope reached into his pocket and pulled out some cash. But Fields said, "I'm sorry, Madam. I gave all my money to the SEBF."

After the disappointed Samaritans left, Hope asked, "Hey, Bill, what's the SEBF?"

"Screw Everybody But Fields!"

Extra: Thomas Robert Malthus (1766-1834) was a British economist who publicly stated that impoverished people should be taken off government relief for their own sake. He felt it morally wrong for a family to reproduce before they could financially sustain themselves. His political enemies said that Malthus didn't care if the poor got smallpox, was an advocate of child murder and simply wanted to take the fun out of life. Charles Dickens (1812-1870) reviled him and Malthus may have been the inspiration for the miserly Ebenezer Scrooge in the writer's short novel, *A Christmas Carol* (1843).

Many free marketers questioned *A Christmas Carol's* philosophy. Why should Scrooge volunteer to give up more of his hard-earned wealth if he was already being taxed to support inadequate institutions? Was it an employer's fault if one of his workers had five children that he could not afford? When Ebenezer lent money, didn't it help his fellow citizens improve their lives and property? If the debtors agreed to Scrooge's terms and then couldn't, or wouldn't, pay him back, was that the businessman's fault? W.C. Fields, who lacked a formal education but loved the works of Charles Dickens, may have felt that the Scrooge at the beginning of the story was a well-meaning entrepreneur and a contributor to society.

Beverly Hills Ad Libber

Twenty-three-year-old Eddie Murphy had to fill in some big creative holes when he replaced Sylvester Stallone in the 1984 comedy *Beverly Hills Cop*. The thirty-eight-year-old Stallone walked off the film when the producers balked at paying for expensive action scenes. The hasty recasting led to huge chunks of dialogue and dark moments being excised from the script. Before shooting certain sequences, the director gave Eddie the merest outline of what was supposed to happen and relied on the innovative young stand-up comic to make it play. In take after take, Murphy came up with spontaneous monologues to con his way into a filled-up exclusive hotel, a posh country club and a heavily secured customs warehouse. The leading man's ad-libbed rifts forced his co-stars to cover their faces or pinch themselves hard; whatever it took for them not to laugh and ruin takes. Critics' complaints about a flimsy murder revenge plot with a typical "shoot 'em up" ending could not stop Eddie becoming the biggest star in America, while the sparse *Beverly Hills Cop* screenplay was nominated for an Oscar.

Extra: In 1980, nineteen-year-old Eddie Murphy of Roosevelt, Long Island, bombarded the Midtown Manhattan offices of TV's *Saturday Night Live* with three phone calls a day, insisting he'd make a great addition to the cast. After six auditions, Murphy was hired, and then it took several frustrating months before Eddie convinced *SNL's* producers that he was ready to carry a sketch. No matter that he'd been working the comedy clubs around New York for four years. "You're too young," they told him. "Learn from us, we have more experience."

Finally his persistence paid off; Eddie debuted on national television as a bitter high school basketball player who'd been a junior for seven years, and was now upset that his team was about to be racially integrated. The studio audience loved him and went into hysterics. Eddie became an instant celebrity, and some of the same people who had been condescending took credit for his discovery.

Extra: After Eddie Murphy became a major movie star, he surrounded himself with a huge paid entourage and worried that he'd lost his creative edge. Unlike other comics, Eddie was not "on" all the time but rather an astute observer of human behavior. When his new employees laughed at whatever he said, the multi-millionaire Murphy intimated that they wanted to keep their jobs. People that expected to meet an aggressive cut-up were sometimes surprised when Murphy displayed a shy demeanor in public. When Eddie played an overweight scientist in the 1996 comedy *The Nutty Professor*, some of his co-workers felt the actor only relaxed when he slipped into his fat suit costume. During breaks in filming, the still disguised Murphy went off on his own to Los Angeles city parks and played with children.

Charlie Chaplin's Advice

Charlie Chaplin always wished to move away from the comedy that made him famous. His serious turns disappointed many of his followers. When future film funny men like Lou Costello or Jim Carrey would get too poignant, they were accused of having "Chaplinitis". Even as the "Little Tramp's" movies got heavier, his comic advice was highly sought after. One time in the 1930s, famed writer Charles MacArthur questioned Chaplin on staging the most basic of scenes, a fat lady slipping on a banana peel. How do you present it on the screen without slipping into cliché? Would it be better to let the audience see the fat lady first and bring in the banana peel at the end of the sequence? With no hesitation, Chaplin said, "No. First you show the banana peel. Then you show the fat lady eyeing it, walking towards it and carefully stepping over it. Then the last thing you see is her falling down the open manhole she didn't notice."

Extra: Charlie Chaplin's screen rival Buster Keaton (1895-1966) once pointed out that audiences didn't like it when comedians were smarter than they were. One time Keaton walked over a banana peel and waved at the camera; the gag got absolutely no laughs at the preview. The scene was redone with Buster slipping on a second banana peel that the comedian didn't notice; he was still gloating over avoiding the first one. The newly edited sequence went over well.

Extra: One morning in the 1970s, comedian Jackie Vernon (1924-1987) was having breakfast in a London restaurant when he spotted his boyhood idol, Charlie Chaplin (1889-1977). Back when he was a kid, Jackie had sent the "Little Tramp" admiring fan letters every week for ten years. The silent film legend never replied so finally Jackie gave up. But now his hero was here in the flesh and Jackie could fulfill his lifelong dream of meeting him. Vernon approached the now wheelchair-bound Chaplin's table. "Mr. Chaplin, I have always admired and wanted to meet you. My name is Jackie Vernon."

The old man repeated the name thoughtfully, "Vernon...Vernon...So why did you stop writing?"

Comics and Monsters

Director Charles Barton put up with many ridiculous antics on the set of the 1948 comic horror film *Abbott and Costello Meet Frankenstein*. Lou Costello, who thought the film's script could have been written by a five-year-old, insisted that the cast participate in a wild pie fight, much to the chagrin of the well-dressed Bela Lugosi, who played Dracula. Costello also put a leash around the neck of Lon Chaney Jr. in his wolfman costume, and then took his hairy co-star for walks around the studio. When Lou was being chased by Glenn Strange, as Frankenstein's Monster, the pudgy comic pelted ad-libs that caused the creature to laugh and ruin takes. A bigger concern to the filmmakers was Bud Abbott, who would get so sloshed by two p.m. that he was incapable of shooting for the rest of the day. Abbott explained that when he was young, a doctor stated that if Bud didn't stop drinking he'd be dead by the age of thirty. The straight man was so worried by the diagnosis, he stayed drunk for the next forty years.

Extra: In 2006, forty-three-year-old director Quentin Tarantino stated that Abbott and Costello Meet Frankenstein was his all-time favorite movie. In Quentin's opinion, the epic meeting between the monsters, who were allowed to be scary, and the silly comics provided the perfect blend of horror and humor.

Laurel and Hardy's Hard Times

Like many Americans, Stan Laurel and Oliver Hardy endured tough times in 1932. The British-born Laurel had tragically lost his son, born two months prematurely, just nine days old. His marriage to his wife Lois was falling apart, and for the rest of his life Stan would deny accusations that he cheated on her. Meanwhile, Oliver Hardy's alcoholic spouse Myrtle was constantly being placed in and escaping from sanitariums. The heavyset, but very graceful actor from Georgia sought escape on golf courses and in the arms of another woman. With all their personal traumas, that year Laurel and Hardy still turned out their only Oscar-winning film, *The Music Box*. The antics of the helpless pair, trying to push a piano up a flight of 131 stairs, proved to be a great tonic for economically struggling audiences during the Great Depression. *The Music Box* continued to make people laugh hysterically for generations to come.

Extra: One time in the 1930s, Laurel and Hardy filmed a scene that required them to run down a narrow alleyway with their wives in hot pursuit. The women would shoot at them, causing two-timing men to come out of the nearby apartment buildings in their undergarments and run away, with Stan and Ollie doing double takes. Before the action commenced, Laurel gathered the extras around. "Listen, fellas, it's costing us a fortune to rent out these apartments so I want to get it right the first time. Now when you hear the shots and run out into the alley, don't linger. We only want you in the scene for about ten seconds."

After the director shouted, "ACTION!" the boys ran down the alley, their wives fired their guns and the men in their undergarments ran out and disappeared quickly, following Stan's instructions to the letter. All except one guy who was about thirty seconds late, ran the wrong way, and bumped into Laurel, which messed up his close-up. "You bloody fool. You ruined the shot!" shouted Stan.

"I'm not in the movie," replied the man.

I'm a Bad Boy

As his popularity rose in the 1940s, Lou Costello found an interesting way to furnish his ranch home in the San Fernando Valley. During the making of one of the Abbott and Costello comedies at Universal Studios, some furniture kept mysteriously disappearing from the set. Following a hunch, the producer called Costello and told him that they needed the chairs and tables to complete the movie. The pudgy star, who was known for his generosity to co-workers, was indignant. What did it have to do with him? Universal was a bunch of cheats! How would Costello and his partner, Bud Abbott, be treated when their careers took a downturn? But the props reappeared at the studio the next day and stayed on hand till the picture was done. Then they immediately vanished in a pattern that continued throughout Lou Costello's employment at Universal.

Blue Buddy Standards

Adults, who took their children to see Buddy Hackett in family movies, were sometimes shocked by his lewd stand-up act. The raunchy comedian, who wrote all his own material, kept a strict moral code when it came to choosing films. In 1952, the little-known twenty-eight-year-old Buddy turned down a chance to replace the late Curly Howard as a member of The Three Stooges because he felt they were too violent on screen. Thirty-eight years later, Buddy threw Martin Scorsese out of his home after the director offered him a role in the R-rated bloody gangster drama *Good Fellas*. Hackett was proud to work in Disney classics like *The Love Bug* and *The Little Mermaid*, but he didn't always behave. In the 1961 comedy *Everything's Ducky*, the funny man worked with a fowl that in one scene was supposed to wobble and fall over like a drunk. After several failed takes, the frustrated director chewed out the duck's trainer; neither noticed Buddy attending to his little white co-star with a whisky bottle and an eyedropper.

The Hard-to-Please Sergeant

Many years after he starred in the 1950s hit TV comedy *Sgt. Bilko*, Phil Silvers was a very difficult guy to buy gifts for. To his pals, the Brooklyn-born comic seemed to have everything; in reality, material goods meant very little to him. Growing up poor, Silvers hated shopping because his sister always haggled to bring prices down — it was so humiliating. The well-off actor often agreed to buy whatever salespeople showed to him, just to get out of stores. One time Phil visited a rich buddy for the weekend in a Rolls-Royce Silver Cloud. The friend saw a golden opportunity to pull off a really great surprise. He asked to borrow the car under the pretext of giving it a tune-up; he then installed a built-in bar, a state-of-the-art hi-fi stereo system, a deluxe color TV and a videocassette recorder. It was all ready by Monday and with great anticipation, he returned the automobile. It turned out to be a rented car.

What's In a Name?

Groucho Marx was incensed when Warner Bros. threatened to sue The Marx Brothers over the title of the 1946 film *A Night in Casablanca*. The wisecracking comedian pooh-poohed the notion that people would mistake the new comedy for Warners classic *Casablanca*, made four years earlier. He wrote the potential plaintiffs a letter stating that the Marxes used the word Brothers professionally long before the Warners; maybe they should countersue. Furthermore, Groucho was certain that moviegoers could tell there was a physical difference between his brother Harpo and *Casablanca's* beautiful leading lady Ingrid Bergman. Also, did Jack Warner own the rights to the name Jack? After all, he was preceded by Jack the Ripper and Jack and the Bean Stalk. After receiving the funny missive, the Warners dropped the issue. Later it was discovered they never objected at all; Groucho Marx made up the whole feud as a publicity stunt.

Moe Watched Out For Larry

In 1958, after twenty-five years of making *Three Stooges* shorts, Moe Howard was a real estate millionaire while his screen partner, Larry Fine, was totally broke. The uptight leader of the famous comedy team often got angry with Larry for being late, not knowing his lines and entering sets at the wrong time, which ruined scenes. Moe, who was five years older than his co-star, had constantly warned the knucklehead not to blow his money by living in hotels and gambling. Now Columbia Pictures had fired them; the fifty-six-year-old Larry was planning to eke out a living managing apartments. It served him right. But Moe remembered when his late younger brother Curly had been sick; the kind-hearted Larry had given him part of his salary. Through hard work and hustle, the rich Stooge kept their movie career alive, remained a worrywart and helped the middle Stooge to continue on with his happy, carefree lifestyle.

Extra: When The Three Stooges were hired at Columbia Pictures in 1934, they made sixty thousand dollars a year divided by three and never got a raise. Head honcho Harry Cohn loved their act and promised Moe Howard that they'd always have a place at the studio while he was boss. By the 1950s, the Stooges were the only comedy team in Hollywood still making twenty-minute, "two reelers"; Moe decided not to rock the boat by asking for more money. Right after Cohn died in 1958, the Stooges were immediately fired. When Moe came back to Columbia to say goodbye to his old pals, he was not admitted on the lot.

Extra: Larry Fine constantly gave money to friends who never paid him back. He made up for it by continuously borrowing from Moe and then forgetting all about it.

Extra: When Larry became a Stooge in 1926, the former violinist was told he'd have to forget about playing his music. Larry happily replied that for one hundred dollars, he'd forget everything.

The Distinct Dummy

To many people, ventriloquist Edgar Bergen and his wooden partner Charlie McCarthy were two distinct individual beings. The self-taught voice thrower based Charlie on a rascally newspaper boy that he had known in his youth. Wearing his cape, monocle and top hat, the dummy got away with sexual innuendos that most adults in the 1930s never dared utter in public. Critics, who charged that Bergen did his best work on radio where people couldn't see his lips moving, were disarmed when Charlie made fun of Edgar for the same thing. For over forty years, Bergen entertained audiences in all different media, and received an honorary Oscar for his wise-cracking creation in 1938. One time when the famous pair appeared on television, the soundman was so absorbed by Edgar and Charlie's banter that he kept moving the microphone back and forth above the head of the one that was currently speaking.

Hope and Roosevelt

Democrat Franklin Roosevelt was the first of eleven presidents Republican Bob Hope entertained. The commander-in-chief loved the comedian on the big screen and appreciated Hope's efforts entertaining the troops during World War II. Their paths crossed when Bob emceed a dinner in the president's honor, a few months before Roosevelt won an unprecedented fourth term in 1944. In front of a crowd of luminaries, Hope told a story about a Marine in the South Pacific who was disappointed that he had not encountered an enemy combatant. At the edge of a jungle, with his gun at the ready, he shouted out, "To hell with Hirohito!"

A Japanese soldier emerged from behind the trees. "To hell with Roosevelt!"

But the Marine lowered his weapon. "Darn it, I can't shoot a fellow Republican."

The president threw back his head and laughed so hard Bob later said he almost considered voting for him.

Extra: In late 1941, Bob Hope started broadcasting his radio show live from army bases as ploy to bring up ratings. The comedian endeared himself to enlisted men by making fun of their officers. Then in December, when America entered World War II, Hope and a number of other stars went on a victory caravan tour and sold war bonds. Unlike his fellow pampered celebrities, who complained about the cramped quarters on their shared train, the ex-vaudevillian Hope felt exhilarated by both the travel and crowds. It was no problem for the energetic Bob, who lived to be a hundred, to go overseas and entertain the troops.

At first, Hope found America's young fighting men to be the easiest audience he ever faced. Jokes that died in the States got uproarious laughter from the homesick G.I.s. In the beginning, Hope stayed out of combat areas, but then he reasoned that those in actual battles needed him the most. Bob flew in planes that could have been shot down and performed in places that had been recently attacked. He was greatly moved by the injuries he saw in hospital wards, and quietly used his vast wealth to help set up several wounded veterans in their own businesses after the war ended. Later, in the 1960s, Hope could not understand the Vietnam conflict, getting in trouble when he repeatedly suggested we should bomb the enemy into submission. Bob continued to perform for United States' troops even after some of the soldiers, who disagreed with his political stances, booed him.

George Burns on Tours

While giving tours of Hollywood in the 1990s, it was a pleasure for me and my customers to see ninety-something George Burns being driven around in a black Cadillac. The comedian always rode shotgun and smoked his trademark cigar. He would roll down the window, say hello and smile for the cameras. The women on the bus frequently commented on his cuteness. Usually Burns rode to Forest Lawn Cemetery to talk with his late wife Gracie or went to have lunch at the Hillcrest Country Club. Since the 1940s, George had sat at Hillcrest's famed "Comedian's Round Table" with legends such as Jack Benny, Danny Kaye, Al Jolson, The Marx Brothers and George Jessel. When we encountered Burns, he was the last survivor of the group. The Hillcrest Board of Directors was always very strict about the club members following their rules. But they amended one policy so that anyone ninety-five and over could smoke.

Extra: Founded in 1897, the Los Angeles Country Club was composed of the city's old money oil people; Jewish show-business types and actors were not allowed. The new moneyed movie folk started the Hillcrest Country Club in 1920, just a few miles away. Ironically, Hillcrest's primarily Jewish membership discovered oil on their property.

Extra: One time George Burns (1896-1996) and Harpo Marx (1888-1964) were playing golf at the Hillcrest. It was a hot day and the two men took off their shirts. A staff member raced over to tell them that their action was against club protocol. They shrugged and complied. Then a grinning George asked if there were any rules against taking off your pants. The employee admitted that there weren't. For the next few hours, several other players were startled by the sight of the two half-dressed comics.

Extra: Always optimistic, when George Burns turned ninety-nine, he signed a new contract with the Riviera Hotel in Las Vegas. He promised to renegotiate in five years if the hotel was still around.

The Unusual Speaking Engagement

One day in the 1950s, George Jessel was having lunch with some fellow comedians when he was approached by a stranger who asked him to speak at his dog's funeral. The famous toastmaster, who often got into trouble professionally because of his outspoken conservative politics and his fierce support of Israel, was insulted. Jessel's speechmaking was reserved for political and entertainment gatherings. This fellow was humiliating him; George's friends would probably rib him about pet eulogies for the next five years. The cash-starved womanizer began to reconsider when the man quietly promised to pay him a great deal of money. Still, George hesitated. Could he really agree to this indignity in front of his pals? His would-be benefactor then stated that he would also donate heavily to George's pet cause, the Jewish Relief Fund. Slowly, Jessel broke into a smile and then said, "Why didn't you tell me your dog was Jewish?"

The Reluctant Stereotype

Marilyn Monroe was disgusted when she read the script for the comedy *Some Like It Hot* in 1959. The thirty-three-year-old Connecticut resident had left Hollywood partly because she had grown tired of stereotypical dumb blonde roles. Now they wanted her to appear as someone too dense to realize that Jack Lemmon and Tony Curtis were disguised as women. Even she had never pretended to be that stupid. Still, Marilyn needed the money. Her acting coach, Lee Strasberg, reminded Monroe that she usually hadn't been close with other ladies. Marilyn should play her character as someone who yearned for female companionship so much that she did not notice her new friends' more masculine attributes. Armed with her teacher's advice, the bombshell unhappily returned to Los Angeles. Though she was resented by her co-workers for constantly being late and blowing her lines, movie audiences loved for Marilyn's sweet and sincere comic performance.

Extra: Thirty-four-year-old actors Tony Curtis and Jack Lemmon (1925-2001) sometimes suffered in silent agony on the set of *Some Like It Hot*. Marilyn Monroe (1926-1962) often took multiple takes to get her lines right, while her dressed-in-drag male co-stars were forced to stand for hours in their uncomfortable high-heeled shoes.

Extra: In one *Some Like It Hot* sequence, Marilyn's only line was, "It's me, Sugar." It took her sixty-five takes. In between camera setups, the frustrated director, Billy Wilder (1906-2002), tried to calm his leading lady down. "Don't worry, Marilyn."

"Worry about what?" she replied.

Later, the blonde, who was very shrewd about her comic abilities, told friends that she functioned as her own director. Once Monroe thought all the elements in a scene were correct, she delivered her dialogue perfectly.

The Great One Could Move

Even though his weight sometimes topped 300 pounds, the heavy-boozing Jackie Gleason moved with great speed and grace when he had to. Christened "The Great One" by his fellow drinking buddy Orson Welles, the forty-six-year-old comic actor embarked on a cross-country train trip to promote Gleason's return to television in 1962. For ten days he'd be surrounded by beautiful dames and the alcohol would be flowing. The publicity tour was a huge success; the often hung-over Gleason managed to keep smiling when he was loudly greeted by fans in each new town. At Union Station in Los Angeles, one of Jackie's entourage, named Billy the Midget, started selling helium balloons on the platform. At one point, the little man was carrying so many products he actually started to float away, when Jackie raced to his rescue and pulled him back to safety. "Nobody gets to San Bernardino before I do, pal!"

Bill Murray Made it in the Shower

When he joined the cast of TV's *Saturday Night Live* in 1977, Bill Murray was getting hate mail till an idea struck him in the shower. The twenty-seven-year-old comic, who replaced the very popular Chevy Chase, had struggled to be funny in his initial weeks on *SNL*. Sometimes the volatile Murray angered the show's writers by blowing his lines; the best material went to Bill's more established castmates. But now, holding onto a gag gift, a microphone-shaped bar of soap, the former medical student Murray had an inspiration. In the season finale, Bill shone as a pretend tacky morning disc jockey that showered with his wife, played by co-star Gilda Radner, while he talked to an imaginary audience. The laughs were enhanced when Murray introduced his spouse's supposedly secret lover, Buck Henry, as a surprise guest who joined the married couple under the running water. The "Shower Mike" sketch was a huge hit with viewers; from then on Bill's fan letters reflected a 180-degree change of heart.

Detective Burns

George Burns and Gracie Allen worried that their careers interfered with their parenting. One night the married comics arrived home late and were distressed to find that all the pictures had been cut out of their dictionary. Burns insisted that he handle it; he asked his boy Ronnie where his daughter Sandy had put the scissors; the kid didn't know. When George asked Sandy the same question, she revealed her brother hid them in a drawer. Even Gracie was impressed by George's detective work, and the kind-hearted straight man was so pleased that he doled out only a minor punishment to his son. For many years afterward, George proudly related the tale about his clever sleuthing to dinner guests until one night the now grown-up Sandy couldn't take it anymore. "Please don't tell the scissors story tonight, Dad."

"Why not, sweetheart?"

"Well, the reason I knew where they were is that I was the one who cut out the pictures."

Extra: The ninth of twelve children, George Burns of New York City (he was born Nathan Birnbaum and renamed himself after a successful baseball player) contributed greatly to the legend and lore of Hollywood. When author Max Wilk did research for his great 1973 book *The Wit and Wisdom of Hollywood*, George related an anecdote to him about a man named Osterman who came from the East Coast to run Paramount Studios in the early 1930s. Actress Claudette Colbert was upset that her stand-in had been fired as a cost-cutting move and threatened to quit her latest picture. Osterman was incredulous. "Miss Colbert, do you mean to tell me you will give up $125,000 unless this girl gets her thirty-five-dollar a week job back?"

The star was adamant, so the executive gave in. Hearing about the incident, George Burns, who along with his wife Gracie Allen (1895-1964) was new to pictures, decided to make his own demand. Their blue dressing room was giving Gracie a headache and it had to be repainted immediately if the comedy team was going to continue working there. "Mr. Burns, do you mean to say you would give up sixty thousand dollars unless your dressing room is made to look a different color?"

"That's right!"

"Mr. Burns, have you ever run a studio?"

"No."

"Well, you're running one now!"

And with that, so said George Burns, Osterman left Hollywood and returned to New York, never to come back. Max Wilk was all set to use the story for publication; the only problem was, according to his information, the Paramount head honcho at that time was named *Otterson*, not Osterman. George explained to Max that he'd used the name Osterman because he didn't want Wilk to be sued since the whole tale was a complete fabrication.

Jack Benny Lived Down to his Reputation

From 1932 to 1965, Jack Benny excelled at playing a beloved miser on radio and television. In real life both a generous man and a worrywart, Jack fretted that people would think he was like his small-screen character. Benny insisted on giving huge tips in restaurants, which caused waiters to give him sad looks, as if they were disappointed that he was not really stingy. Each year Benny gave lots of money to charity, but there were times that the former vaudevillian lived down to his reputation. Once, Jack was about to leave a posh hotel in a cab when he realized he had left his wallet in the restroom. He raced back to where he'd been, crouched down to look in the stall, and sure enough, he saw his little pocketbook on the floor. Not wanting to repay the ten-cent fee, Jack tried to crawl underneath the door and was straining to reach his money, when he was startled by laughter. Another man had come in to use the facilities. "Mr. Benny, I'm so glad everything I heard about you is true!"

Extra: Jack Benny (1894-1974), who made a lucrative career out of pretending to be cheap and eternally thirty-nine years old, once praised the shtick of little-known comedian Jacob Cohen (1921-2004). Born in Babylon, Long Island, Cohen grew up a sad child who claimed his mother woke up each morning at eleven a.m. and never made him breakfast. At the age of twenty-two, he gave up his dream of being a stand-up comic and got a job selling aluminum siding. ("I was the only one who knew I quit," Jake said.)

Twenty years later, the frustrated tin man returned to the stage, determined to create a distinct image that would separate him from the crowd. Benny caught Jake's act and thought it was wonderful. "Everyone can identify with what you're going through, keep it up," Jack told Cohen.

The encouraged younger funny man continued to entertain audiences, delivering rapid-fire one-liners such as, "My wife wanted to make love in the back seat and she wanted me to drive."

Cohen, who made a great living with his "no respect" routine, borrowed the moniker of a fictional cowboy star mentioned on Jack Benny's radio show back in 1942, and renamed himself Rodney Dangerfield.

Growing Up Stooges

Growing up in Brooklyn, two of The Three Stooges, Shemp and Moe Howard, got a taste of their future. In 1911, the boys enrolled in trade school; sixteen-year-old Shemp took a plumbing course and Moe, two years younger, studied to be an electrician. They learned how to install a button that quietly opened their apartment door from the outside, useful for sneaking in late without their old man hearing. One time the two dressed-up teens returned home well after midnight, but their contraption did not work. Moe snuck around the back, climbed through the bathroom window and in the darkness fell into the bathtub that someone had left full of water. Sopping wet, he crawled out laughing his head off, and a moment later, his brother followed him and made an equally loud splash. That night it earned each of them a smack in the face from their Pop; years later, they performed similar antics on camera for much better pay.

De Forest Enjoyed Belushi

Sixty-two-year-old De Forest Kelly saw John Belushi's TV parody of William Shatner's Captain Kirk five years after it aired on *Saturday Night Live*. The thirty-two-year-old comedian, who would sadly die of a drug overdose within a year, visited the set of the 1982 movie *Star Trek II* and invited Kelly to see the footage. The gentlemanly Atlanta-born actor had by that time played Doctor McCoy, alongside Shatner as Captain Kirk, off and on for sixteen years. Kelly always bristled when someone outside the *Star Trek* family criticized his co-star. Yet he was curious to see the young man's skit, he'd heard that it was hilarious. When De Forest watched the video, he was astonished; every one of Kirk's mannerisms, from his dramatic pauses to his intense delivery of dialogue, had been perfectly mimicked. Later that day, an annoyed William Shatner wondered why the usually professional Kelly kept looking at him and breaking into laughter.

Extra: When John Belushi (1949-1982) rehearsed to play Captain Kirk on *Saturday Night Live,* he performed so badly his bosses considered removing the *Star Trek* skit from the program. Belushi didn't resemble William Shatner physically, and perhaps the young comic was simply not up to the task. But John said he could do it. On show night he was right on the money; the *Star Trek* sketch was one of the most well received moments in *SNL* history and perhaps Belushi's proudest moment as an actor.

Not So Crazy After All

Jonathan Winters thought he was hearing things when he returned home from the funny farm in 1963. The thirty-eight-year-old comedian institutionalized himself after drinking too much coffee to counter his heavy boozing; Jonathan blamed insomnia as the main cause for several wild stunts he committed in public. Winters' antics included trespassing on and climbing to the top of a schooner ship in San Francisco Bay; standing in the middle of busy Sunset Boulevard directing traffic; and causing a panic when he pulled out an authentic-looking toy grenade in a Hollywood watering hole. After several restful months at the sanitarium, Winters couldn't be sure about these strange sounds. "Yes, I want you, Johnny," the voice repeated.

The man on the phone turned out to be director Stanley Kramer, who offered him a major part in the classic comedy *It's a Mad, Mad, Mad, Mad World,* and for the next few months, Winters got big money in exchange for his craziness.

Conductor Groucho

Groucho Marx was miffed when his older brother Harpo and writer Ben Hecht excluded him from their musical quartet in 1940. The cigar-smoking comic, who played the mandolin in his spare time, had never been so insulted! How dare they imply Groucho wasn't musically inclined? A week later, in Hecht's Beverly Hills mansion, the players were rehearsing upstairs when a glaring Groucho popped his head through the door. "So I'm not good enough for your sessions, am I? Amateurs!"

After he left, the foursome momentarily considered inviting their pal to join them, then snobbishness won out and they resumed the session. Suddenly, their soft chamber melody was drowned out by a thunderous sound from below. They raced downstairs and were stunned to see one hundred men squeezed into the living room; Groucho was wildly conducting a full orchestral symphony with the entire Los Angeles Philharmonic.

Racing with Jackie

New York bar owner Toots Shor once thought he'd make an easy ten bucks out of one of his favorite patrons, comedian Jackie Gleason. The two buddies had agreed to a race starting from Toots' establishment; they would each run around the block and the first one back to the saloon would win. Though he moved with extreme grace for a big man, the three-hundred-pound Gleason had no chance. Perhaps to save humiliation, Jackie insisted that both men take off in opposite paths. Fifteen minutes later, an out-of-breath Toots Shor staggered to the finish line and was stunned to see "The Great One" sitting at the bar stool, nursing a drink. "I need your money for the tab, pal."

Witnesses insisted that Jackie had come racing in from the other direction. Shor scratched his head and paid Gleason off, wondering how the hell he did it; Toots never even passed Jackie on the sidewalk. A few days later, Shor picked up the newspaper and read a story, which revealed the secret of the escapade; Gleason had hailed a cab.

Red Skelton the Loner

Comedian Red Skelton felt very little need to socialize during the twenty-one seasons his TV show ran. Like his famed clown character, Freddy the Freeloader, the Indiana-born Skelton was a natural loner. Why should he spend time with fellow comedians, who were more interested in topping his performances rather than being his friend? Let others hang around Hollywood nightclubs, and give the impression to their fans that they were out-of-control drunks. In the turbulent 1960s, the very conservative Red felt even more isolated from younger comics whose humor seemed raunchy and inappropriate. His most important relationship was with his audience. One rare night when he ate out, Red observed a comedy writer entertaining his dinner mates. Appreciative of the man's talents, Skelton walked up to his table and stated, "I wish you worked on my show."

The scribe was startled. "But I do."

Dorothy Kept Up With the Boys

For twenty-two years and through seven movies, Dorothy Lamour was sometimes an unwilling straight woman for Bing Crosby and Bob Hope. Beginning with *Road to Singapore* in 1940, the twenty-six-year-old former Miss New Orleans realized that her two co-stars adlibbed so much, there was no point in learning the script. Well, she loved both men; the money was good; but boy, they acted like jerks sometimes. When she complained, Bing told her to wait for a pause and shout out a line. Bob could be even worse, saying her only function was to look good in a sarong. The kindly Lamour, who always claimed that making pictures with the boys was more hilarious than the finished films, managed to hold her own. Once after Crosby and Hope kept stepping on her words, Dorothy smiled at the camera revealing black teeth; the brunette refused to brush until the two stars promised she would get to speak.

Greta Garbo's Strange Encounter

Three ghostly figures induced Greta Garbo to restate her famous quote from the 1932 movie *Grand Hotel.* The twenty-eight-year-old Swedish beauty never allowed visitors while she worked on MGM movie sets. Interlopers caused her to lose concentration when she made faces on camera, shattering the illusions she worked so hard to create. But somehow these three clownish apparitions, with their ghoulish makeup, had come charging into Garbo's workspace. She hadn't seen them at the studio before; there was something unusual, almost frightening about them. What did they look like normally? "I want to be alone!" she cried, and then beat a hasty retreat to her dressing room.

Her antagonists, who were actually new contract players at Metro, were at first bewildered by her reaction, and then they began to laugh and ran off. "C'mon, let's see who else we can scare around here!" Moe said to the other two Stooges.

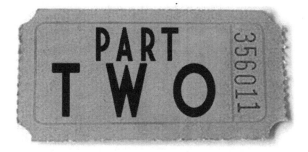

SCIENCE FICTION
AND HORROR

"What terrified me will terrify others; and I need only
describe the spectre which had haunted my midnight pillow."
– Mary Shelley

"My wife has good taste. She has seen very few of my movies."
– Boris Karloff

The Gambling Predator

After the release of *Rocky IV* in 1985, the joke around Hollywood was that the picture's star, Sylvester Stallone, should fight a space alien in the next sequel. The concept inspired the movie *Predator* two years later, with Stallone's screen rival Arnold Schwarzenegger taking his place. Not wanting to battle the creature alone in a blazing hot Mexican jungle, the famous body builder asked the screenwriters to create a part for his buddy, wrestler Jesse "The Body" Ventura. In between setups, the two future state governors boasted in front of the crew that each had bigger biceps, which led to a wager involving a bottle of champagne. The gleeful Ventura knew he would win; the wardrobe department had privately informed him that his arms were bigger. But Jesse had to pay off when it turned out that the earlier measurements were falsified at Schwarzenegger's request.

Who Lives in the *Star Wars* Galaxy?

Early in their careers, the loud, boisterous Frances Ford Coppola became a mentor to the quiet, introspective George Lucas. Although Lucas sometimes resented the older director's pushy persona, he shared Coppola's opinion that the movie studios, which controlled the purse strings, imposed too much power over filmmakers. Lucas put these relationships on the screen in a science-fiction tale. The reserved, heroic Luke Skywalker was based on George Lucas, while the cocky, reckless, always-in-debt Han Solo was inspired by Frances Ford Coppola. And the powerful intergalactic empire was modeled after the Hollywood studios. George Lucas' quest for his creative freedom paralleled young Luke Skywalker's struggle to win his liberty, and both achieved their goals thanks to the *Star Wars* movies.

Extra: The transition from old to new Hollywood may have happened in 1967 when Warner Bros. studio founder Jack Warner (1892-1978) cleaned out his desk. On the same day, a twenty-three-year-old ex-USC film student named George Lucas, showed up at Warner Bros. for his first day of work. With not much going on, Lucas quickly fell under the spell of the five-years-older Francis

Ford Coppola (the only other person on the lot besides George that was under thirty and wore a beard), who was directing the musical *Finian's Rainbow*, starring Fred Astaire. The charismatic Coppola, who had become a legend at UCLA film school and dressed in combat fatigues like Fidel Castro, recruited Lucas to be a crew member on Francis's next project, a low-budget road picture called *The Rain People* (1969). George resented his new boss for spending weekends partying in New York, while insisting that his film crew stay cooped up in various small towns at Howard Johnson hotels, without female companionship. But he was thrilled when Coppola stood up to pigheaded studio executives. Lucas made a documentary about his *Rain People* experience called *Filmmaker*, which was later shown to aspiring film students. George eventually admitted that working for Francis was a great time despite the rugged conditions.

Extra: In 1971, George Lucas wrote and directed the bleak science fiction film *THX 1138* for Coppola's production company. The new management team at Warner Bros. provided Francis with the needed financing, and planned to distribute his friend's picture; the wily Coppola appeased both sides. "I'm telling you, this kid Lucas is making a great film," he told the Warner brass. At the same time he reassured Lucas, telling the younger man that his new bosses had low expectations.

After the suits saw the completed *THX 1138,* they were furious. "Francis, what is this?"

"I don't know; I've never seen it," replied the bewildered producer.

The studio execs infuriated George Lucas by editing parts out of the movie, causing him to exclaim, "They're cutting the fingers off my baby!"

Extra: After *THX* failed at the box office, Lucas was encouraged by his friends to do something more commercial. How could he hook audiences while working within a very low budget? George felt that moviegoers would share his love of the top forty songs that he heard on the radio growing up. And at USC Lucas studied anthropology; he concluded that young American males were the only members of the species who cruised around in cars to pick up girls. George combined those elements with his own small-town upbringing into a coming-of-age screenplay called *American Graffiti* (1973). The new project was green lit by executives at Universal Studios after they were assured that it was not an Italian story about feet.

Extra: After a very difficult twenty-eight-day shoot in Northern California, *American Graffiti* was screened for a young audience in San Francisco that went crazy for it. Lucas and his producer Francis Ford Coppola waited as the Universal executives walked up to them after the show. They expected to be congratulated, but instead were accused of making a movie that Middle America would not want to see. The suits were unimpressed by the positive reaction of the audience, who in their minds were George's planted hippie friends. Coppola argued back, getting right up in their faces, offering to buy the movie and distribute it himself; Lucas said nothing. Just like Warner Bros. had done with *THX*, the executives at Universal made what Lucas considered to be unwarranted cuts. *Graffiti*, however, was one of the most profitable movies in history. Lucas made millions, which gave him the time to write the *Star Wars* screenplay that helped to set him free of the Hollywood system.

Extra: Several of George's and Francis's real-life traits were written into the characters of Luke Skywalker and Han Solo. George's enjoyment of racing cars was transferred to Luke's love of space pods. One scene, where Young Skywalker argued with his disapproving uncle about becoming a Jedi Knight, mirrored George's heated discussions with his father when Lucas announced he wanted to be a filmmaker. Likewise, Han Solo was constantly in debt and being chased down by creditors, yet like Francis Ford Coppola, it never seemed to bother him. In 1982, Francis attended his friend and fellow director Martin Scorsese's fortieth birthday party. The happy occasion was marred by Scorsese's distress over the recent box office failure of his latest offering *The King of Comedy*, about an out-of-control TV talk show fan. "Francis, I'm broke! They cut up all my credit cards today! What am I going to do?"

Calmly, Coppola replied, "Marty, shut up. I owe fifty million dollars; it's no big deal."

Extra: After *Star Wars* (1977) became the biggest hit in Hollywood history, Coppola suggested that he and Lucas turn "The Force" (the metaphysical power Luke Skywalker attains in the movie) into a new, lucrative religion. George dismissed the idea as ridiculous, but his friend may have been onto something. After thirty-four-year-old Ewan McGregor played a young version of Luke's mentor Obi-Wan Kenobi in *Star Wars Episode III: Revenge of the Sith* (2005), he was approached by a serious *Star Wars* fan in costume. "Mr. McGregor, I'm a Jedi Knight in training, could you advise me?"

The Forgettable Actress

Thirty-six-year-old director Brian De Palma had a specific actress in mind to play the mousey girl with telekinetic powers, who you don't want to make mad, in the 1976 horror film *Carrie*. But to Brian's surprise, a determined Sissy Spacek wowed him with her screen test and grabbed the part. The twenty-seven-year-old Texas-born tomboy insisted on doing her own stunts, which included being physically attacked while standing nude in a girls' locker room, getting drenched by fake blood at the prom and actually lying in a grave so Spacek's real hand could shoot out terrifyingly and grab co-star Amy Irving's arm. Several of the actresses who were supposed to be taunting Carrie on camera were very shy but the leading lady's boldness helped them lose their inhibitions. *Carrie* became De Palma's biggest commercial hit and the filmmaker later claimed he couldn't remember who his first choice for the role was.

Extra: Twenty-six-year-old Nancy Allen, who played Carrie's chief teenage tormenter, was surprised how horrifying the completed film was. Brian De Palma made her character so over the top, she'd assumed that *Carrie* was a comedy. One scene called for her gym teacher (Betty Buckley) to slap Allen hard in the face. Director De Palma was so unhappy with Allen's reaction that he ordered thirty takes. Three years later, Nancy became Mrs. Brian De Palma.

Visions of *Blade Runner*

Ridley Scott felt there was only room for his own vision when he directed *Blade Runner* in 1982. The filmmaker's controlling attitude alienated many of his co-workers on the set. Forty-year-old leading man Harrison Ford, who during production went from feeling like a partner to a pawn, complained that his android hunting character was overshadowed by the movie's visuals. Rebellious crew members openly wore t-shirts that stated, "Will Rogers never met Ridley Scott." The forty-five-year-old director stuck to his guns; *Blade Runner* overcame initial bad reviews and weak box office to later gain a huge cult following. One staunch defender of Scott's work was Philip K. Dick, who had written the novel that the movie was based on. The science-fiction author said that the bleak futuristic city presented on the screen was exactly how he envisioned it. An ironic compliment since Ridley Scott never bothered to read his book.

Extra: Humorist and movie star Will Rogers (1879-1935), was famous for saying, "I never yet met a man I didn't like." The actual quote was, "I bet you if

I had met him and had a chat with him, I would have found him a very interesting and human fellow, for I never yet met a man that I didn't like. When you meet people, no matter what opinion you might have formed about them beforehand, why, after you meet them and see their angle and their personality, why, you can see a lot of good in all of them."

Rogers was referring to Russian revolutionary and Marxist theorist Leon Trotsky (1879-1940).

Extra: Philip K. Dick (1928-1982) came across diaries of SS men stationed in Poland during World War II. The Nazis' casual lack of empathy toward other people made the author believe they were only human on the outside. His reading inspired him to write the 1968 novel *Do Androids Dream of Electric Sheep?*, which was turned into the movie *Blade Runner*.

Extra: *Ben-Hur* (1959) cost fifteen million dollars and at the time was the most expensive movie ever made. For years afterwards, The Roman epic's Oscar-winning star Charlton Heston speculated that Hollywood would never produce another film like it; it was too expensive to build massive sets and hire thousands of extras. But Heston was proven wrong in 2000 when director Ridley Scott and executives at DreamWorks Studios decided that there had been too many recent science fiction films. What this generation hadn't seen was a Roman spectacle and advancements in computer technology made the costs feasible. The result was the eighty-million-dollar production of *Gladiator*. Ridley Scott, who had nearly had come to blows with Harrison Ford during the making of *Blade Runner* (1982), had a similarly tense relationship with *Gladiator's* leading man, thirty-six-year-old Russell Crowe. The New Zealand-born actor was not allowed to join his mates for soccer games during production. "They have me wrestling tigers and sword fighting, and they're worried about me playing football?" he asked incredulously.

Crowe also worried that Scott wasn't putting his performance in its best light. In turn, Ridley couldn't fathom why Russell failed to see that the overall look of the movie was more important than any individual portrayal. Proving John Wayne's old adage that actors hate directors until the picture comes out, when Crowe won his Best Actor Award for *Gladiator* at the Oscars, he said, "The bloke responsible for me getting this is Ridley Scott."

Scott, who lost out on the Best Director award that year to Steven Soderbergh for the war-on-drugs crime thriller *Traffic*, was less conciliatory in his statements. During the making of *Gladiator*, the company sadly lost Oliver Reed (1937-1999) from a fatal heart attack, after a wild booze binge. For some of Reed's scenes, the filmmakers grafted a computer-generated image of the heavy drinking actor's face onto a stand-in's body. The seamless special effect fooled audiences; after the Oscars, Ridley Scott cryptically commented about the amazing advancements in digital technology, "Stars like Russell Crowe don't have to worry about being replaced by computers…yet."

The Image-Conscious Terminator

Arnold Schwarzenegger was unsure if playing the title role in the 1984 science fiction thriller *The Terminator* would be good for his image. The future California governor was well aware that one of his idols, former actor turned President Ronald Reagan, usually had taken nice-guy roles. Did Arnold really want to risk his standing with the public to portray a murderous robot with very little dialogue? Schwarzenegger had a meeting with Mike Medavoy, the head of Orion Pictures. "Listen Arnold, you should play a bad guy once. When I was a kid I saw Richard Widmark as a killer in a movie called *Kiss of Death*. He pushed an old lady in a wheelchair down the stairs and laughed like a maniac. I'm telling you people never forgot it. Be a villain once, make an impact and then you can switch to heroic parts."

Arnold agreed to sign onto the movie that would make him a superstar. Medavoy never mentioned that in 1948, after Widmark did his evil turn, some elderly ladies stopped the actor in the street and slapped his face.

I'm a Lover, Not a Biter

Forty-nine-year-old Bela Lugosi failed to capitalize on his success after playing the title role in the 1931 horror classic *Dracula*. The English-challenged Hungarian actor turned down the chance to follow up with Frankenstein's monster because the part had no dialogue; his replacement, Boris Karloff, became a star. The five-times-married Lugosi embarked on a checkered horror film career, which made it difficult to maintain his extravagant lifestyle. During long bouts of unemployment, roller skates became Bela's main mode of transportation. Bitter about being typecast as vampires, mad scientists and their deformed assistants, Lugosi sadly became a morphine addict. In his last days, he fantasized that his rival Karloff was a bogeyman out to destroy him. As the years passed, people forgot that *Dracula* was originally marketed as a love story, which came out on Valentine's Day. At the time, Lugosi received more love letters from females and was a bigger sex symbol than Clark Gable.

Extra: Most Dracula scholars believe that the fictional vampire character was based on Vlad the Impaler (1431-1476). In his reign as Prince of Wallachia (Southern Romania), the real Dracula (Latin for *son of Dragon*) doled out cruel, torturous death to his political enemies, including the poor and disabled so they would not be a burden to others. Driving a stake through people was not uncommon in the fifteenth century, and many of his countrymen considered the Impaler to be a hero.

Extra: Bela Lugosi (1882-1956) became a sex symbol when he played Dracula on Broadway in 1927. Nurses were on hand during the performances to provide smelling salts for audience members (usually females) who fainted. One of the stage vampire's biggest fans was cinema icon Clara Bow (1905-1965), who watched him from the front row for two consecutive weeks. Lugosi and the famous flapper (a 1920s term that referred to brash young women with bobbed hair who drank and smoked, listened to jazz music and flaunted sexual behavior) had a love affair, which ended the actor's three-day marriage to a wealthy San Francisco widow. The resulting scandal with Bow raised Bela's profile in Hollywood, and helped him land the Dracula movie part in 1931.

Extra: Although he was always professional and cordial toward Boris Karloff (1887-1969), it was hard for Bela Lugosi not to be a bit envious of him. Forgotten by Hollywood producers (some who thought he had died years before), Lugosi scraped by in the early fifties by doing-one man shows as Dracula. One night Bela was strolling through a small town when a young boy eagerly approached him with an autograph book. "You see," he told a companion. "They know me everywhere."

Lugosi took the pad from the boy and then hesitated before signing. "And what is my name young man?"

"Boris Karloff," the kid immediately replied.

The Adventures of Super Hair

Forty-eight-year-old Gene Hackman did not want to go bald or get rid of his mustache for his role as Lex Luthor in the 1978 movie *Superman*. He was unmoved when director Richard Donner explained that the comic book villain had no hair on his head and everyone knew it. Donner shot around Hackman till he was needed and when they met again, the filmmaker was sporting his own handsome mustache. He told Gene that he would only have to wear a bald cap in just one scene, but he had to shave. Richard would reciprocate by losing his stash as well. Reluctantly, Hackman agreed and the make-up man was called in to do the job. Then it was Donner's turn. Richard reached up and ripped off his facial hair, which had been provided by the prop man. For a moment, Donner thought the red-faced star would choke him, then Gene burst out laughing, and the Man of Steel got to face his clean-shaven nemesis.

The Lazy Super Dad

Marlon Brando wanted to work as little as possible when he played Jor-El, the Kryptonian father, in the 1978 movie *Superman*. The fifty-three-year-old actor told the film's producers that he only needed to do a voiceover and some object could stand in his place. After all, he would be part of an alien race; nobody knew what they looked like. Perhaps the extraterrestrial could appear as a green bagel. His bosses were both bemused and alarmed. They pointed out that Marlon's son would look human and be played by an earthling. A grinning Brando agreed to show up on the set. For his ten minutes of screen time, the star made an estimated nineteen million dollars while not bothering to learn his lines. In his most dramatic scene, Marlon held his baby above his head, speculated on the child's future, and then placed him on the space ship to escape the doomed planet. Brando hadn't bothered to learn his lines; his dialogue was penned on the bottom of the super infant's diaper.

Extra: The first *Superman* movies were low-budget serials made in 1948 starring Kirk Alyn (1910-1999) in the title role. The cheaply made Saturday Matinee cliffhangers got surprisingly good reviews. Alyn was only given credit for playing Clark Kent; the studio claimed that no actor was qualified to play the Last Son of Krypton so he'd appear as himself. One scene required the Man of Steel to rescue two would-be victims from a burning building. After the first take the director said, "That was great, Kirk. But could we do it again without you straining so much? I mean, you're super strong, lifting a couple of humans should be easy."

Alyn, a body builder in real life, was indignant. "What do you expect? These people are heavy!"

"People? Oh my goodness, baby, I'm sorry, we forgot to get you the dummies!"

Extra: In 1973, Marlon Brando (1924-2004) starred in the controversial and sex-charged drama *Last Tango in Paris*. This time around, the actor wrote some of his non-memorized lines on the bottom of his shoe, and in a few scenes hopped around awkwardly on one foot in order to read them.

Extra: Thirty-nine-year-old Jack Nicholson looked forward to working with the great Brando when they co-starred in the 1976 western, *The Missouri Breaks*. But Marlon, who eventually became Jack's next-door neighbor in the Hollywood Hills, disappointed Nicholson by reading cue cards, thus not making eye contact in their shared scenes. Later Brando hired an assistant to read the dialogue out loud into a radio transmitter from Marlon's trailer, the actor could then hear them through an earpiece. Once, Brando was about to speak his lines when the device inadvertently picked up a police broadcast. The confused performer came out of character. "Oh my God! There's been a robbery at Woolworths."

Horror on the Cheap

In the 1930s, executives at Universal Studios found horror movies were a perfect antidote to the huge salaries demanded by film stars. Actors, hired to play mostly silent horrible creatures under several cakes of make-up, could be replaced without the public caring. British-born Boris Karloff was forever grateful when he landed the career-making role of Frankenstein's Monster. The forty-four-year-old part-time truck driver's legendary performance as the sometimes-sympathetic demon, paved the way for Boris to get more parts and a better lifestyle. But in later years, Karloff revealed some unhappiness about the *Frankenstein* pictures. "I was only in three but I get blamed for all nine. Every time a new one comes out I get the fan mail and some other bloke gets the check."

Each year on Halloween, Boris would sigh and then gently tell the many children who came to the door of his Beverly Hills mansion that he would not go trick-or-treating with them.

Extra: Boris Karloff turned down the chance to reprise his role as Frankenstein's Monster for the fourth time in *Abbott and Costello Meet Frankenstein*. He feared the creature would lose his dignity in a comedy. Actor Glenn Strange (1899-1973), who played the demon in *House of Frankenstein* (1944) and *House of Dracula* (1945), donned the green make-up once again for *Abbott and Costello*. When Karloff died in 1969, newspapers around the world published obituaries of him accompanied by Strange's picture.

Extra: Karloff's influence was felt in Berkshire, England, during the making of Hammer Films' *The Curse of Frankenstein* (1957). Fearing that any resemblance to Universal Studios' version of the monster would cause a lawsuit, make-up artist Philip Leakey (1908-1992) worked hard to make thirty-five-year-old actor Christopher Lee's version of the reanimated brute gruesome and unique. Lee, a former officer in the Royal Air Force, became so angry at Leakey's painful experiments on his visage that he threatened to run Philip through with his sword. The fearful face artist disappeared for several days, which delayed the production. Later, a calmer Lee complained about his job to co-star Peter Cushing (1913-1984), who played Baron Frankenstein. "Being the creature is horrid. I have no lines."

"You're lucky. I've read the script," replied Cushing. *The Curse of Frankenstein* was critically panned and highly profitable.

Extra: Moviemakers have found the horror genre to be a potentially low-budget, high-profit way of breaking into the business. Standing in a long line at a hardware store, Tobe Hooper imagined taking a chainsaw off the wall and cutting his way to the front; the gruesome notion inspired the thirty-one-year-old to write and direct *The Texas Chainsaw Massacre* (1974). Twenty-eight-year-old short film and commercial director George Romero found a local butcher in Pittsburgh, who was willing to supply blood and guts for Romero's zombie thriller *Night of the Living Dead* (1968). Forty-five-year-old Wes Craven combined a nasty bully named Freddy that he knew in grade school, with a frightening old hobo Craven saw hanging around his Cleveland neighborhood to create the dream killer Freddy Krueger for *A Nightmare on Elm Street* (1984). And forty-year-old Val Lewton was given credit for saving RKO Pictures (the studio was teetering on bankruptcy because of the overspending Orson Welles) by producing the highly lucrative *Cat People* (1944). Lewton kept the budget way down by showing suggestive shadows rather than the actual humanoid felines.

Shatner Aged Well

William Shatner resisted producer Harve Bennett's pleas that he let go of his leading-man image for the 1982 science fiction film *Star Trek II: The Wrath of Khan*. The fifty-one-year-old actor was full of ideas that Bennett found objectionable. In the scene involving the death of Mr. Spock, played by Leonard Nimoy, Shatner proposed that the extraterrestrial first officer should not be seen on camera; they should just show Bill as Admiral Kirk reacting to the loss. And why did the story have to focus on the aging former starship captain having a grown-up son? Bennett pointed out that some great film actors got older on screen. Who? "Well, uh, Spencer Tracy. You remind me of him."

Shatner smiled, backed off his demands and gave a mostly fine, understated performance. Later, Bennett found out that he lucked out with his answer; Shatner had worked alongside the aging Spencer Tracy in the 1961 ensemble courtroom drama *Judgment at Nuremberg,* and idolized him.

Extra: Thirty-seven-year-old director Nicholas Meyer used different methods to guide both his hero and villain through the 1982 movie *Star Trek II: The Wrath of Khan.* Ricardo Montalbán (1920-2009), who played the genetically engineered super-bad guy Khan Noonien Singh, had initially been over the top when he delivered his dialogue. The nervous Meyer suggested to the twenty-five-years-older Ricardo that he'd tone it down; Khan was a madman, but many crazy people were soft-spoken and that made them even more dangerous. To his relief, Montalbán, who at the time was a huge TV star on *Fantasy Island* (1978-1984), was grateful for the input. The veteran actor displayed no ego and did exactly what his younger instructor asked of him. With William Shatner in the role of Khan's sworn enemy Admiral James Kirk, Meyer's approach was to let his leading man do several bombastic takes until he got tired and bored. Then finally Shatner would give the low key line reading that ended up in the finished film.

Vincent Price was of Two Minds

Actor Vincent Price was of two minds regarding his career in horror films. The St. Louis-born Price, who was both a gourmet cook and art collector, always felt a bit embarrassed when he made low-budget chillers. On the other hand, appearing in creature features helped older stars stay popular with young audiences. Besides, they were a kick to make; Vincent enjoyed the creepy jobs much more than those stodgy Biblical epics where everyone was always on their best behavior. While working on the 1958 low-budget thriller *The Fly,* the forty-seven-year-old Price kept breaking into laughter and ruining takes when he looked at the cheap-looking human/insect. Vincent continued to make mischief after the movie was completed. One day two female teens enjoyed a matinee screening of *The Fly.* They screamed loudest at the end when a familiar face they had just watched on screen stuck his head in between theirs and asked, "So how did you like the show?"

Extra: Often in search of extra publicity, Vincent Price (1911-1993) once took the place of his own dummy likeness at the Hollywood Wax Museum. The horror star stood motionless, held a hypodermic syringe, waited patiently for unsuspecting people to walk by and then reached out and squirted them with water.

The Two Sides of Godzilla

Audience reactions to the 1956 thriller *Godzilla, King of the Monsters!*, about a dinosaur-like creature awakened by nuclear testing, differed by the countries in which it was shown. The Americanized version included ten minutes with actor Raymond Burr as a reporter whose advice on how to deal with the creature is sought by brilliant scientists. A combination of the Japanese words meaning whale and gorilla, Godzilla was portrayed by a very hot, uncomfortable actor in a two-hundred-pound rubber suit. He could walk about three hundred feet, had a cable operator behind him to control eye movements, and shot radioactive breath from his mouth which was made out of hot wax. The producers chose to dub the Japanese actors instead of using subtitles, which led to some awkward lip synching. Taken very seriously in Japan as a somber symbol of the dangers of atomic warfare, *Godzilla* became a huge success in the USA while providing many unintentional laughs.

Rotten Tomatoes

The makers of the 1978 comedy *Attack of the Killer Tomatoes* paid homage to the low-budget, campy science fiction flicks of the 1950s. Following the typical plot conventions of its genre, the film had scientists and the military teaming up to stop a horrifying menace. Amateur actors gave widely panned performances as eccentric characters, ranging from an underwater expert who always wore his scuba suit on land to a master of disguise who infiltrated the enemy's lair, and then was exposed when he asked them to pass the catsup. When a helicopter accidentally crashed into one of the sets, the quick-thinking crew converted the wreckage into a spectacular-looking special effect, a bit out of place in a movie where the villains were made out of papier-mâché. Although many critics complained that for a bad picture to become a classic it had to be unintentionally bad, *Tomatoes* became a cult favorite just like the movies it poked fun at.

Steve McQueen hid from the Blob

Years after it was made, Steve McQueen had different emotions about starring in the 1958 cheap sci-fi flick, *The Blob*. Sometimes he was resentful; *The Blob's* producers had offered the struggling twenty-eight-year-old actor a choice between three thousand dollars or 10 percent of the profits; Steve took the one-time cash payment to make rent, and then fumed for years as the movie made millions. Other times he was embarrassed; if McQueen's fans brought up *The Blob* he denied that he was ever in it. Hard to do when the darn thing was always being shown somewhere on the TV late show. Once in a while, Steve expressed pride; for the first time on screen, McQueen displayed his trademark scowling broodiness. When *The Blob* hit the theaters, he knew he was on his way. But mostly Steve had to laugh; man, it was crazy to be praised for playing a bug-eyed teen that ran around warning people about a giant man-eating pile of Jell-O.

Bad Movie, Good Money

Fifty-four-year-old Michael Caine turned down a chance to receive an Oscar in person, when he agreed to star in the 1987 clunker *Jaws: The Revenge*. The third sequel, generated by the 1975 classic *Jaws*, about a man-eating shark that answered the dinner bell every time someone went swimming, reached a new low in ridiculousness. The thirty-foot fake-looking beast somehow swam thirteen hundred miles from Cape Cod to the Bahamas in three days, so he could intercept the family he was dedicated to feed on. One mercifully discarded plot point had the great fish under the control of a voodoo doctor. Filming in the Bahamas forced Michael to miss the Academy Award ceremonies where he won the Best Supporting Actor award for *Hannah and Her Sisters*. When asked about *Jaws: The Revenge*, the British-born actor claimed that he had never seen it, but he was certain it was terrible. But Michael had seen the house that his paycheck from the movie helped him build, and it was wonderful.

Extra: When Michael Caine was a struggling actor, he sometimes met very wealthy people. They would tell him, "Michael, being rich doesn't make you happy."

After Caine became a well-to-do movie star, he concluded that those people were wrong!

The Wolf Man's Temper

Lon Chaney Jr. mystified employees at Universal Studios with his wild mood swings, when he played the title role in the 1941 horror classic *The Wolf Man*. The thirty-five-year-old actor would go from pleasantly chatting with a crew member to sneaking up behind an actress and grabbing her with his hairy claws, causing his victim to scream in fright. Or Chaney could destroy dressing rooms by suddenly challenging drinking buddies to shin kicking contests. Some of Lon's friends speculated that the former plumber was bitter that his first wife had left him; others thought that Chaney Jr. feared he'd never live up to the acting pedigree of his famous father. Lon's personal demons seemed to aid his performance; *The Wolf Man* was a huge hit. Years later, one of his co-stars gave a mundane explanation for Junior's behavior: "Lon was a nice guy, but when he was stuck in the wolf costume the only things he could eat were liquids with a straw, and when his back was turned we spiked them with hot peppers."

Extra: Known as "The Man of a Thousand Faces," silent film star Lon Chaney Sr. (1883-1930) excelled at applying his own make-up, which made him virtually unrecognizable. Chaney once stated that he didn't exist in between his pictures. He was especially skilled at portraying characters that were crippled, which required him to slither on the ground while making painful body contortions. In the 1920s, there was a saying, "Don't step on it, it may be Lon Chaney."

The Monster's Back-Up Plan

Forty-four-year-old Boris Karloff had a good reason to defy his bosses when he played the monster in the 1931 horror classic *Frankenstein*. The British-born actor had been ordered to stay hidden at Universal Studios; Boris's bosses assumed that the sight of him would be too traumatic for their pregnant secretaries. There was also the publicity value of not showing himself till the picture opened. Karloff, who had known unemployment and starvation, was happy for the job even if it meant eighteen-hour hot days in sixty pounds of padding and makeup. He expected *Frankenstein* to be a hit, but tonight the former ditch digger was working on his backup plan; he needed to eat in case the movie career didn't work out. They had finished working late; Boris hadn't had time to remove the costume. No one recorded how many Los Angeles drivers hit the brakes when they saw a seven-foot tall creature planting vegetables in his garden.

Extra: Some historians claimed that author Mary Shelley's (1797-1851) horrifying 1818 novel *Frankenstein* was based on the work of Johann Konrad Dippel (1673-1734). The theory was controversial; there was no proof that the German-born alchemist Dippel robbed graves or was thrown out of his village for boiling cadavers in order to reanimate them. Another unlikely rumor stated that Johann blew up a tower in 1734 using nitroglycerin; the explosive chemical wasn't even synthesized until 1847. Many scholars disputed claims that the British-born Shelly had any knowledge of the legends surrounding Dippel when she wrote her book. In the summer of 1817, Mary had been on her way to Lake Geneva and could have stopped to visit Dippel's birthplace, but it rained so ferociously that more likely she passed by without seeing it. The young writer later claimed that both her frightening story and its title came to her in a waking dream; it was just a coincidence that Dippel's real-life family home, where he conducted his experiments, was called Castle Frankenstein.

Screaming Success at the Box Office

The absence of gore in the 1996 comic thriller *Scream* caused fear behind the scenes. Screenwriter Kevin Williamson crafted a clever tale about teenagers who followed slasher movie rules to evade a deadly disguised maniac. Shortly after shooting began, the producers fretted that *Scream's* parody elements were overshadowing the film's suspense. The killer's ghost face mask looked like a joke in the early footage. Executives also worried about their only name actress, Drew Barrymore, getting bumped off at the beginning of the story. Sure it raised the stakes by showing all the characters were vulnerable, but was Barrymore's early demise worth alienating her fans? The cast and crew comforted their bosses by increasing the blood splattering and the body count. Released at Christmas time against Oscar-nominated competition, *Scream's* tongue-in-cheek approach delighted horror buffs, who helped turn the low-budget picture into the surprise hit of the year.

Extra: A movie star's job is usually 5 percent acting and 95 percent promoting. Shortly after twenty-one-year-old Drew Barrymore agreed to play the heroine in *Scream*, the actress had a change of heart. Drew suggested that the movie would be more exciting if she was killed right away. The reluctant producers consented only after Barrymore promised she would fully push their product on talk shows and press interviews.

Let's Do Lunch

A lunch with Arnold Schwarzenegger caused James Cameron to change his opinion about casting for the 1984 sci-fi thriller, *The Terminator*. The thirty-year-old director disagreed with his bosses that Arnold was the right man to play the film's hero, who goes up against a homicidal robot. Cameron planned to insult the Austrian bodybuilder and end the work relationship before it started. But the thirty-seven-year-old Schwarzenegger was charming, suggested some great ideas for the movie and had muscles rippling beneath his shirt; might as well be nice or the famed weightlifter could break him like a twig. It was bad enough that James had no money on him and Arnold had to pick up the tab. Maybe Schwarzenegger could play the Terminator; it made more sense than the producers' other suggestion. The filmmaker wondered how anyone in their right mind could see former football star O.J. Simpson as a killer.

PART THREE

OSCAR TALES

"That statue looks just like my Uncle Oscar."
— Margaret Herrick (1902-1971), the Academy's chief librarian
who supposedly gave the award its nickname.

"And the winner is . . ."
— Kirk Douglas, being politically incorrect at the 2003 Academy Award
ceremony. He was supposed to say, "And the Oscar goes to . . ."

Jack Wasn't Rude

Director James Brooks faced a casting challenge before he could start filming the 1997 comedy *As Good as It Gets*. Who would star as the rude, obsessive-compulsive, bigoted novelist that redeems himself when he falls in love with a single-mom waitress? Brooks flirted with hiring Jim Carrey, but ultimately chose Jack Nicholson as the only actor in Hollywood who could be totally obnoxious, yet get the audience's sympathy. The sixty-year-old Nicholson surprised himself by winning his third Oscar; at one point during the shoot, he felt he wasn't doing a good job and asked Brooks to replace him. After the award ceremonies, Jack was asked if he was similar to his character. The New Jersey-born Nicholson took umbrage to the question; of course he was polite, just as his mother raised him to be. "Naw, rudeness is for amateurs. I prefer going right from polite conversation to extreme violence."

Extra: Thirty-three-year-old Dennis Hopper had been given $500K to direct and star in the 1969 hippie biker movie *Easy Rider*. Rip Torn, five years older than Hopper, was cast in *Easy Rider* as an alcoholic Texas lawyer. Torn, who later played a cantankerous wheelchair-bound coach in the 2004 comedy *Dodgeball: A True Underdog Story*, thought his *Rider* character was underwritten, and after a nasty verbal altercation with Hopper, walked off the movie. Into the fray stepped the little-known, thirty-two-year-old Jack Nicholson, who after appearing in fourteen low-budget movies had been unable to make his car payments. As far as Jack was concerned, he was done with acting; from now on he would write and direct. But *Easy Rider's* producers, as a personal favor, asked him to replace Rip Torn and go in front of the camera one last time. "Watch Dennis, make sure he doesn't blow our money or kill Peter Fonda." (The twenty-nine-year-old Fonda co-starred in and co-produced *Easy Rider*, and at times tried to have the volatile Hopper fired.)

Jack proved to be a calming influence on the set; he kept Dennis in line with lots of inebriation. One morning the two men woke up in a tree, and they couldn't remember how they got there. The completed *Easy Rider* became a huge counter-culture hit, and the very surprised would-be-retiree Nicholson found himself catapulted into sudden superstardom.

Extra: In 1974, thirty-seven-year-old Jack Nicholson found out that the woman he believed to be his seventeen-years-older sister was actually his mother.

The All-American Awards

When the Academy Awards began in 1929, there were bigger values in Hollywood than cutthroat competition. Filmed on location in New York City, MGM's *The Crowd* told the story of a New Yorker who toiled away his life in a large, impersonal office and then ended up in obscurity. The film was considered such a downer that theater owners were offered two different versions, either a realistic or happy ending. The somber movie looked like a sure thing to land the first Best Picture award, until its own studio boss campaigned against it. Louis B. Mayer, a former junk dealer who had risen up to be the most powerful man in the picture industry, argued for less insulting themes on screen. It wasn't America's fault if *The Crowd's* main character lacked the drive and ambition to become successful. The winner instead was *Wings*, from rival studio Paramount, which celebrated World War One flying aces, and met with the Russian-born Mayer's approval.

Extra: The filming of *Wings* (1927) was anything but smooth. Director William Wellman (1896-1975) was fired by angry investors for going over budget, and then rehired when they realized it would cost more to start the picture over again from scratch. On location in San Antonio, the director and crew spent hours getting ready to recreate a brutal World War I battle. Minutes before the scene was to be shot, Wellman stood in a high-observation tower alongside a city official and his young daughter. The little girl recognized a school chum from the crowd below, excitedly picked up Wellman's red handkerchief and started waving it so her friend would see her. Two thousand extras, brandishing guns and swords, charged into the fray before the cameras were in place.

Louis B. Mayer's Consolation Prize

The Academy Awards were started for want of a house. In 1926, the boss of Metro-Goldwyn-Mayer, Louis B. Mayer, assigned his set builders to construct his new beach home in Santa Monica. The mogul was miffed when his employees rebuffed him; the extra-curricular job violated their union rules.

Mayer became concerned that Hollywood's non-organized actors, writers and directors would follow suit and start their own labor guilds. Louis formed the Academy of Motion Picture Arts and Sciences as an arbitration board to settle disputes between management and workers. The new association would also give out annual special awards for achievements in the motion-picture industry; Louis theorized that arranging a competition for arrogant filmmakers to win medals was the best way to keep them in line. Eventually, the Hollywood artists became organized, despite Mayer's best efforts.

In the long run, the tycoon may have been lucky his ocean residence was put together by someone else. A few years earlier, the very thrifty Charlie Chaplin enlisted his own lowly paid studio carpenters to build his Beverly Hills mansion. They were used to erecting temporary structures, and the "Little Tramp's" new palatial residence sometimes fell apart from the inside.

Acting out Frustrations

In 1994, roommates Ben Affleck and Matt Damon found themselves in the same boat with thousands of unemployed, twenty-something actors living in LA: no good parts being offered and too much time on their hands. The two Boston grammar school buddies decided to create jobs for themselves in the movie business. They dug out an unproduced play Damon wrote when he attended Harvard, about a genius janitor named Will Hunting, and extended it into a screenplay. More comfortable performing than writing, Ben and Matt physically played out their ideas before they put them down on paper. Over four years, they paired down a messy one-thousand-page government-espionage thriller into a simple tale of rich human relationships. After several rejections, Miramax Films green-lit the script with its two little-known authors cast in leading roles. *Good Will Hunting* won the Oscar for Best Original Screenplay in 1997, and Affleck and Damon became so-called overnight successes. They were thrilled and grateful, but still complained about their choice of projects. Damon cheerfully noted that once you become famous, studio executives send you old scripts other film stars turned down twenty years ago.

Extra: Twenty-four-year-old Matt Damon and his two-years-younger buddy, Ben Affleck, struggled mightily to stay attached to the *Good Will Hunting* script, after they sold it in 1994. The guys quickly burned their entire six-hundred-thousand-dollar fee, mostly on video games, matching Jeep Cherokees, and all-night poker parties. Meanwhile, *Hunting* sat on the shelf at Castle Rock Entertainment. Affleck and Damon wrote new drafts of the screenplay, adding obscene sex scenes just to get a reaction from the executives who held their project in limbo; they were ignored. Finally, the movie was put in turnaround (a Hollywood term meaning screenwriters can take their script to a second buyer; the first purchaser gets compensated for their development costs. A screenplay in turnaround is generally thought not to be very good) and *Good Will Hunting* was picked up by Miramax Films. The movie was finally good to go after a major star, forty-three-year-old Robin Williams, agreed to work with the two unknowns. (Williams won an Oscar for playing a washed-up shrink who helps Damon's Will Hunting take full advantage of his math skills.) Even after filming started, there was a failed attempt by one of *Good Will's* producers to have the script rewritten, and to fire Ben and Matt.

Beauty and the Jerk

Walt Disney tried and failed many times to adapt the 1756 French short story *Beauty and the Beast* into an animated movie. He could never figure out what to show on screen when Belle and the transformed prince were trapped in the castle. But in 1991, lyricist Howard Ashman suggested giving voices and personalities to the enchanted inanimate objects, such as the candlestick and the teapot. The results were a delightful, Academy Award-nominated hit. The producers were extremely proud that the monstrous Beast was shown to be a noble hero, while the handsome, arrogant Gaston, based on the shallow jerks that sometimes inhabit the L.A. dating scene, was the villain of the piece. They knew their goal was accomplished at *Beauty and the Beast's* Hollywood premiere, when a girl in the front row said of Gaston, "Oh please, I just broke up with him!"

Under the Freezing Moon

Director Norman Jewison felt the moon was a powerful symbol of love that could magically affect all our lives. His romantic notion was displayed on screen in the 1987 comedy *Moonstruck*, starring Cher as a conflicted Italian bookkeeper who must choose between two brothers as potential suitors. For the sixty-one-year-old Jewison, who was going through a new romance in his own life, the whole production was pure poetry. However, his forty-one-year-old leading lady, exhausted after making three films that year, was less sentimental. Jewison pushed the reluctant Cher, who wore a light dress and high heels, into doing one of the film's big scenes outside at three in the morning. The freezing-cold Brooklyn night caused her physical pain and made her cry, which added to her character's anguish over betraying the man she was promised to, and helped Cher win the Academy Award for Best Actress.

Titanic Undertaking

James Cameron pushed the motion-picture industry into new levels of spending when he made the two-hundred-million-dollar epic *Titanic* in 1997. The forty-three-year-old director's attention to the authentic details of the doomed ocean liner, that had struck an iceberg and sunk in 1912, had caused his already expensive production to go way over budget. The executives at 20th Century Fox suggested cutting certain scenes, then relented when the volatile former truck driver Cameron threatened to walk off the picture. Despite a few critics' complaints that *Titanic* was overlong, schlocky and historically inaccurate, the tragic love story took in a staggering $1.7 billion at the box office, and tied the 1959 Roman saga *Ben-Hur* with a record eleven Oscars. James's bosses were more relieved than euphoric, figuring they had dodged a financial bullet. Meanwhile, the self-proclaimed "King of the World" declared that high costs for pictures were here to stay. "Listen, we need to raise ticket prices by five bucks. People would be mad for six months and then come back to the theaters." Cameron paused. "Of course I wouldn't want one of my movies to come out during those six months."

Extra: James Cameron both joked about and justified putting Marxist theory into *Titanic*. The director pointed to statistics; there were many more deaths amongst the less well-to-do people in the lower berths. But there was no hard evidence that on the real-life ship the passengers in third class were deliberately blocked from reaching the upper decks, or that the wealthy bribed their way to safety. The emphasis was on rescuing the women and children. The richest man onboard the ship, real estate builder John Jacob Astor (1864-1912, played in the movie by fifty-six-year-old German-born actor Eric Braeden) died after making sure his pregnant wife was safe in one of the lifeboats. (Astor asked to go along due to her delicate condition, but he was denied.) Third-class women had a greater survival rate on the Titanic than first-class men.

Extra: During the filming of *Titanic*, James Cameron saved most of his screaming for the film crew. His philosophy was you couldn't get great performances out of the actors by yelling at them. In one sequence, Kate Winslet couldn't get away from a huge wave, was submerged underwater and nearly drowned. Moments after the twenty-three-year-old leading lady was rescued, Cameron calmly said, "OK. Let's do it again."

Extra: James Cameron's initial pitch for *Titanic* to the nervous executives at 20th Century Fox was, "Romeo and Juliet on a doomed ship." There was a tense pause and Cameron said, "Also, fellas, it's a period piece, it's going to cost $150,000,000 and there's not going to be a sequel."

Extra: For a major Hollywood production, *Titanic's* star salaries were relatively low. Twenty-four-year-old Leonardo DiCaprio made the most at $2.5 million. The biggest expense of the film was building the ship; it required the construction of an entirely new studio in Rosarito Beach. Cameron's attention to historical detail was evident down to the replicas of the original woven carpets, the grand staircase, the Picasso paintings and the 1911 touring car that Jack and Rose made love in. When the costs really began to mount, a contrite Cameron stated he was willing to forfeit his share of the profits. James's bosses dismissed his offer as an empty gesture; they were sure there wouldn't be any profits. The executives' decision turned out to be a $100 million miscalculation. (Once the movie became the biggest hit ever, Fox probably would have reinstated Cameron's bonus anyway.)

Stung by the Critics

The Gondorf brothers were two real-life con men who fleeced rich marks out of fifteen million dollars between 1906 and 1915. Their antics inspired the 1973 film *The Sting*, which re-teamed Paul Newman and Robert Redford after their great success in the 1969 comedy western *Butch Cassidy and the Sundance Kid* The stylish *Sting* hooked the audience and set up an Academy Award Best Picture victory, but many critics felt they had been scammed by an unimportant, formula story designed to recycle the two stars' previous movie. The thirty-six-year-old Redford angrily defended *The Sting*, pointing out that he had very few scenes with the twelve-years-older Newman. Their relationship was more pupil-teacher than the buddy-buddy equals they had been in *Butch Cassidy*. Couldn't a film be relevant just by entertaining people? Ironically, Redford didn't see *The Sting* until 2004, thirty-one years after its release.

Extra: The Gondorf brothers, Fred and Charley, helped originate one of the classic con jobs of all time. They placed "For Sale" signs around the Brooklyn

Bridge and made hundreds of dollars (a ton of money at the beginning of the twentieth century) from gullible buyers.

Extra: Paul Newman (1925-2008) and Robert Redford began a friendly, yet competitive relationship when they costarred in *Butch Cassidy and the Sundance Kid* (1969). Newman stood up for his new friend when some studio executives wanted to replace Redford with someone better known. Four years later, the older star was reticent about playing Redford's con man teacher in *The Sting*. By then Redford had equaled him in fame and made wisecracks about Newman's age; in return, the very punctual Paul ripped Redford for constantly being late to the set. After their two incredibly successful pictures, Newman and Redford became neighbors in Connecticut and their families socialized regularly. They shared a love of liberal politics, philanthropic causes and a desire to top each other with wild practical jokes. (Redford, who thought Newman's love of racing was boring, once went to a junkyard, bought a damaged sports car and had it delivered to Paul wrapped in a blue ribbon. A few weeks later, Robert's "present" was molded down into a very ugly garden sculpture and returned to him.) The two superstars were friends until Newman's death, stayed linked to each other in many cinemagoers' minds, and never acted together in another movie.

The Improbable Sensei

Fifty-two-year-old Pat Morita's Hollywood career was on life support when he landed the role of Mr. Miyagi in the 1984 movie *The Karate Kid*. His co-star Ralph Macchio, who had expected to work with a more physically imposing actor, compared his little sensei to Yoda, the tiny Jedi Master from the *Star Wars* series. Morita, an invalid as a child, found the grueling Karate training sessions interfered with his morning diet of cigarettes, coffee and Grand Marnier. With no reference in the script, the former standup comic suggested that Miyagi be a World War II veteran whose family was killed to explain an uncharacteristic drunken rant. Very convincing as a wise old teacher, Pat found himself in a surprise hit, established a life-long friendship with Macchio and was nominated for an Oscar. After years of feeling like a personal and professional screw-up, Morita was amazed by fans who stopped him in the street to seek advice about life.

Extra: Pat Morita (1932-2005) suggested that his *Karate Kid* character be a veteran of the 442nd Infantry Regiment in World War II. After Japan's attack on

Pearl Harbor in 1941, second-generation Japanese Americans, or Nisei, trained for military service in Hawaii. Two-thirds of the units were island locals who displayed some Mr. Miyagi-like characteristics. They averaged five foot three and 125 pounds, often drank, usually dressed casually, liked to gamble and sing, and spoke Pidgin English. The islanders got into several fights with their more serious counterparts, who came from other states. As far as the locals were concerned, the well-spoken mainlanders were a bunch of stuck-up jerks. The army considered disbanding the unit, then, in a desperate move to change attitudes, ordered the new troops to visit a Japanese internment center in Arkansas. The Hawaiians, many of whom had never left home, arrived in the mainland wearing aloha shirts and grass skirts as they played their ukuleles. Their lighthearted mood ended when they saw whole families, many of whom had been uprooted from their homes, incarcerated behind barbed wire or buried in camp graveyards. The Hawaiians realized that their stateside comrades' attitudes were due to worries over their imprisoned loved ones. The battling factions banded together, fought valiantly in Europe and became the most highly decorated combat force in US military history, up until that time.

Extra: Right before Pearl Harbor, the majority of gardeners, butlers and chauffeurs who worked for movie stars were of Japanese descent. Gasoline rationing in World War II, combined with domestic staffs being sent off to internment camps, left many well-to-do residents living in expensive mansions high up in Bel Air and Beverly Hills, feeling isolated and trapped.

Extra: A former child invalid who spent time in a Japanese internment camp, the financially struggling Pat Morita was about to lose his house when he got the Mr. Miyagi role. He loved his sensei character but claimed karate didn't make any sense. "Why would you want to chop a brick in half? Better to leave it intact, pick it up and smash your enemy in the head."

Patton was Overwhelming

Karl Malden worried that he would be overwhelmed by supporting George C. Scott who played the title role in the 1970 World War II classic *Patton*. Right before filming started, the fifty-eight-year-old Malden paid a visit to Omar Bradley, the real-life general he would depict on screen. Why was Bradley so soft spoken when the lower-ranked Patton carried on with his controversial antics? Perhaps in the film it would be more realistic if Karl lost his temper with Scott in their shared scenes. The retired army man quietly responded that the extra star on his helmet meant he never had to raise his voice. Malden was low key throughout the picture, allowing his fellow actor to dominate with an unforgettable, Academy Award-winning performance. After Bradley saw the completed movie, he told Malden that it would have been an honor to serve under General George C. Scott.

Extra: The movie *Patton* showed the general slapping a battle-fatigued soldier, then being forced to humble himself in front of his men, who are eager to see him humiliated. In real life, George S. Patton (1885-1945), after finding out the man he hit was truly shell-shocked, deeply regretted his action. Afterward, General Dwight D. Eisenhower (1890-1969) ordered Patton to apologize to his troops. Patton stood in front of three thousand soldiers who cheered wildly each time he opened his mouth. After several minutes of not being able to get any words out, the commanding officer's eyes welled up in tears. "The hell with it!" he said and walked away, never making a statement.

Extra: George C. Scott (1927-1999) felt his Oscar-winning performance as George S. Patton didn't capture the complexity of the man. Scott refused to shoot the film's opening, which required him to speak to his troops while standing in front of an American flag. The actor felt the stirring text, which was a compilation of real-life Patton speeches, would overshadow the rest of his performance. The leading man relented only after director Franklin J. Schaffner (1920-1989) lied to him that the sequence would be placed at the end. Both current and former servicemen, who went to see *Patton* in darkened movie theaters, were overwhelmed with emotion at their first sight of Scott in uniform. When an off-screen voice said, "Ten Hut!" some of them stood up and saluted.

Doris Helped Rock

Thirty-five-year-old Doris Day got her career back on track when she was paired with Rock Hudson in the 1959 romantic comedy *Pillow Talk*. After making several bland musicals, Day found playing a virtuous single woman, who shares her phone line with a cad, a refreshing change. The thirty-four-year-old Hudson had been a fan of Day's since he served in the Navy during World War II; as he sailed out of San Francisco, toward an uncertain future, listening to the ex-band singer's records had driven him and his shipmates to tears. In person, Doris's bubbly personality and impeccable timing helped the dramatic actor get over his fear of comedy. Day's performance in *Pillow Talk* became the butt of jokes; various comedians claimed that they knew her before she was a virgin. But the public embraced her new wholesome image; Doris was nominated for an Oscar and became the biggest box-office draw in the United States.

Schindler's Oscar

After coming up short three times, Steven Spielberg finally took home the Best Director Oscar for *Schindler's List* in 1993. The forty-seven-year-old had delayed filming the Holocaust story for ten years, thinking he could not do it justice. Spielberg had been uncertain of *Schindler's* financial prospects and had taken no pay. During production, Steven had gotten depressed by the dark subject matter; several times, he had called his buddy, Robin Williams, long distance from Poland, asking the famed comedian to cheer him up by performing monologues over the phone. And now, for the first time in his life, Spielberg held an actual Oscar statue in his hand. A reporter asked the moviemaker whether he was disappointed that his leading man Liam Neeson had not won for his outstanding performance as Oskar Schindler. "Of course not, Liam should just be happy to have such a great role."

How then would Spielberg have felt if he hadn't won? Clutching his statue like a newborn, the director smiled and admitted he would have been crushed.

Extra: The climactic scene in *Schindler's List* involved the title character, played by forty-one-year-old Liam Neeson, breaking down and crying because he did not do enough to save Jews from concentration camps. In real life, opportunistic German businessman and Nazi Party member Oskar Schindler (1908-1974) initially cut down on costs in 1939 by hiring forced Jewish Labor to work at his Poland-based enamelware plant. Schindler lived well and socialized with powerful SS (Nazi Party "Shield Squadron," which were responsible for many crimes against humanity) leaders. Oskar became appalled in 1943 when some members of his staff were murdered by German soldiers. From then on, he used stealth, charm and bribery to save eleven hundred downtrodden employees and their families from certain death. When Schindler took over an abandoned munitions plant in Czechoslovakia, he persuaded friends in the High German Command to let him take all his workers with him. Oskar's labor force produced no weapons to help Hitler win the war; the whole enterprise was designed to keep his personnel out of gas chambers. In 1945, Schindler, to avoid capture by the Allied Army, quietly left his factory disguised as a Jewish prisoner, without displaying any histrionics. The ex-millionaire's heroism cost him nearly every penny he had made, and he died bankrupt.

Francis Ford Coppola Redux

Francis Ford Coppola once joked that the only way he would do a second *Godfather* film was to do "Abbott and Costello Meet the Godfather". The always unconventional director insisted that the 1974 sequel switch back and forth between the new Michael Corleone saga, starring Al Pacino, and the old world tale showing the rise of the young Robin Hood-like Vito Corleone, played by Robert De Niro. When preview audiences became confused by the dual narrative and complained the film jumped around too quickly, Francis resisted suggestions from worried Paramount Studios' executives to dump De Niro's scenes. He chose instead to make the segments longer so viewers would become more emotionally involved with the two stories. *The Godfather Part II* opened to lukewarm reviews but after a few months, opinions changed. Coppola was astonished when he won Oscars for directing and screenwriting, and was praised for his artistic courage.

Extra: When Francis Ford Coppola directed the original *Godfather* in 1972, he wanted twenty-nine-year-old Robert De Niro to play the hotheaded Sonny Corleone. But the three-years-younger Al Pacino, Coppola's choice for the role of Sonny's younger brother Michael, was not winning any fans at Paramount Studios. Al inspired no confidence among the suits when he avoided eye contact in meetings and stared at the floor. Fearing that Pacino would be blown off the screen, the regretful Coppola decided not to hire De Niro for the first film.

Famous and Unnoticed

Without fanfare, Samuel Leroy Jackson of Chattanooga, Tennessee, became the highest grossing actor in cinema box office history. His Oscar-nominated turn as a philosophical, Jheri-curled gangster in the 1994 crime drama *Pulp Fiction* brought the forty-six-year-old to the attention of both executives and moviegoers. While other stars would insist on huge salaries and top billing, Jackson would take on small roles if he thought the films worthy. He could be counted on to come to work without an entourage or a prima donna attitude. By 2005, the sheer volume of his appearances on screen allowed him to surpass Harrison Ford in ticket sales, yet Jackson still remained under many people's radars. One time Samuel was at a public event with his good friend, actor Laurence Fishburne. A woman politely approached Fishburne for an autograph and with Jackson standing right there told Lawrence, "I loved you in *Pulp Fiction!*"

Extra: Thirty-one-year-old director Quentin Tarantino was determined to have specific actors in *Pulp Fiction* (1994). Forty-six-year-old Samuel Jackson had previously auditioned for Tarantino's earlier crime thriller, *Reservoir Dogs* (1992). He didn't get the part, but Quentin promised Sam another role, which he wrote for him in *Pulp*. The filmmaker also went all out to land Uma Thurman for *Pulp Fiction's* drug-taking mob boss's girlfriend. After the twenty-four-year-old actress initially turned him down, Tarantino got Thurman to agree to work for him by reading Uma's lines to her over the phone. But the biggest prize for Quentin was getting forty-year-old John Travolta to play the ill-fated hit man, Vincent Vega. After receiving the *Pulp Fiction* script, Travolta, who had just come off a string of box-office flops, was invited to Tarantino's West Hollywood apartment. When the puzzled star arrived, he said, "You know, Quentin, this place seems familiar. My God, I think I used to live here."

"I know, man, that's why I moved in! I'm your biggest fan!"

The very flattered Travolta agreed to do what turned out to be his comeback movie for well below his normal fee, and was nominated for an Oscar.

By My Beard

Director Norman Jewison literally pulled his hair out when he chose the little-known Topol to star in the 1971 musical *Fiddler on the Roof*. Stuck for months on location in Communist Yugoslavia, the Israeli actor and soldier suffered through a horrible toothache, and openly cried about being separated from his family. Topol's sentimentality perfectly fit the role of a loving father who accepts his daughters' untraditional choices of husbands. The stressed-out Jewison, who worried that people would not buy a film where the characters burst into song, would often find himself smiling at Topol when he completed one of his on-camera monologues. *Fiddler* was a huge hit and Topol's Oscar-nominated performance was even more appreciated when people found out he was only thirty-five. His much older look in the movie was achieved by Jewison tearing white hairs out of his beard, and pasting them to his leading man's eyebrows.

Extra: *Fiddler on the Roof* takes place in 1905 and shows the violent Russian anti-Semitic pogroms, or riots, that took place under the harsh rule of Tsar (meaning monarch) Nicholas II (1868-1918). Many of the Russian Jews fled to the United States, and a few of the exiles entered and rose to the top of the fledging film industry. Shortly after "Bloody Nicholas" was overthrown during the 1917 Russian Revolution, he was sent a cable by movie mogul Lewis J.

Selznick (1870-1933). The tycoon stated that he bore the former ruler no hard feelings for the mistreatment that the Selznick family had suffered at the hands of Nicholas's policemen when Lewis was a boy. In fact, Selznick had prospered in America, and now was in a position to hire the out-of-work ex-Tsar to act in movies. Unfortunately, the imprisoned Nicholas and his family were killed by the Bolsheviks (Marxist revolutionaries) before he could reply.

Roommates

Two former New York roommates, Gene Hackman and Dustin Hoffman, each won Oscars. The soft-spoken forty-one-year-old Hackman got the role of a violent drug-busting cop in the 1971 thriller *The French Connection*, after five other potential leading men turned it down. Gene prepared by going on patrols with real policemen in New York City; at one point, Hackman, who was sickened by seeing the underworld up close, physically detained a suspect. The forty-two-year-old Dustin Hoffman had criticized the award process when he won as a divorced dad in *Kramer vs. Kramer* in 1979, then was thrilled to get a statue for his turn as an idiot savant in *Rain Man*, nine years later. Both Hoffman and Hackman could look back and laugh at their struggling younger days when they followed producers into bathrooms, slid their photo headshots under the stall doors and then ran away.

Extra: After Meryl Streep took the role of the husband-leaving, child-abandoning wife and mother in *Kramer vs. Kramer* (1979), she expressed distaste for her leading man. The thirty-one-year-old actress told the story of how he approached her at an audition, burped, grabbed her breast and said, "Hi, I'm Dustin Hoffman."

Like his divorced dad character, Hoffman had a closer relationship during filming with eight-year-old Justin Henry, the actor who played his son, than with his make-believe wife. In a tense restaurant scene where Mrs. Kramer tells her ex that she intends to get custody of their child, Hoffman angrily felt that Streep, who made nervous mannerisms with her hands, was trying to upstage him. Dustin improvised by smashing a glass of wine against the wall. Meryl reacted fearfully on camera, and both actors ended up in the winner's circle on Oscar night.

"I Die?"

Many movie actors focus on their own parts to the exclusion of anything else in the script. Sessue Hayakawa was perfectly cast as the brutal prisoner of war commandant opposite Alec Guinness playing the captured, somewhat mad, Colonel Nicholson in the 1957 drama *The Bridge on the River Kwai*. After several months of filming, in the blazing Sri Lanka sun, it came time to shoot the climactic scene. When director David Lean called action, Alec Guinness walked toward his fate, while Hayakawa stood still.

"Sessue, follow him!" said Lean.

"Follow?"

"Yes, your character follows him and then he dies."

The sixty-eight-year-old actor, who had been a big star in the silent film days, was startled. "I die?"

Hayakawa had only bothered to learn his own dialogue, and ripped out the rest of the pages in the screenplay. Sessue's bewildered expression was perfect for the moment, and he got nominated for an Oscar.

Extra: Born in Japan, young Sessue Hayakawa (1890-1973) planned to be a naval officer. At the age of seventeen, a friend dared him to swim to the bottom of a lagoon, and he ended up with a punctured eardrum. Disqualified from military service, Sessue was made aware of the great shame he'd brought upon the Hayakawa family and tried to commit seppuku. A barking dog outside the garden shack, where Sessue was stabbing himself, alerted his father in time to save his bleeding son's life.

Extra: Sessue's second career choice was to be a banker; he enrolled at the University of Chicago to study political economics. Always a man of multiple interests, Hayakawa became the quarterback of his school's football team. He once was penalized for knocking down one of the opposing players using jujitsu.

Extra: In 1914, on a trip to Los Angeles, Sessue became intrigued by acting, and was seen on stage by movie producer Thomas Ince (1882-1924). The mogul offered the young man a job in pictures. Sessue thought the idea ridiculous. He still planned to be a banker and tried to get rid of Ince by saying he'd only do movie work for the vast sum of five hundred dollars a week. The inexperienced performer was shocked when his price was met.

Extra: In the 1917 western *The Jaguar's Claws,* Sessue played a Mexican bandit. Five hundred cowboy extras got drunk on the Mojave Desert set and were unable to work. The frustrated five-foot-eight actor challenged all of them to a fight. Two big, burly types took Sessue up on it and were soundly thrashed. The other men, full of newfound respect for their co-worker, performed their jobs from then on without incident.

Extra: By 1919, Sessue became one of the most popular stars in the world and was making two million dollars a year. Women swooned at Hawakaya's dashing good looks, while critics praised his minimalist acting style. The young sex symbol drove a Pierce-Arrow, built a huge castle in Hollywood and threw lavish parties where the booze flowed. At a time when Americans commonly used the phrase "The Yellow Peril," which referred to fears of Asian immigrants taking away jobs and the expansion of the Japanese military, Sessue's fame rivaled that of Charlie Chaplin and Douglas Fairbanks.

Extra: Bad business deals, huge gambling losses, plus a lack of success in talking movies drove Hawakaya temporarily off the public's radar. In 1940, the traveling artist found himself trapped in German-occupied France. For the next few years, he made his living by selling water colors. Later, the American Consulate investigated Sessue's activities during World War II and discovered that he had secretly joined the French underground resistance and aided Allied flyers.

Extra: Most people who worked with Sessue in his later years remembered him as a gentleman of few words. Some stated that he spoke English perfectly, while others said the actor was forgetful, monosyllabic and had to learn his lines phonetically. The married Sessue often traveled with two beautiful Japanese ladies that attended to his every need. A few years after Hawakaya was Oscar-nominated for *Bridge on the River Kwai* (1957), he became a Zen priest and returned to Japan. He eventually retired from films to teach drama.

Extra: The real Bridge on the River Kwai was part of the Burma Siam Railway, pushed by Japan to fortify their occupation of Burma in 1943. Its construction resulted in the deaths of thirteen thousand prisoners of war. Director David Lean (1908-1991) considered an accurate depiction of the structure's history far too brutal to show on screen.

Extra: Alec Guinness' (1914-2000) Colonel Nicholson character in *The Bridge on the River Kwai* was based on senior Allied officer Philip Toosey (1904-1975). In actuality, Toosey did everything he could not to cooperate with his Japanese captors. His acts of sabotage delayed the building of the real Bridge on the River Kwai. Some ex-POWs, who served with Toosey, were outraged when they saw how he was portrayed in the movie. It was pointed out that if a leader collaborated with the enemy like Colonel Nicholson did in *Bridge*, his own men would have quietly killed him.

The Backwoods Sudden Star

Raised in the Arkansas woods, forty-one-year-old Billy Bob Thornton felt like a loser before he wrote, directed and starred in the 1996 drama *Sling Blade*. The chronically unemployed Thornton had almost died of starvation, lost his house in a fire, and had come down with a mysterious heart ailment that no doctor could diagnose. One day Billy Bob was staring at his reflection in the mirror when he was drawn back into his childhood; Thornton imagined a super strong, mentally challenged outsider that became the central role in his film. With the help of friends who worked for nothing, Billy Bob completed his low-budget project, which made his spirits lift. Interviewers found him pleasant, colorful and thankfully free of his character's homicidal tendencies. *Sling Blade* became a surprise hit, took home the Oscar for best screenplay and turned its little-known leading man into one of Hollywood's most in-demand actors.

Gone With the Old Director

Olivia de Havilland was distraught when director George Cukor was fired from the 1939 classic *Gone with the Wind*. The twenty-three-year-old beauty fretted that her goody-two-shoes Melanie Wilkes character would be overwhelmed by co-star Vivien Leigh, as the fiery, temperamental Scarlett O'Hara. Cukor was a sensitive artist who understood women, unlike his macho replacement Victor Fleming. Olivia phoned the now unemployed filmmaker, who agreed to meet with her secretly. For the remainder of the shoot, unknown to her bosses, de Havilland's unpaid mentor advised her on the role. The fictional Melanie became a stronger woman who held her own with Scarlett onscreen, and Olivia was nominated for an Oscar. Only after filming finished did she find out that Vivien Leigh also paid clandestine visits to the same coach. The English actress thought Scarlett compared unfavorably to Melanie, and had asked for Cukor's help to make the charming Southern Belle a nicer person.

Extra: George Cukor (1899-1983) was replaced on *Gone with the Wind* by Victor Fleming (1889-1949). The new director had flown small planes while serving in World War I, raced cars and hunted tigers in India, which were all tame accomplishments compared to making the Civil War epic. Fleming decided that the movie needed to focus on the characters' reactions to the cataclysmic events and keep the bloody conflict in the background. Victor fought constantly with leading lady Vivien Leigh; at one point, she refused to do an important scene because her Scarlett character was too rotten. Clark Gable (1901-1960), who personally looked up to Fleming, was easier for Victor to get along with. However, when the script called for Gable's Rhett Butler to cry, the Hollywood he-man threatened to retire from his profession before he would do it. Both actors eventually completed their assignments, but the stressed-out Victor Fleming ended up hospitalized with a nervous breakdown and had to be replaced by Sam Wood (1883-1949), who finished the picture.

Extra: Right after Vivien Leigh (1913-1967) completed her last scene in *Gone with the Wind*, she went to audition for the leading female part in director Alfred Hitchcock's *Rebecca* (1940). After playing a strong and willful Civil War survivor, there was no way for Leigh to slip into being the timid second wife of a rich widower. George Cukor laughed at Vivien when he saw her *Rebecca* screen tests; by all accounts, she did poorly. A few months later, Leigh received an Oscar and thunderous acclaim for her performance as Scarlett.

Extra: The night of the 1939 Oscars, Olivia de Havilland was stunned when the Best Supporting Actress Award went to her *Gone with the Wind* co-star Hattie McDaniel (1895-1952). Olivia ran into the kitchen of the Biltmore Hotel where the ceremony was being held and started sobbing. Irene Mayer Selznick (1907-1990), the wife of *Gone with the Wind* producer David O. Selznick, followed her backstage and grabbed de Havilland's arm. "Listen, you'll have plenty of chances. Get out there and be gracious."

The actress dried her eyes, composed herself and went backstage smiling to congratulate McDaniel. Selznick was proven correct; de Havilland went on to win two Oscars. Meanwhile, Olivia's leading man was also crushed that night; Clark Gable as Rhett Butler lost to Robert Donat (1905-1958) who played a British school teacher in *Goodbye, Mr. Chips*. "Don't worry, Pa," Clark's actress wife Carole Lombard (1908-1942) said to him as they left the Biltmore. "Someday we'll have one of those statues on our mantle."

Gable, who'd given away the award he'd won five years earlier for *It Happened One Night,* shook his head. "No way, Ma. I can't take the disappointment. I'm never coming to one of these damn things again."

His spouse hit him on the arm. "You big jerk! I was talking about me."

All the Cohn's Men

Columbia Pictures head Harry Cohn argued with director Robert Rossen that the 1949 drama *All the King's Men* was not fit to be released. The bombastic mogul felt the adaptation of Robert Penn Warren's story, about a tyrannical politician, was unwatchable. The preview audiences were either leaving early or staying to the end to boo. As far as Cohn was concerned, the whole thing was a blankety-blank loser that should be shelved. Rossen defended his work while at the same time calling his boss foul names, which Harry respected; Cohn agreed to give Rossen more time to edit the picture. The filmmaker cut all but the most exciting part of each scene. Much to Cohn's surprise, the new and improved *King's* got outstanding reviews, did fine business, and won the Academy Award for Best Picture. The director later admitted that he instructed his Oscar-winning lead actor Broderick Crawford to base his gruff dictatorial candidate on Harry Cohn.

Ingrid Bergman Didn't Appreciate *Casablanca*

Throughout the filming of *Casablanca* in 1942, leading lady Ingrid Bergman felt she was working on a loser. The unfinished script gave her no clue as to which of her leading men she was supposed to be in love with: Humphrey Bogart, playing her ex-fiancé whom she jilted in Paris, or Paul Henreid, as the husband she mistakenly thought was dead. Play it in between, she was told. Bergman felt very little connection to Bogart; that *Casablanca* won the Academy Award for best picture made little impression on her. Other roles meant more, and for years Ingrid lamented that all anybody wants to talk about is "that thing I did with Bogart."

But in the late 1960s, Bergman was invited to a college retrospective of her films; she watched *Casablanca* with an enthusiastic young crowd. After the screening, Ingrid walked up to the podium and seemed surprised as she smiled at the audience and said, "Wow, that was a really good movie!"

Extra: Ingrid Bergman (1915-1982) was rumored to have had affairs with many of her leading men. Of her *Casablanca* co-star Humphrey Bogart (1899-

1957) the Swedish beauty said, "I kissed him, but I never really knew him." One possible reason for the lack of off-screen passion was Bogart's possessive and sometimes violent third wife, Mayo Methot (1904-1951), who watchfully stood behind the camera during her husband's love scenes.

Left-Wing Fortunes

As fame and fortune came to Peter O'Toole, he found it hard to maintain his left-wing leanings. In his youth, the Irish actor had been attracted to the Communist Party because he felt it understood the plight of the working man. Not only that, they had an excellent equity theater where he received valuable stage training. But at age twenty-eight, O'Toole broke through with his Oscar-nominated performance, playing acclaimed writer T. E. Lawrence in the 1962 drama *Lawrence of Arabia*. Suddenly, Peter found himself living in a mansion with lots of servants; like many new movie stars, he felt guilty. Once, before an important national election, he gave household staff instructions that they should all vote for the Socialist Party. Everyone agreed except his driver. "Sack me if you like, but I am a Conservative."

O'Toole admired the man's honesty and sent him off to the nearest polling station in the actor's Rolls Royce.

Extra: Peter O'Toole struggled to get through the role of legendary British writer and soldier T.E. Lawrence (1888-1935), who fought alongside Arab revolutionists against the Ottoman Turks in World War I. *Lawrence of Arabia* took so long to make that in one scene the Irish actor started walking down some stairs, and then aged a year before he reached the bottom. O'Toole was a heavy drinker, partly to relieve intestinal pain. On location in the Jordanian desert, alcohol was scarcely available, and at times it looked as if Peter would not make it through the *Lawrence* shoot. It didn't help his confidence that the director, David Lean, was a stern taskmaster and rarely complimented his cast for simply doing its job. After long, hard days spent in blistering desert heat without reassurance, the inexperienced O'Toole would beat himself up for doing bad work and considered walking off the picture. But although some critics found the completed film drawn out and boring, *Lawrence of Arabia* was generally well received with O'Toole getting an Oscar nomination for his performance. The new superstar laughed when writer Noel Coward (1899-1973) stated that if Peter looked any prettier on screen, the movie would have been called "Florence of Arabia".

Kirk Douglas's Lucrative Disappointment

Kirk Douglas dreamed of playing Randall Patrick McMurphy in the 1975 movie *One Flew Over the Cuckoo's Nest*. In 1962, the forty-six-year-old Douglas bought the rights to the novel about an irresponsible convict trying to evade prison in a mental institution. After *Cuckoo's Nest* flopped on Broadway, with Douglas in the lead role, Kirk tried to sell it to Hollywood. The studio executives thought he was nuts; who would pay to see a movie about lobotomies and electroshock therapy? After thirteen frustrating years, Kirk's actor-son Michael expressed interest in producing the property. The younger Douglas surprised his father by getting the four-million-dollar project financed, and then crushed him by telling him that at fifty-nine, Kirk had grown too old for the lead role. Watching Jack Nicholson give his Oscar-winning performance as McMurphy was one of the worst disappointments in Kirk's life, even though he earned far more money owning a piece of *Cuckoo's Nest* than he ever did being a movie star.

Please, No Autographs

Jane Fonda often found it difficult to reconcile her position as a movie star with her personal philosophy. At one point, the well-paid daughter of Henry Fonda deliberately chose to live in a rundown shack near a freeway. While delivering her Oscar-winning performance as a prostitute in the 1971 drama *Klute*, the thirty-four-year-old actress faced a moral dilemma. Her co-star and boyfriend, Donald Sutherland, showed her a letter from a fan requesting an autograph for his daughter. Fonda was adamant that he should not; an autograph would imply that movie actors are somehow superior to others. Did Donald want this girl to get the wrong impression? Sutherland bowed to Jane's wishes and wrote a detailed reply stating his reasons for refusing. The man wrote him back, "Dear Mr. Sutherland, thank you for your letter. We think you are full of it, but we ripped off your signature and gave it to our daughter."

Gardner's Mad Dash

Executives at MGM Studios worried about thirty-one-year-old Ava Gardner, on location in Africa, when she starred in the 1953 adventure film *Mogambo*. The North Carolina-born daughter of tobacco farmers was putting to rest the notion that she couldn't act; Ava was perfect as an uninhibited playgirl who falls for Clark Gable's big game hunter. But her off-screen antics were even more outrageous than her character's. Word had gotten back to her bosses that Gardner had lifted up the loincloth of an African tribesman, in order to show co-star Grace Kelly what was underneath. A letter was sent asking Ava to refrain from embarrassing Metro; she just smirked. Uh uh, honey. No way were a bunch of stuffed shirts going to stop her fun. Ava was nominated for an Oscar, and some Kenyan natives, used to living among wild animals, always remembered the untamed beauty who laughed and then ran naked through their village.

Extra: Clark Gable once said that Ava Gardner (1922-1990) was a great guy that played cards, drank whiskey and cursed like a sailor. He just happened to be trapped in the body of the world's most beautiful woman.

Don't Practice What You Preach

Warren Beatty was fired up to direct and star in the 1981 drama *Reds*, which told the story of John Reed, the founder of the American Communist Party. The forty-four-year-old sex symbol Beatty had scored big at the box office with the 1978 comedy *Heaven Can Wait*, and now wished to tackle much more serious subject matter. Leery of the politics, but wanting to be in the Warren Beatty business, Paramount Studios' executives reluctantly agreed to pony up twenty-five million. Warren led a large cast through a punishing nine-month schedule in which it recreated the 1917 Russian Revolution. The completed *Reds* got great reviews, won a Best Director Oscar for Beatty, but struggled to earn back its costs. The leading man's passion for his project inadvertently drove up the film's expenses; at one point during the production of *Reds*, several extras became so inspired by one of Beatty's anti-capitalistic speeches that they went on strike.

The Fighting Flirt

Forty-six-year-old Wallace Beery told director King Vidor he would not do his own fighting in the 1931 boxing drama *The Champ*. When he was a young man, Beery had once worked in a circus, and had been bit by leopard. After Wallace became a big star, he didn't care if his co-workers despised him, which was a good thing, because most of them did. There was no way Wallace would take any physical risks. Vidor thought Beery was perfect to play a washed-up loser who comes through for his son, and agreed to his terms. One day, King noticed Beery doing some heavy flirting with two gorgeous female extras, which gave him an idea. The director invited the two girls to work on *The Champ* set;

they were given seats in the front row during the prizefight sequence. As Vidor predicted, the actor's ego took over. Beery waved off his double, did some very convincing punching in the ring and ended up taking home an Oscar.

Victory Jog

The low-budget 1981 sports drama *Chariots of Fire* raced to a surprise Academy Award Best Picture victory over the heavily favored *Reds*. Based on the true story of two beleaguered British athletes preparing for the 1924 Olympics, the underdog *Chariots*, with its cast of unknowns, was initially rejected by every studio in town. By contrast, *Reds*, which told a sympathetic version of the birth of American communism, was a star-filled three-hour production featuring Warren Beatty, Jack Nicholson and Diane Keaton. The completed *Chariots* became a phenomenon; scores of TV parodies popped up showing determined comedians and costumed characters running on beaches. Meanwhile, the ponderous *Reds* struggled to gain box-office traction. Still, *Reds* was the critical favorite; most observers were surprised on Oscar night, except for an astute pundit who remembered that many Academy voters were also joggers.

Mrs. Miniver Was Worth It

When Greer Garson accepted the title role in the 1942 drama *Mrs. Miniver*, she felt the German soldier that menaced her in the movie was too sympathetic. With her country under attack, the thirty-three-year-old Londoner wanted to give up Hollywood stardom, return home and drive ambulances. The only reason Greer agreed to do the picture was that the British government felt that it would be great propaganda. And now any hawkish message would be undermined by the nice Nazi. Garson's cautious bosses at MGM pointed out that America was neutral; they couldn't take sides. Their attitude changed when Germany declared war on the US in December; Greer's on-screen antagonist was allowed to become evil. Years later, Garson lamented that *Mrs. Miniver* trapped her into being typecast as sacrificing British mothers. But her Oscar-winning performance helped persuade many Americans to support England's war effort.

Extra: In the 1940s, Greer Garson (1904-1996) became the queen of the MGM lot. Once, she attended a party at the home of studio head Louis B. Mayer (1884-1957). The Oscar-winning actress was standing a few feet away when she overheard the mogul speaking to some of the other guests. "The legs, the body, the beautiful red hair. Such a magnificent specimen. She is such a great addition to our team. I am so proud of her."

Garson blushed and walked up to the little gathering. "Oh, thank you, Mr. Mayer!"

It turned out her boss was talking about his new horse.

Joe Pesci to the Rescue

As the intimidating Tommy DeVito in the 1990 crime drama *Good Fellas,* the five-foot-four Joe Pesci won an Oscar and made an unforgettable impression on moviegoers. The actor's turn as the swearing wise guy who exploded into sudden violence may have helped defuse a potentially dangerous situation. One time Pesci was driving in Las Vegas when he saw a man accosting an attractive-looking woman on a street corner. Racing to rescue the damsel in distress, Joe rolled down his car window. "Take your hands off her, man!"

With a shocked expression, the man seemed to recognize the little movie mobster; he took off in a hurry and didn't look back. The woman wiped her forehead and gave Pesci a smile. As she came closer, Joe got a better look at her features, decided he was no longer needed there and drove away. "Wait, I wanted to thank you!" a masculine voice shouted after him.

Sergeant York Was Not a Turkey

Director Howard Hawks worried that people wouldn't believe the events in the 1941 biopic *Sergeant York,* starring Gary Cooper. Even though it took place near the end of World War I when the enemy was willing to surrender, the story of a pacifist hillbilly, who single-handedly captured eighty German soldiers in 1918, seemed outlandish. Hawks turned the York character into a turkey hunter, who used gobbling sounds to root out the enemy of their hiding places. The sequence was made amusing when the bewildered hero marched his POWs into a camp of U.S. soldiers, who refused custody. The real Alvin York, much more gregarious than the quiet Oscar winner that played him, admitted that the movie version of his life was greatly exaggerated. But American audiences in 1941, grimly aware that they soon might have to fight the same foe again, enjoyed the results and made *Sergeant York* the highest-grossing film that year.

Mrs. Robinson Was Worth It

Though she was nominated for an Oscar, Anne Bancroft didn't always appreciate her role as the seductive Mrs. Robinson in the 1967 comedy *The Graduate*. The thirty-six-year-old beauty from the Bronx had gotten spoiled working in high-budget studio films. What a comedown, getting paid peanuts to do bedroom scenes in a shabby production. Bancroft, who was only six years older than her *Graduate* love interest Dustin Hoffman, fretted that their woman/boy sequences were in bad taste. When the movie came out, the happily married actress became an annoyed sex symbol. It was maddening to Bancroft that her other work was ignored, or when insecure younger actors were intimidated in her presence. But one night in the 1990s, when she was vacationing in Italy, some adoring men in a café recognized Mrs. Robinson. They came to Anne's table, kissed her hands and feet, lifted her up in the air and made the whole thing worth it.

The African Water Queen

During the making of the 1951 classic *The African Queen,* on location in the Congo, Katharine Hepburn constantly nagged Humphrey Bogart about his drinking. The forty-four-year-old actress had seen firsthand the damage too much alcohol had caused her beloved Spencer Tracy. The cynical Bogart, who was seven years her senior, would listen patiently to her speeches about temperance, then ask her to pour him another drink. Director John Huston highlighted their personal differences in a scene where Hepburn's busybody missionary infuriated Bogart's boozing riverboat captain by throwing his liquor bottles overboard. The wonderful chemistry between the stars onscreen was apparent for all to see and resulted in Bogie winning his only Oscar. Ironically, during production, the Africa-loving Kate came down with dysentery while her co-star, who longed to return to civilization, protected himself by brushing his teeth with scotch.

Extra: Katharine Hepburn (1907-2003) got so sick during the making of *The African Queen* that the producers worried about how her green skin would look in Technicolor. At one point, she was ordered by the doctor on location to undergo seventy-two-hours' bed rest. Always a trouper, Kate came back to work early so the picture wouldn't have to shut down. Hepburn's toughness on *African Queen* infuriated her unhappy bosses, who were hoping to offset their production costs by receiving thousands of dollars in insurance payouts.

Extra: Thirty-year-old Anthony Hopkins met Katharine Hepburn during the filming of *The Lion in Winter* (1968). Playing her own distant ancestor, Eleanor of Aquitaine (1122-1204), brought Hepburn her third of her four Oscars. In her free time, when she wasn't lecturing Hopkins about his alcoholic demons, she was shocking him by swimming nude (twice a day) in the freezing Irish Sea. Hepburn explained that it was such an awful experience, she had no choice but to feel great afterwards.

Twenty-three years later, Gene Hackman, who had grown tired of violent parts, turned down the role of the murderous but brilliant Hannibal Lecter in *The Silence of the Lambs* (1991). The producers then passed over Louis Gossett Jr., fearing the publicity of casting a black man as a cannibal, and unexpectedly chose the five-foot-nine Hopkins. Despite appearing in *Silence* for only twenty-four chilling minutes, the now more sober Welshman took home the Best Actor Oscar. After the ceremonies, Hopkins stated that his serial killer's controlled madness had been partially inspired by Katharine Hepburn.

The Nutty Professor

In writer Tom Schulman's original script for the 1989 drama *Dead Poets Society*, Robin Williams' imaginative English teacher was supposed to die of leukemia. Director Peter Weir convinced the reluctant Schulman to jettison the illness, and then had his hands full restraining Williams from going overboard with his improvised monologues in front of his prep-school pupils. The motor-mouthed comedian used his best material off camera, which caused shooting delays as the laughing crew fought for composure. Critics' complaints that the thirty-eight-year-old Williams played himself, and boys reading poetry was not exactly the stuff of revolutions, did not stop *Dead Poets* from being a worldwide hit. Tom Schulman took home the screenwriting Oscar even after the real-life English professor whom the movie was based on stated publicly that Robin Williams was a nut.

A *Rocky* Budget

The low budget of the 1976 boxing drama *Rocky* forced its makers to improvise. A touching first date between Rocky and his love interest Adrian was switched from a static restaurant to an otherwise empty ice-skating rink. The scene became more romantic, and with no extras, much cheaper. The producers also couldn't afford to hire enough fans to carry Rocky out of the arena after losing his championship bout. It was decided instead that Adrian should push her way through the crowd and into the ring to embrace him. At one point, the production completely ran out of money; the *Rocky* crew pilfered camera equipment from former New York University student, Martin Scorsese, to complete the picture. *Rocky's* triumph at the box office and Best Picture Oscar surprised and thrilled its creative staff. Success made it easier to ignore nitpickers' complaints that they could see the microphones above the cameras cast shadows onscreen.

Extra: In 1975, twenty-nine-year-old Sylvester Stallone was living with his pregnant wife in a one-hundred-dollar-a-month Hollywood apartment. The struggling, mostly unemployed actor had no car and barely a hundred bucks in the bank. Yet he couldn't resist buying an expensive ticket to watch the heavyweight title boxing match on close-circuit television. The fight featured the unknown thirty-six-year-old Chuck Wepner going up against the three-years-younger world champion Muhammad Ali. Stallone, along with the rest of the audience, was amazed by Wepner's tenacity. The man was taking all the bloody punishment Ali could dish out, yet he kept coming. The heavy underdog lasted late into the fifteenth round before finally being knocked out. The excited Sylvester went home and (with the idea of himself playing the lead) wrote the *Rocky* script in three days.

Extra: The first draft of the *Rocky* script was not film-worthy. The boxer's manager Mickey, later played by actor Burgess Meredith (1907-1997), was depicted as an unlikable racist, and the ending had a disillusioned Rocky throwing the fight. But as Stallone tweaked the story to make it more inspirational, he began to get some serious interest from Hollywood producers. The problem was that they wanted somebody other than Sylvester to play the lead part. Stallone wavered when he was offered three hundred and fifty thousand dollars for the script outright. The conflicted screen writer asked his pregnant wife what to do.

"Have you ever seen $350,000?"

Sylvester, a formerly troubled youth who had been voted by his high-school classmates in Philadelphia the most likely to end up in the electric chair, shook his head, "No, never."

"Well, you won't miss it then."

Stallone held out until he received $1.1 million to make the film with himself in starring role.

Extra: When making the decision whether or not to green light *Rocky*, United Artists Studio head Arthur Krim (1910-1994) watched an earlier Sylvester Stallone outing, *The Lords of Flatbush* (1974). The New York-based mogul thought the Stallone kid was an interesting actor. With his blonde hair and blue eyes, he sure didn't look Italian though. One of Krim's underlings suggested maybe the young man was from northern Italy. Arthur nodded and approved going ahead with the thirty-year-old Stallone playing Rocky. A few months later, when *Rocky* was well into production, Krim was furious to find out that the man he liked in *Flatbush* was actually Stallone's twenty-six-year-old co-star, Perry King.

Extra: *Rocky* was never intended to be a series. But after some box-office failures in other roles, Stallone chose to bring the character back. In each of the sequels, Rocky's career trajectory matched the current popularity of the man who played him. In *Rocky II* (1979), the fighter's recent glory is quickly forgotten by the public. In *III* (1982) and *IV* (1985), he is on top of the world, and in *V* (1990) reflecting Stallone's personal decline as a movie star, the Italian Stallion was down and out.

The Godfather Refuses

When Marlon Brando won the Oscar for Best Actor for the 1972 movie *The Godfather*, he shocked America when his proxy who came on stage to refuse the award. The stand-in stated she was a Native American called Sacheen Littlefeather, who, at the podium, complained about the film industry's treatment of her people, as several in the audience booed. The professional actress was later revealed to be the daughter of a white mother and an Apache and Yaqui Indian father whose birth name was Marie Cruz. Rock Hudson, who was the next presenter, stated that sometimes the best eloquence is silence. Brando took his advice. He ignored several calls to explain his views publicly. The forty-eight-year-old star stayed holed up in his mansion high in the Hollywood Hills. A rumor spread through the film industry that Marlon was camped out in his projection room running John Wayne movies backward so the Indians would win.

Extra: When asked by the media what he thought of the Sacheen Littlefeather incident, sixty-four-year-old John Wayne (1907-1979) was strongly critical of Marlon Brando. If the man had something to say, why did he have to hide behind a girl dressed up in an Indian outfit? Everybody complained that

Native Americans didn't get enough work in movies, and then Brando hired a fake one (as Marie Cruz was wrongly thought to be at the time). And why the hell should anyone use the Academy Awards as a soapbox? Later, Wayne, who had a wonderful sense of humor, privately confessed to friends he found Marlon's action hysterically funny.

The Audrey Tour

Twenty-two-year-old Audrey Hepburn had little acting experience when she played a princess who falls in love with a fibbing reporter, in the 1953 romance *Roman Holiday*. On location in Rome, director William Wyler and leading man Gregory Peck kept the newcomer spontaneous on camera. Her shocked reaction was genuine when Peck pretended to lose his hand in the Mouth of Truth, an actual statue that according to legends bit off the body parts of liars. Another sequence called for her to end the relationship with Peck and start crying; she delivered tears when Wyler yelled at her after several failed takes. The completed picture was a huge hit and led to an Oscar victory and international stardom for Audrey. Years later, tour guides at the Forum in Rome would excitedly point out the spots where Julius Caesar was buried, Mark Antony gave speeches and Audrey Hepburn emoted.

Extra: Many leading men prefer buddy movies over romances, concerned that their female co-stars will steal the show from them. Shortly after meeting Audrey Hepburn (1929-1993), actor Gregory Peck (1916-2003) insisted (despite her lack of movie-star pedigree and against his agent's advice) that Hepburn's name should be placed alongside his above the title (Gregory Peck and Audrey Hepburn in *Roman Holiday*). The higher credit may have made the difference in Audrey getting the Best Actress Oscar, rather than Best Supporting for *Roman Holiday*.

Extra: A year after he starred in *Roman Holiday*, thirty-eight-year-old Gregory Peck played a reckless mosquito fighter bomber who falls for a refugee nurse in *The Purple Plain*. Not wanting to be upstaged, Peck approved of a totally inexperienced leading lady, a Burmese beauty named Win Min Than, in what would be her only film. Right before their big kissing scene, Peck was shocked to see her eyes bulging; she was suffering from extreme facial convulsions. It turned out Win's jealous husband made her chew a large portion of garlic before the sequence.

Amadeus Was Here

New York actor F. Murray Abraham didn't mind spending months in Prague when he starred in the 1984 largely fictionalized Mozart biopic *Amadeus*. In the Communist-controlled city, you could turn the camera 360 degrees and it still looked like the eighteenth century. So what if there were a few inconveniences?

One night a friend of Abraham's, who was staying in the same building, was consumed with searching the actor's apartment for electronic listening devices. F. Murray, who would win an Oscar for his performance as Mozart's obsessed rival Salieri, couldn't care less if the secret police heard them, and just wanted to go to dinner. But when his buddy found a mysterious plate under a decorative rug, he exclaimed to Abraham, "I told you, man!" and attempted to disable the suspected bug by triumphantly wielding a butter knife to undo the screws.

When they suddenly heard the loud crash of a chandelier hitting the floor of the room beneath them, the two shocked men then beat a hasty retreat to the nearest restaurant.

Who Cares If it is not Real?

The lavish 1984 production of *Amadeus* angered some classical music scholars with its portrayal of Wolfgang Mozart. The film's depiction of the former child prodigy as a foul-mouthed juvenile was a stretch; in reality, Mozart enjoyed toilet humor but was too well bred to act that way in front of royalty. And his supposed rival Salieri was a talented composer, not the jealous mediocrity displayed onscreen. There was no evidence to prove that he plotted Mozart's demise. In 1791, the final year of his short thirty-five-year life, Wolfgang was hired to write a death requiem (not as shown in the movie by Salieri, but instead by a Viennese Count who passed off others' work as his own). Some who defended the picture pointed out since it was narrated by a madman in an insane asylum, dramatic license was allowed. *Amadeus* won eight Oscars including Best Picture, and proved once again that historical accuracy was not necessary to achieve great cinema.

Extra: Shortly after Antonio Salieri (1750-1825) died, a rumor spread through Austria that the Italian composer had admitted to the murder of Wolfgang Amadeus Mozart (1756-1791). The most widely accepted theory of Mozart's demise was rheumatic fever, and no foul play was suspected at the time. The negative portrayal had begun during Wolfgang's life when the Mozart family occasionally accused Salieri of using his influence with the Royal Court to stop Mozart from obtaining important posts. There was more evidence that Antonio admired Wolfgang and tried to help him. When Salieri was appointed Kapellmeister, or head music maker, in 1788, he revived Mozart's *The Marriage of Figaro* (1784). The comic opera, which had originally been banned in Vienna because it made fun of the aristocracy went on to become one of the always-struggling-for-money Wolfgang's most famous works. Salieri's attending doctors and nurses later claimed that Antonio's death-bed confession never happened. Yet the gossip about enmity between the two men persisted for centuries, and inspired fifty-three-year-old Peter Schaffer to write the play *Amadeus* in 1979.

The Exile Who Never Left

Forty-four-year-old Forest Whitaker became a believable Idi Amin in the 2006 drama *The Last King of Scotland*. On location in Uganda, the Texas-born former football player captured the spirit of the late dictator, who ordered the deaths of thousands and was rumored to be a cannibal. Forest gained sixty pounds, learned Swahili and tricked himself into believing that English was his second language. He stayed in character in his general's uniform at all times, which intimidated his castmates; at one point Forest went alone into the wild and rehearsed his dialogue with some indifferent giraffes. Despite the producers' fears that their star was praising Amin too much in interviews, *Last King* was well received; Forest took home an Oscar and moved on to other parts. Meanwhile, back in Africa, some news-deprived villagers, who had seen the actor giving speeches in person, remained convinced that he was their exiled leader.

Belated Attraction

Twenty-three-year-old Richard Beymer was uncomfortable playing Natalie Wood's doomed lover in the 1961 classic *West Side Story*. Richard had heard a rumor that Wood, two years younger but a much bigger star, had wanted him fired and replaced by her husband, Robert Wagner. The Ohio-born Beymer believed it; every time he had seen her around Hollywood, the former child actress had always seemed like such a prima donna. Each day before shooting their romantic scenes, the modern Romeo and Juliet would greet each other with a curt good morning, and rarely exchange a word when the camera was not rolling. *West Side Story* was a box office smash and won the Oscar for Best Picture, but many critics complained about the lack of chemistry between the lead couple. Beymer agreed his performance as a love-struck ex-gang leader was lacking. A few years later, Richard saw the now-divorced Natalie at a club on the Sunset Strip. She was sexy and friendly, and he finally felt attracted to her.

Extra: Twenty-eight-year-old Tony Mordente, who played the hot-headed gang member Action in *West Side Story,* dreaded his new assignment. Director Robert Wise (1914-2005) had asked Tony to go to Natalie Wood's (1938-1981) Beverly Hills mansion to help get her up to speed with her acting and dancing. Thus far, the leading lady had not endeared herself to either Mordente or his castmates. On the first day of work, Natalie had let everybody know who the big movie star was. Wood had shown up late, wearing an expensive skin-tight dress and a monkey-fur hat. With her French Poodle, entourage and lighthearted air kisses, Natalie reeked of phony Hollywood. The former child star was always running off to see her analyst, and never apologized for messing up simple steps. Did it even matter to the spoiled brat that her fellow dancers now had to redo routines over and over with the same fierce energy? But shortly after he got to know her, Mordente realized his assumptions about Wood were all wrong. Natalie was a bubbly and friendly girl that didn't have a snobbish or mean bone in her body. If anything, she was too concerned about what her fellow *West Side Story* workers thought of her; the company had mistaken Wood's insecurity and shyness for laziness and indifference. The ambitious actress confessed to Tony that she was having problems with Richard Beymer, her love interest in the film. Natalie had nothing against Richard personally; he just wasn't helping her to give a good presentation. Mordente explained that even if Beymer was miscast, it was her job to love him convincingly onscreen. Tony and Natalie became great friends, he helped her to be passable with the choreography and she delivered a heart-wrenching performance.

Extra: In 1968, Natalie Wood was one of four co-leads who starred in the adult spouse-swapping satire *Bob and Carol and Ted and Alice.* Her fellow actors were impressed by Wood's down-to-earth demeanor on the set. On location in a Las Vegas casino, Natalie gave an interview where she made fun of her past studio queen image. Sure, a few years back she demanded extra perks in her contracts, but to the twenty-nine-year-old Russian beauty, all that star behavior seemed silly now. Hollywood was no longer glamorous; on *Bob and Carol,* Natalie was even doing her own make-up. As Wood was talking, a fan walked by and complimented her mink stole. "Sable, darling," corrected the icon.

Extra: When Robert Wise directed *West Side Story*, he was faced with the challenge of making cinemagoers believe that street hoods would suddenly burst into song. He insisted to reluctant studio bosses that the movie's prologue be shot expensively on location in New York. The musical started with panoramic views of Manhattan taken from a helicopter, then seamlessly closed in on the dancing gang members. Later, all the interiors were filmed on Hollywood sound stages. The only giveaway that the company was no longer in the Big Apple came during the violent rumble scene. Written on the wall, behind the on-camera knife fight, there was graffiti that clearly said, "GO LAKERS!"

Bette's Resentment

Thirty-year-old Bette Davis deeply resented William Wyler when he directed her in the 1938 drama *Jezebel*. The New England-born Davis relished the challenge of playing a duplicitous Southern belle in the 1850s. But why did the older-by-six-years Wyler humiliate her in front of the crew, demanding that she do constant retakes? Didn't this arrogant man realize she was now a big enough star to have him fired? After Davis complained that the filmmaker never complimented her work, he sarcastically kept saying her acting was marvelous until she begged him to stop. Despite coming down with bronchitis and throwing several fits on the set, Bette won the Oscar for *Jezebel*, which she said was the proudest moment of her career. She praised Wyler for getting a great performance out of her, and later acknowledged what everyone at the studio already knew; throughout the production, she and Willy had engaged in a torrid love affair.

Extra: Bette Davis (1908-1989) met her fourth and final husband Gary Merrill (1915-1990) on the set of *All About Eve* (1950). She would later say that he was a tough guy, but none of her spouses were macho enough to be Mr. Bette Davis. When they divorced in 1960, a tearful Davis told a judge that the couple had gotten into a fight while driving through Connecticut. Merrill had stopped the car, picked her up and thrown her out. She had landed face first in a snowdrift. "I might be there still, if I hadn't been rescued by a local farmer."

Merrill stood up and said angrily, "Your honor, you're not going to believe this malarkey, are you? I never threw Bette out of the car in Connecticut. It was Vermont where I threw her out!"

Shortly afterward, a much calmer Bette stood out on the courthouse steps, brandishing a long cigarette holder as she spoke with the press. She was asked if she'd ever marry again. "Well, gentlemen, it's tough with my career and all, but never say never. I do however have three conditions." She took a puff from her cigarette. "First he must have at least fifteen million dollars. Second, he must immediately sign half of it over to me. And finally," she paused for dramatic effect, "he must promise to be dead within the year!"

Her criteria were never met.

GREAT MOVIE ANECDOTES

"The movies are the only business where you can
go out front and applaud yourself."
— Will Rogers

"Egotism — usually just a case of mistaken nonentity."
— Barbara Stanwyck

Who Cares About *Double Indemnity?*

Unlike many other egotistical Hollywood actors, Barbara Stanwyck was unique in that she cared about the whole movie, not just her own part. In 1944, director Billy Wilder challenged Barbara to play against type in the crime-thriller *Double Indemnity.* She shone as a seductive villainess who convinced Fred MacMurray's insurance salesman character to help murder her husband. When the film was completed, the two stars watched the final cut at Paramount Studios. Both had been worried that playing nasty characters would hurt their images, but after the screening, they were giddy. Stanwyck, who would receive an Oscar nomination for her performance, remarked that the movie was wonderful. What did MacMurray think? "Oh, I don't know how the movie is, but I'm great!"

Extra: In 1925, a housewife in Queens named Ruth Snyder convinced her husband to sign a huge life insurance policy. Then she teamed with her lover, a corset salesman named Judd Grey, to murder her spouse. They made several botched attempts before finally succeeding. After they were caught, the killer couple blamed each other; the jury believed both of them, which led to Snyder and Grey being sentenced to the electric chair. Their crime inspired author James Cain (1892-1977) to write the serial novel *Double Indemnity* in 1943, which a year later was turned into the classic film.

Extra: Barbara Stanwyck's (1907-1990) mother died when she was two; her father abandoned her two years later. Her rough upbringing didn't stop Barbara from having a hugely successful sixty-year acting career in movies, stage and television. The twice-divorced Brooklynite was loved for her kindness and respected for her demanding professionalism. Best known to later audiences for playing the tough matriarch, Victoria Barkley, on the 1965 TV western, *The Big Valley*, Barbara once had some advice for her co-star Linda Evans. "You need more presence."

The beautiful twenty-three-year-old Evans, who had leaned on the thirty-one-years-older Stanwyck emotionally since her real mother died, asked what she meant. "I'll show you."

Linda was about to do a scene where her character, Audra Barkley, walked through a door. Right before the cameras rolled, Barbara kicked her small-screen daughter in the rear; Evans came flying onto the set with a startled, wide-eyed expression. "Now that's presence," said the smiling Barbara after the director yelled cut.

The two women remained close friends for the rest of Stanwyck's life.

The Pitch-Black Classic

In the early 1930s, Warner Bros. ripped controversial story ideas right out of the day's headlines, and then produced them at a breakneck pace with the cheapest production values possible. One example was the 1933 crime drama *I Am a Fugitive from a Chain Gang*, starring Paul Muni as an unemployed man who is falsely arrested and suffers cruel punishments. The producers ignored leaders of Southern states who complained the harsh treatment of convicts was necessary. In the final scene, Muni's character was asked how he survived. An accidental power outage plunged the set into darkness just as the actor whispered, "I steal."

Rather than do a retake, the penny-pinching studio bosses decided to release what they had. *Chain Gang* was a huge box-office success and helped lead to improvements in prison conditions, with the pitch-black ending considered a classic.

Extra: *I Am a Fugitive from a Chain Gang* was based on one of Georgia's most famous convicts, Robert E. Burns (1891-1955). After serving as a medic in World War I, the shell-shocked veteran was unable to make ends meet and became a drifter. The New Jersey-born Burns was convicted of robbing an Atlanta grocery store in 1922; he and two accomplices split $5.81. The prisoner twice escaped from brutal chain gangs, and then wrote a story about his experiences in 1930 that eventually was turned into the Paul Muni film. While still a wanted man, Burns showed up at Warner Bros. in Burbank to briefly work on the movie. After *Chain Gang* was released, public opinion turned in Robert's favor and he was eventually exonerated.

After M*A*S*H

In 1970, 20th Century Fox executives got a bargain when they hired Robert Altman to make the big-screen version of *M*A*S*H*. Altman's bosses were shocked at the loose atmosphere their authority-hating director created on the set. Robert instructed the *M*A*S*H* cast to live in their tents on the Fox backlot, and experience as much fun and frolic as their fictional doctor counterparts. In a war movie where dialogue took precedence over action, the only gun fired was by the referee during the football game scenes. When the completed *M*A*S*H* became a massive unexpected cash cow for Fox, Altman's grateful employers planned to give the lowly paid artist a share of the profits. But the rebellious filmmaker couldn't resist badmouthing the studio in public, and as a direct result never saw an extra dime.

Extra: The very left-wing Robert Altman (1925-2006) hated the television series *M*A*S*H* (1972-1983). The director felt that the anti-war message put forth in his film was diluted by the weekly comedy. Another detractor of the program was author Richard Hornberger (1924-1997), who wrote the 1968 novel *M*A*S*H* under the pseudonym Richard Hooker. The real-life Hornberger, a former army surgeon, was much fonder of Altman's feature film, which adhered closely to his book. The doctor came to his negative opinion of the series from a much different angle. Hornberger had written about his own madcap experiences during the Korean conflict. He felt the small-screen version was too liberal. The main character should have been a pro-military hawk like Richard; after all, he was named Hawkeye.

Christmas in July

20th Century Fox Studio head Darryl Zanuck was unsure about the 1947 Yuletide classic *Miracle on 34th Street*. Would the public buy a picture about the mental health of a department-store Santa? A famous memo writer, Zanuck, suggested to his creative staff that the mother character, played by the beautiful twenty-seven-year-old Maureen O'Hara, was too cold to be likable. Maureen was transformed into a jilted ex-wife, giving her strong motivation to protect her young daughter from fanciful beliefs in fairy tales. Another note from Zanuck warned the filmmakers about overdoing the scenes in which the employees of Macy's sent their customers to a rival department store; simple dialogue could get the point across. Preview audiences cheered when Kris Kringle was declared sane in the courtroom. The tale of keeping faith was an immediate hit, despite Darryl's lack of it. Zanuck released *Miracle* in July and told his marketing team not to disclose that it was about Christmas.

Extra: One reason that important movies of the 1940s didn't open up in summer is because very few cinemas had air conditioning.

Extra: The toughest casting choice for the makers of *Miracle on 34th Street* was who would play the little girl who didn't believe in Santa Claus. An assistant director remembered an amazing child prodigy from Santa Rosa, California, who could cry on cue. Her name was Natasha Nikolaevna Gurdin, renamed Natalie Wood after director Sam Wood. At eight, Natalie possessed none of the typical child-star precociousness. She earned the respect of her *Miracle* co-workers with her professional demeanor, and became known on the set as "One-Take Natalie". (In real life, the talented little tyke absolutely believed in Saint Nick, and was surprised to see her co-star Edmund Gwenn [1877-1977], who won an Oscar for his kindly portrayal of Kris Kringle, at *Miracle*'s wrap party without his white whiskers).

Extra: As head of 20th Century Fox Studios, Darryl F. Zanuck (1902-1979) supervised the making of thousands of movies. Among his many classics were *The Grapes of Wrath* (1940), *How Green Was My Valley* (1941), *Miracle on 34th Street* (1947) and *All About Eve* (1950). In 1962, Zanuck promoted his twenty-eight-year-old son Richard to be his successor, and then fired him nine years later. The younger Zanuck was appreciative for the learning opportunity and bore no resentment toward his old man. Richard formed his own independent company and co-produced the thriller *Jaws* in 1975. His share of the profits from the man-eating shark picture was a greater sum than Darryl earned in a lifetime.

Miracle Hassles

The use of New York locations increased the budget of the 1947 Christmas classic *Miracle on 34th Street*. Hundreds of extras were hired to pretend they were shopping at Macy's after business hours, due to fears that actual customers might be startled by the movie maker's bright lights into tripping and falling down escalators. *Miracle*'s set builders also constructed a costly replica of Bellevue. The famed mental hospital's staff members were upset at being portrayed as cruel in earlier movies and denied the film's fictional Santa Claus the use of their psycho ward. Another bottom-line hassle involved a bickering couple on 34th Street. The lady of the house got big bucks for allowing the film crew to shoot the Macy's Thanksgiving Day Parade from her window. When her spouse came home, he was furious that his view of the spectacle was blocked. He accused his wife of being greedy; she responded by calling him an idiot. Domestic tranquility and the work environment were restored when the husband received equal pay.

Respectful With a Cause

Thirty-three-year-old Nicholas Ray decided to move the problem of juvenile delinquency from the wrong side of the tracks to the middle classes when he directed the 1955 drama *Rebel Without a Cause*. Nicholas researched the film by riding in cars with Los Angeles gang members who instructed him on the proper way to handle a switchblade, and why you shouldn't have a rumble with a lot of people around. Ray's message was that young people with no right to vote were justified in lashing out at society, and the film was a huge success with teenagers. But the movie's star felt differently. Right before his untimely death and just prior to the picture's release, twenty-four-year-old James Dean, who was to become an eternal symbol of alienated youth, stated he hoped that *Rebel's* young audience would see it was important to treat people respectfully, and not act like punks.

The Grateful Gangster

In 1936, Warner Bros. purchased the Broadway play *The Petrified Forest,* about a John Dillinger-like gangster on the run, as a vehicle for Edward G. Robinson. Thirty-six-year-old Humphrey Bogart had been chosen by co-star Leslie Howard to play the bad-guy role on stage, and the loyal Englishman insisted again that Bogie repeat the part in Hollywood. The Warners' brass thought it over: Leslie Howard, Bette Davis, maybe Edward G. was one too many egomaniacs on the same set; they reluctantly agreed to replace Robinson with the unknown New Yorker. The studio publicity machine worked overtime to create the impression that the upper middle-class doctor's son Bogart was as sinister in real life as the gun-toting character he portrayed. Humphrey Bogart went on to become a movie star, and sixteen years later, the grateful actor named his only daughter Leslie.

Extra: Leslie Howard (1893-1943) is best remembered for playing the gentlemanly Ashley Wilkes in the 1939 classic *Gone with the Wind.* The London-born Howard disdained his most famous role, complaining that his nineteenth-century Southern costume made him look like a sissy hotel doorman. In real life, Howard was a respected writer, avid sportsman and very popular with the ladies. In 1916, Howard joined the British Cavalry and was wounded in battle. Twenty-seven years later, the very brave actor once again became a German target. Leslie conducted some intelligence-gathering missions on behalf of the British government. Howard's covert actions, combined with the anti-Nazi propaganda films he personally produced, made it imperative for the enemy to eliminate him. A plane carrying Leslie was fatally shot down by the Luftwaffe (German Air Force) on a return flight to London from Lisbon.

Extra: The five-foot-eight Humphrey Bogart (1899-1957) was so convincing as a tough guy on screen that it sometimes landed him in trouble. One time he was dining out with his third wife, Mayo Methot (1904-1951), when an idiot walked up to his table.

"So you're Mr. Tough Guy, Humphrey Bogart. You don't look so tough to me! Why don't we step outside?"

Bogart sighed. "Sit down, pal. Have a drink."

"No, I don't want a drink. I told my friends at the bar I could beat you."

The man kept badgering until the weary star turned to his wife. "Hey, Mayo. Take care of him."

Mayo took off her shoe and beat the hell out of him.

The Lost Patience of El Cid

Charlton Heston felt he was more than tolerant toward Sophia Loren while filming the 1963 epic *El Cid*, about the legendary eleventh-century Castilian hero Rodrigo Diaz and his vengeful wife. A former Northwestern University student, Heston, prided himself on his historical research. He had deep concerns about the script and at first appreciated his Italian leading lady's helpful suggestions. But as the production dragged on, Heston began to tire of Loren's ever-increasing tardiness, plus her resistance to letting her character age over the movie's twenty-year time period. One day when Sophia was hours late to the set, Heston had enough and decided to stop speaking to her. But they were filming the scene where the already dead *El Cid* was placed on his horse to fool the Islamic hordes, so the actress assumed her co-star was just staying in character.

Extra: Many years after Charlton Heston (1923-2008) starred in *El Cid* (1963), he reflected that it was understandable if an actress was a little late to the set. Unfortunately, there were fewer roles for them, they were frequently employed more because of their beauty than talent and it took longer for them to get made up. His twenty-nine-year-old *El Cid* leading lady had become an international star, despite her lack of English skills. Why shouldn't Sophia protect herself from unflattering camera angles and aging onscreen? And while making *El Cid*, Sophia was a trouper who braved the freezing cold of the

Spanish winter during their love scenes for long hours without complaint. In 1995, Heston was proud to introduce Loren at the Golden Globe Ceremonies when she won the Cecil B. DeMille Lifetime Achievement Award.

Young Mr. Fonda

Henry Fonda reluctantly allowed 20th Century Fox to test him for the title role in the 1939 biopic *Young Mr. Lincoln*. When the make-up and wardrobe departments had completed their work, the thirty-four-year-old looked in the mirror and saw his personal hero, complete with the trademark stovepipe hat. The illusion worked until the actor heard his own voice come out of Lincoln's mouth. Suddenly, Fonda felt embarrassed and out of his league. He tore off the costume and raced out of the studio. A few months later, Hank was summoned to the office of director John Ford, whom he had never met. The Maine-born, Irish filmmaker was furious with him; Henry wasn't being asked to play the great emancipator but a young inexperienced lawyer from Springfield, Illinois, for goodness' sake. After Ford finished his foul-mouthed diatribe, Fonda felt too ashamed to refuse him. For many Americans, Fonda – the lifelong liberal Democrat – gave the definitive portrayal of the man who would become the first Republican president.

Extra: James Stewart (1908-1997) and Henry Fonda (1905-1982) met each other in 1932 while they were performing on Broadway and became lifelong friends. They often roomed together, shared a love of model planes, went on double dates and hunted for bobcats in the Santa Monica Mountains. The two stars were willing to give up their careers and put their lives on the line for their country during World War II. Their relationship survived Stewart falling in love with Fonda's ex-wife Margaret Sullavan (1909-1960). Likewise, Fonda was able to get over losing the Oscar for his acclaimed performance as Tom Joad in *The Grapes of Wrath* in 1940. It was OK with Hank that his buddy Stewart beat him out with a lightweight acting job in *The Philadelphia Story*. Henry just figured the Academy was making up for overlooking Jimmy in *Mr. Smith Goes to Washington* a year earlier. But there was something that almost ruined their friendship. Once, in the 1930s, the very liberal Fonda got into a heated argument with the equally conservative Stewart, which turned into a brawl. After rolling around on the ground and throwing a few punches, they promised and kept their word never to discuss politics again.

The Video-Store Redemption

The Mansfield Ohio Correctional Institution was a tense place during production of the 1994 prison drama *The Shawshank Redemption*. Thirty-six-year-old Tim Robbins prepared for his role as an imprisoned man, who claimed he was innocent of murdering his wife, by sitting in a cell for hours bound in leg irons. His co-star Morgan Freeman, older by twenty-one years, simply imagined what it was like to be incarcerated and keep on keeping on. Freeman felt writer/director Frank Darabont was too in love with his words and thus should not be filming his own script. Darabont also tangled with the Humane Society when they complained about the onscreen mistreatment of maggots. When the picture was finished, a very disappointed Morgan Freeman thought they were hurt at the box office because people couldn't pronounce the title. *Shawshank's* slow-moving but immensely positive word of mouth helped turn the picture into one of the most popular home-video rentals ever up until that time.

Bat Invaders

The makers of the 2005 blockbuster *Batman Begins* thought the key to restoring the wobbly franchise was to create an awesome new Batmobile. Unlike the Caped Crusader's past movie vehicles, which were modified existing cars, the new model was designed from scratch. The Dark Knight's ride came complete with forty-four-inch Humvee tires, could go zero to sixty in six seconds and performed its own stunts without camera tricks or computer enhancements. On location in Chicago, the spectacle of the sixteen-foot-long armor-plated gas-guzzler caused massive traffic jams. The high-tech automobile worked flawlessly and helped its masked owner to reconnect with audiences. The only delay during filming came when a drunk crashed his car into the Batmobile. The driver explained he thought Earth was being invaded by an alien spaceship.

Extra: Created in 1939, Batman's alter ego Bruce Wayne was named after a real-life nighttime adventurer. Brigadier General "Mad" Anthony Wayne (1745-1796) led patriot troops in a daring midnight raid at Stony Point, New York, in 1789. Using only bayonets in order not to give away their presence, the Continental forces shockingly took what seemed to be an impregnable British fort in less than an hour. The fiery Wayne had urged his men to go on even after he was shot in the neck by a musket ball. The Battle at Stony Point was a major morale booster for the American side, which had lately experienced heavy losses, during the Revolutionary War (1775-1783). The fallen leader recovered from his wound and received a — rare at that time — medal from Congress. Wayne, who was later called "Mad" for his raging temper, was praised for the great mercy he showed to the captured prisoners. In some versions of *Batman* comics, Bruce Wayne is revealed to be the general's direct descendant.

Extra: Cartoonist Bob Kane (1915-1998) was thrilled watching *The Mark of Zorro* in 1920. The movie's star Douglas Fairbanks (1893-1939) was great as a seemingly harmless rich ninny who transformed into a dashing masked avenger at night. Ten years later, the illustrator enjoyed seeing a mystery film called *The Bat Whispers*. Haunted house pictures, with their creaking doorways and loud screams, were a great fit for the early sound movies. And it was eerie how the filmmakers told the story through the eyes of the villainous Bat, as he snuck up behind his victims. The two different cinematic concepts were later combined into one character by Kane when he created Batman in 1939.

We Don't Want a Hit

Executives at United Artists were unimpressed viewing the initial footage of Sean Connery playing James Bond in the 1962 spy thriller *Dr. No*. The thirty-two-year-old Scottish actor, whose receding hairline was carefully hidden by a toupee, seemed to change his accent in almost every scene. Sure, the former Mr. Universe runner-up was a formidable presence, but did Connery have the sophistication to play the suave super spy 007, a role originally meant for Cary Grant? The studio kept the completed film on the shelf for many months before releasing it in England where it was a smash. Well, it had to be a fluke; Bond was British, after all. Six months later, they released it in the USA where it did great again. *Dr. No* led to a hugely successful James Bond franchise and made Sean Connery an international star. It failed only in Japan, where movie-theater owners translated *Dr. No* to read, "We don't want a doctor!"

Extra: After six outings as James Bond, the forty-six-year-old Sean Connery made a bold, image-changing move by revealing his baldness onscreen. The public got their first glimpse of his new look in the 1976 drama *The Man Who Would Be King*. On location in Casablanca, the Scotsman rejected the use of a chauffeur and limo, choosing instead to drive himself in a Volkswagen Bug. One day dressed in a sweatshirt and shorts, the white-bearded foreigner was stopped for questioning by the local police. Sean had left his passport back at the hotel and looked like a suspicious character to the authorities. Just as he was about to be locked up, Connery shouted, "007! I'm 007!"

They recognized the ex-make-believe super spy and let him go.

Judy Garland Believed In Oz

Sixteen-year-old Judy Garland had a tough time taking her job seriously in the 1939 MGM musical *The Wizard of Oz*. The character of Dorothy was actually much younger in L. Frank Baum's book, causing some at Metro to push for the unavailable ten-year-old Shirley Temple for the part. Director Richard Thorpe had Judy running around in a blonde wig and baby-doll make-up giving a campy performance. It was hard for the fun-loving teenager not to laugh at some of her hammy co-stars dressed up in their ridiculous costumes. Thorpe's job was deemed inadequate and he was replaced by George Cukor. The new director, who left after three days to begin making *Gone with the Wind*, told Garland to lose her childish get-up and be herself. From then on, the Minnesota-born actress played her farm-girl role with sincerity, and for generations audiences believed that she believed in the wonderful Land of Oz.

The Battle of the Munchkins

The actors who played the Munchkins in *The Wizard of Oz* were hard working and much maligned. In the 1960s, the often-inebriated Judy Garland became a favorite TV talk show guest and would trash her former co-stars from the 1939 classic. She would make up tales about them being drunk, swinging from chandeliers, getting into knife fights, making lewd propositions to her, and being rounded up for their scenes in butterfly nets. In real life, the New York-based Leo Singer Midgets had won the lucrative *Oz* contracts in a hard-fought battle with another group of little vaudevillians managed by dwarf actor Major Doyle. There was much animosity between the two rival bands of performers. The cigar-chomping Doyle was in his apartment on Fifth Avenue, still fuming over the job losses, when a phone call instructed him to look out the window. Three busloads of tiny entertainers mooned him and then it was on to California.

The Real Maria Loved the Sound of Music

Sixty-year-old Maria von Trapp had a great time watching Hollywood change her life history for the 1965 musical, *The Sound of Music*. The escape from the

Nazis in the film was so exciting. Audiences would be bored to find out that the von Trapps left Austria in 1938 with a tourist visa; no one had tried to stop them — the train station was actually right behind their family estate in Salzburg. And they made her seem like such a wonderful governess and mother. Nobody wanted to hear how in real life, Maria, the driven leader of the von Trapp Family Singers, verbally battled with her stepchildren when they wanted to quit their music careers. While constantly touring around America, the kids complained so much to her about living out of a bus for eighteen years. The best thing about the picture was this handsome Christopher Plummer who played her late husband, Captain von Trapp. So romantic was this movie! In truth, young Maria had at first loved her seven stepchildren far more than her twenty-five-years-older spouse. When introduced to the thirty-six-year-old Plummer on *The Sound of Music* set, Maria, who once intended to be a nun, shocked the actor by greeting him with a big kiss on the lips. "My God, darling, I wished my real husband had looked as good as you!"

Extra: Although in real life Maria Augusta Kutschera (1905-1987) admitted she had not been in love with her husband Captain Georg (pronounced GAY-ork) Ludwig von Trapp (1880-1947) at the time of their 1927 wedding, she said that she eventually learned to love him more than she ever loved before or after.

Extra: Maria actually came to the von Trapps to be a tutor to one of the children, not a governess to all. The entire family disputed *The Sound of Music's* portrayal of Georg as a cold man who did not welcome the newcomer into his household.

Extra: In the early 1950s, when Maria von Trapp performed on stage with her singing stepchildren, in between songs she entertained audiences with stories of her past life in Austria. How her late husband Georg had been a former captain in the Austro-Hungarian Navy, as distinguished in his country as General Eisenhower was in the United States. How when the Austro-Hungarian Empire broke up in 1918, it left Austria without a coast and Georg without a job. How von Trapp recognized that his children's singing ability was enhanced by their new Governess, Maria Kutschera, and his financial desperation had allowed Georg to overcome his distaste for a show-business career. And how after Hitler annexed Austria in 1938, the family fled from Salzburg, first to Italy and then America; they were forced to leave behind all their belongings. The von Trapps later learned that Heinrich Himmler (1900-1945), the head of the

Gestapo himself, had moved into their family home. Maria's charming tales led to the development of the 1959 Broadway musical, *The Sound of Music*.

Extra: The producers of the big-screen version of *The Sound of Music* (1965) were unsure if they wanted to hire thirty-year-old Julie Andrews for the part of Maria von Trapp. The British-born singer had made a name for herself on Broadway, as a cockney flower girl who gains refinement in *My Fair Lady* (1956). But Jack Warner had broken Julie's heart by choosing Audrey Hepburn for the film version of *My Fair Lady* (1964), claiming that the stage performer Andrews was not photogenic. Julie instead had made her movie debut playing the flying nanny title role in *Mary Poppins* (1964) for Walt Disney. It was a strict Hollywood tradition that you never show an incomplete film to your competitors, but Walt was giddy about his new star who would go on to win an Oscar for *Poppins*. Disney delighted in granting the request from 20th Century Fox to see rough cuts of Andrew's work. *Sound of Music* director Robert Wise was impressed enough to offer Andrews the lead, but Julie wasn't certain. She had made fun of the Broadway version of *Music* during a television special in 1962. It sounded so saccharine; a singing nun and seven children running through the Austrian Alps. Wise pointed out that *The Sound of Music* would be in direct box-office competition with *My Fair Lady*. "Let's do it," Andrews said immediately.

Extra: *The Sound of Music's* interiors were filmed in Los Angeles while the exteriors were shot in Austria. The movie nuns were confused by having to run through abbeys at Fox and coming out the door in Salzburg. Seven-year-old Kym Karath, who played the youngest of the von Trapp children, gained a lot of weight eating cream cakes during the six-month stint in Europe. For the final scene, when Christopher Plummer as the captain led the family to their escape through the Alps, the Canadian actor had to carry the heavy child for several hours. After many takes, Christopher screamed at director Robert Wise to get it right, his back was breaking. Although Plummer would come to appreciate the film in later years, during the shoot he became dispirited and complained constantly. He referred to the picture as "The Sound of Mucus."

Extra: *Sound of Music* director Robert Wise said it was good that Plummer was distant toward the children; it helped them to be scared of him onscreen. Conversely, leading lady Julie Andrews was as warm as she needed to be. Julie helped the young actors get over their nerves by making funny faces. When the production was held up by rain, Andrews entertained the bored crew by bursting into song or doing pratfalls. It was her idea that Maria should sometimes be cross or exhausted having to take care of so many kids; that she be more spirited than sweet. But even Julie couldn't always maintain her good humor. For the opening sequence where Maria ran through the hills and sung, Wise used a helicopter to get an overhead shot. The force from the blades kept blowing Andrews over; in between takes, she would spit out dirt and grass, and then curse like a sailor.

Extra: The first reviews of the film were extremely negative. The premiere party was like a wake. But the initial slow business turned into a phenomenon as *The Sound of Music,* in 1965, became the most successful film of all time, surpassing even *Gone with the Wind* (1939). Struggling Hollywood studios, including Fox, saw financial salvation in musicals. But subsequent movies with songs, such as *Doctor Doolittle* (1967) and *On a Clear Day You Can See Forever* (1970), lost millions of dollars. Bitter executives, who failed to cash in or were fired because of putting out inferior products, blamed *The Sound of Music* for ruining the picture business.

Unscripted *Strangelove*

The most memorable moments from the 1964 war satire *Dr. Strangelove or: How I Learned to Stop Worrying and Love the Bomb,* were not written into its Academy Award-nominated screenplay. George C. Scott accidentally tripped and fell while the camera was rolling; the action fit the character of his excitable general and remained in the film. Peter Sellers' hilarious limp-wristed president was causing his co-stars to break up laughing, thus ruining takes, until director Stanley Kubrick told him to take a more serious tone. The comic actor Sellers was transformed into a still-weak leader who came off saner than his military staff. When Sellers, who was already playing two other roles, sprained his ankle, former rodeo clown Slim Pickens replaced him as the gung-ho Major King Kong. The cowboy showed up to the London location in his trademark ten-gallon hat and alligator shoes, and never realized he was performing in a comedy. Slim played it straight when he rode a nuclear missile down to Earth, whooping, hollering and waving his hat like a rodeo cowboy.

Extra: Louis Burton Lindley Jr. (1919-1983) quit school to join the rodeo at age twelve. His father hated the boy's career choice and did not want to see his son's name on a program. Louis was told his new job would only pay "Slim Pickings," meaning very little money, and adopted the phrase as his stage name (it was accidentally printed as Pickens). He became a very successful rodeo clown or bullfighter. Slim entertained the folks in the stands until an angry bull, mounted by a cowboy, would come out of the chute. If the two-ton animal threw the rider, the funny man would selflessly get between them until his fellow performer was saved. Slim later said his dangerous profession was great training for his future film-acting career. For twenty years, Pickens appeared to have a good time in front of paying customers, while breaking nearly every bone in his body.

Extra: After director Stanley Kubrick (1928-1999) purchased the rights to the 1958 nuclear war novel *Red Alert*, he felt the only way to present such horrific material onscreen was satirically. For *Dr. Strangelove*, Kubrick hired Peter Sellers (1925-1980) to play multiple roles so that everywhere the camera turned it showed the fate of the world in the zany comedian's hands.

The Unhappy Islanders

During the making of the 1975 thriller *Jaws* on location in Martha's Vineyard, an uneasy relationship existed between the visiting filmmakers and the island residents. One scene involved a group of amateur fishermen capturing a shark that was not responsible for the deaths in the story. Some locals were hired to make the real-life big catch. After several days of disappointing results, the frustrated producers had a frozen tiger shark shipped in from Florida. The shooting process required the stinky beast to be hung up for long periods over a boat dock, infuriating the people who lived nearby. In retaliation, the production staff was besieged by dead sharks tossed on the porches of their rented houses. Where were all these sharks when they needed one? As the long months dragged on, the desperation of the *Jaws* cast and crew to finish their jobs and return home was transferred effectively onto the fictional embattled Great White Shark hunters in the movie.

Extra: The idea for the best-selling novel *Jaws* (1974) came from author Peter Benchley (1940-2006) wondering what would happen if a man-eating shark started feeding off the shore of a small beach town, and then hung around for a while. Benchley was amused by critics who mistakenly saw all sorts of hidden meanings and symbolism that he hadn't intended in the story. Communist Cuban leader Fidel Castro said the book's plot was about the corruption of American capitalism. Others suggested that *Jaws* represented President Richard Nixon (1913-1994) covering up his knowledge of the 1972 Watergate Hotel and Office Building break-in. In later years, Benchley said while he never regretted writing the book, he came to believe that in real life, sharks were victims and unlikely to attack people unless provoked.

Extra: Earlier movies that took place at sea were usually made in a studio tank. But twenty-nine-year-old director Steven Spielberg insisted that *Jaws* be filmed in the Atlantic off the New England island, Martha's Vineyard; if Steven turned the camera 180 degrees, the frightened audience would see nothing but water. Almost immediately, the cast and crew were locked in a logistical nightmare. For several days, a thick fog rolled into the bay, making it impossible to shoot anything. Then, when the haze lifted, local boaters sailed out into camera range, providing some unwanted background scenery. When the sailors were asked to leave, they retorted angrily that the *Jaws* Company did not own the ocean. The moviemakers relocated to isolated areas, leading to inconsistencies; the sea looked choppy and flat in the same scenes. To make matters worse, the mechanical shark (real Great Whites were impossible to train) was an inefficient piece of equipment. Nicknamed *Bruce* (after Spielberg's lawyer), the twenty-five-foot metal beast worked perfectly in fresh water during pre-production. But when it counted, in salt water, the fake monster sank like a stone. Sometimes the creature's eyes crossed, and its mouth never seemed to close properly. The ten-week schedule turned into six months and Spielberg's beleaguered behind-the-scenes staff renamed the production "Flaws."

Extra: The seemingly endless, stressful production of *Jaws* sometimes got to its three leading men. Roy Scheider (1932-2008) was angry that his police-chief character was taking a back seat to his more colorful co-stars; he felt like a straight man. Roy also resented having Spielberg's phobia of water transferred to him onscreen. To relieve tension, he started a food fight with some members of the crew. Meanwhile, Robert Shaw (1927-1978), who played the shark-hating fisherman Quint, was bored out of his mind during the months he lived on the island, despite some local gang members shooting out the windows of his rented house. Shaw, who was once quoted as saying, "Can you tell me one great actor who doesn't drink?" had his own ways of blowing off steam.

One day when they were filming out on the ocean, Robert lamented to his castmate, Richard Dreyfuss, that he would like to give up alcohol. He then became furious when Richard threw his supply of booze over the side of the boat. Remembered as a wonderful man when he was sober, after a few drinks Shaw would hurl venomous insults at Dreyfuss, stating that the short, insecure twenty-eight-year-old had no future in Hollywood. For his part, Richard already thought he was working on a turkey; Dreyfuss complained throughout the shoot that *Jaws* would ruin his career. Richard also denied *Jaws'* director Steven Spielberg's claims that the actor hooked up with many young women who lived on Martha's Vineyard.

Extra: As the *Jaws'* budget ballooned to ten million dollars, Spielberg was miserable. Every visit to the island by a Universal executive made Steven fear he would get fired. The frustrated young director toyed with having the film climax with a school of sharks preparing to attack the two survivors as they swam back to shore; the producers talked him out of it. Steven also battled constantly with *Jaws'* novelist Peter Benchley, who had been hired to write the screenplay; the author questioned Spielberg's filmmaking ability. The ending that was chosen, the shark exploding after biting an oxygen tank, caused Benchley to object that it was preposterous; Spielberg then ordered Peter removed from the set. (Later, Benchley conceded that from both a cathartic and emotional standpoint, Steven understood better than he what the audience, after two hours of riveting fear, needed to happen.)

Extra: *Jaws'* slow progress gave its actors more time to rehearse and develop chemistry with each other onscreen. Roy Scheider, forced to imagine the malfunctioning shark he was supposed to be seeing for the first time, ad-libbed the funny line, "You're going to need a bigger boat."

After some drunken misfires, Robert Shaw delivered a chilling speech involving his character Quint being aboard the USS *Indianapolis* (the Navy ship that delivered the atom bomb that was dropped on Hiroshima, Japan, in 1945). The boat was sunk by torpedoes and Quint described watching many of his crewmates devoured by sharks. Robert was so compelling in the scene that executives at Universal considered making a film about the real-life terrifying ordeal. One night the inebriated Shaw, who had called *Jaws* a piece of crap written by committee, had a moment of clarity. In a slurry voice, he told the producers that the movie would be a smash hit. He wanted to exchange his entire two-hundred-thousand-dollar salary for an ownership percentage of the film. Robert was told to go back to sleep. Unlike his two *Jaws'* co-stars, Roy Scheider and Richard Dreyfuss, who would go on to solid careers if not major stardom, the colorful Shaw would sadly die of heart failure three years later, at the age of fifty-one.

Extra: When he got enough film, Spielberg left Martha's Vineyard without throwing the customary wrap party for the film crew. Back in Los Angeles, he realized in order for the picture to work, Bruce's onscreen appearances had to be limited, otherwise audiences would laugh the fake-looking beast out of the theater. With help of editor Verna Fields (1918-1982), he used thirty-four-year-old composer John Williams' music plus Quint's harpoon barrels to announce the monster's presence. Spielberg later said that the dysfunctional shark forced him go Hitchcockian, meaning he raised the *Jaws'* suspense level by showing less.

Extra: At one of the early free previews of *Jaws*, Spielberg was so nervous he could not sit down. By that time, Steven was so tired of watching and hearing the same material over and over he had no idea whether the film was good. What if *Jaws* was a flop? Would he ever work again? Eighteen minutes into the screening, the shark killed a boy in a bloody attack. Suddenly, a man in the front row got up from his seat and ran past Spielberg into the lobby. The startled director followed him and watched in amazement as the invited patron threw up on the carpet, went to the bathroom, cleaned himself up and then returned to his seat. For the first time in months, Spielberg relaxed, figuring correctly that if the movie made people sick and they still wanted to watch, it would be a hit.

Extra: The normal way to market a movie in the 1970s was to put it in a few first-run theaters and spend money on newspaper ads. But Universal Studios, wanting to strike gold immediately, gave *Jaws* massive distribution combined with a heavy dose of thirty-second television commercials, similar to a political campaign. It quickly raced to all-time box-office records and made Steven Spielberg into a rich and famous director. Hardly anyone noticed when the shark bit into one of its victims and his teeth bent back.

Extra: When Steven Spielberg first heard John Williams' primal two-note motif for *Jaws*, he thought the composer was kidding. The director listened to the score several times before he thought it was right for the film. After the 1975 Academy Awards, Spielberg expressed bitterness that both John Williams and editor Verna Fields won Oscars, while Steven himself had not even been nominated. As the years passed and the director's fame increased, he graciously credited Fields and stated that Williams' music was responsible for at least half of *Jaws'* success.

Extra: After twenty years in Hollywood, Alfred Hitchcock finally became super rich when he personally financed the low-budget, horrific *Psycho* (1960). His agent Lew Wasserman (1913-2002) convinced Hitchcock to trade the ownership rights of the movie in exchange for shares of stock in Universal. The transaction made him the third-biggest owner of the studio. While directing his last film *Family Plot* (1975), Hitchcock would get to work early, sit in his chair and joyfully read the *Wall Street Journal.* This new picture *Jaws* was a smash, thus adding millions to the seventy-six-year-old Englishman's portfolio. One day Alfred's morning routine was upset by an uninvited young man hovering around the set. Hitchcock, who seemed to have eyes in the back of his head, called a security guard to have the intruder removed at once. The interloper turned out to be the source of Hitchcock's happiness; it was *Jaws'* director Steven Spielberg who wanted to meet his idol.

A Lasting Kiss

In 1950, when Hollywood onscreen kisses were limited to three seconds, director Billy Wilder decided to play a practical joke on actors William Holden and Nancy Olson while filming a love scene in the classic *Sunset Boulevard.* They started making out and Wilder let the action go beyond the allotted time without calling cut. The performers stayed in character. Holden decided to go further and kiss her neck. Olson's face turned red and she let out a deep sigh. She unbuttoned his collar button. He responded by unzipping the back of her dress. Still no cut. More unbuttoning. More unzipping. The film crew, who were in on the joke, watched in silent amazement as the artificial couple began ripping off each other's clothes, continuing to devour each other with increasingly passionate embraces. Finally, someone yelled, "CUT!"

It was William Holden's wife.

The Ecstatic Doctor

Director David Lean made full use of Omar Sharif's good looks for a violent scene in the 1965 Russian Revolution drama *Doctor Zhivago.* Lean had come under fire for hiring the thirty-three-year-old Egyptian actor to star as the Russian poet. David dismissed the critics, especially the male ones, as simply being jealous. Sharif had the quality of a romantic dreamer, exactly what Lean wanted. A turning point in the movie took place when the White Russians bloodily suppressed the Communist insurgents. Just as the soldiers on horseback charged the crowd, there was a cut to a close-up of Zhivago. Sharif was instructed to imagine he was doing a love scene. His look of ecstasy amid the thundering sound of hoof beats was interpreted as an expression of horror by the audience. In the next cut, the dragoons were gone; the dead bodies lay in the streets, with the carnage never shown onscreen.

We'll Always Have Paris

Some unruly actors dampened the good mood of English-challenged William Dieterle when he directed *The Hunchback of Notre Dame* in 1939. Up to then, the German filmmaker's instructions were being carried out flawlessly. In blistering Los Angeles' heat, covered in tons of make-up, Charles Laughton was wonderful as the deformed bell ringer. Playing the gypsy Esmeralda, Maureen O'Hara was excellent in her dialogue and dance scenes. And hundreds of costumed extras were performing without a hitch. The mammoth production had gone smoothly until that day; there was a bunch of chimpanzees, orangutans, and gorillas running around their seventeenth-century Paris set. Dieterle, who always wore white gloves to protect himself from germs, demanded to know what these smelly, noisy creatures were doing there. It turned out that a hard-of-hearing assistant misunderstood the director's request for some more *monks*.

The CGI Schizophrenic

Thirty-seven-year-old Andy Serkis expanded an off-screen job into the role of a lifetime when he provided vocals for the computer-generated Gollum in the 2002 fantasy *The Lord of the Rings: The Two Towers*. Director Peter Jackson was bowled over by Andy's vocal performance as the ring-craving, deformed hobbit who is friendly one minute and murderous the next. He asked Serkis to be on hand and rehearse with his castmates so that *Two Towers'* computer animators could study his movements. Joining an exhausted company in New Zealand, the five-foot-eight actor injected some fire into the second installment of the history-making *Lord of the Rings* trilogy. Whether it was rock climbing, jumping into freezing streams or having physical altercations with his co-stars, Andy's intensity never lagged. His fellow performers, who knew that the work they did with Serkis was a run-through and that the digital Gollum would be added in post-production, felt guilty if they didn't match Andy's energy when the cameras weren't rolling. Gollum arguably became the most memorable character in rhe *Rings* films. Although Andy complained about the lack of scripts for three-foot-six addicts, it was fun when people would ask him to mimic his alter ego. Slipping into his creepy voice and split personality, Serkis could dish out insults to his fans that he could immediately take back.

Extra: Andy Serkis' idea for Gollum's garbled voice in *The Lord of the Rings: The Two Towers* came from the sound a cat would make by coughing up a hairball. The deformed hobbit's desperate, conniving personality was based on the actor's observations of heroin addicts.

Raising James Dean

Twenty-three-year-old James Dean was ordered to rub people the wrong way in his 1955 debut film *East of Eden*. The adaptation of John Steinbeck's modern retelling of Cain and Abel featured bad son Dean trying to win the love of his Bible-thumping father, played by Raymond Massey. The very professional Massey threatened to quit the film when Dean ad-libbed obscenities while he was reading scripture. Another time the young actor upset the crew when he showed up drunk for a heavy dialogue sequence. Jimmy also infuriated his bosses at Warner Bros. by recklessly riding his motorcycle around the studio and sneaking girls onto the lot at night. *Eden's* director Elia Kazan quietly encouraged much of the bad behavior; he felt that Dean had limited skills as a performer and needed special help. The filmmaker was as surprised as anyone when his Machiavellian tactics helped to turn the novice leading man into a superstar.

Meet Me Every Christmas

Twenty-one-year-old Judy Garland complained strongly about some song lyrics in the 1944 musical *Meet Me in St. Louis*. The four-foot-eleven star felt she was ready for more adult roles; Judy did not want to play an innocent teenager who deals with being uprooted from her home in 1904. It was a bunch of sentimental hogwash for old folks. And the director was driving Garland crazy; after each take he asked her to do it again. At one point in the production, Judy missed three weeks of work due to exhaustion. And now they wanted her to sing these dark words, which Garland felt had no place in the picture. Thanks to her objections, the line "this might be your last" was changed to "let your heart be light." Later, Judy said *Meet Me in Saint Louis* was one of her favorite films; she married the director, Vincente Minnelli, and the song she initially rejected, "Have Yourself a Merry Little Christmas" became a perennial holiday classic.

No Food at the Circus

Seventy-one-year-old Cecil B. DeMille expected his hired hands to keep up with him when he directed the 1952 extravaganza *The Greatest Show on Earth*. On location in Sarasota, Florida, with the real Ringling Brothers Barnum and Bailey

Circus, the energetic DeMille was an imposing figure. He was constantly on his feet barking orders at temperamental actors whether they were human, elephant or panther. One day the company was getting ready to film a crowd scene when Cecil motioned to a pretty extra in the back of the room. "Young lady, come up here. Take the microphone and tell your co-workers what's so important you would interrupt this multi-million dollar production. Don't be shy."

Her face turned beet red. "Well, I was just asking when is this old baldheaded blankety-blank going to let us have lunch."

After the laughter died down, the chastised filmmaker politely thanked her and yelled out, "Lunch!"

Extra: *The Greatest Show on Earth* featured a rare screen appearance of one of the few circus clowns the public knew by name, Emmett Kelly (1898-1979). Unlike others in his profession who used slapstick to make audiences laugh, Kelly's "Weary Willie" character was a sad tramp who won sympathy. Trudging along slowly with his broom in hand, Emmett would fruitlessly try to sweep up the pool of light that followed him. Once, at the Ringling Brothers Circus, the unhappy-looking star came across a young fan who offered him popcorn. Kelly's expression showed that he was touched at the boy's kindness. He took the box and pulled out one kernel, examining it carefully like he was a jeweler appraising the most precious stone in the kid's collection. Then after a long pause, Emmett handed the single piece of popcorn to his benefactor, kept the box for himself and slowly walked away. (After the laughter died down, the honest clown returned the popcorn to its owner.)

The Unrealistic Dozen

Forty-three-year-old Lee Marvin found his military expertise of limited use when he made the 1967 World War II thriller *The Dirty Dozen*. After John Wayne was offered the part and passed, Marvin accepted the role of a rebellious army major in charge of twelve murderers who volunteer to go behind enemy lines on a suicide mission. Lee knew something about combat; he had been wounded and saw fellow Marines die in a deadly ambush in 1944. It stretched credibility that the script had Marvin unarmed, yet still able to wrestle a bayonet away from one of the killers under his command. The actor was appeased when it was pointed out that the fictional screen story was so implausible one more ridiculous scene wouldn't matter. Filled with plenty of killings and explosions to distract audiences from the plot holes, *The Dirty Dozen* was a huge hit and turned its surprised leading man into the biggest action star in the U.S.

A Brunette is a Blonde's Best Friend

Director Howard Hawks wanted level-headed Jane Russell to star alongside Marilyn Monroe in the 1953 comedy *Gentlemen Prefer Blondes*. 20th Century Fox head honcho Darryl Zanuck told Hawks to forget it; Russell was unavailable. The filmmaker asked the mogul if he could borrow his phone. Fourteen years earlier, Howard had discovered the eighteen-year-old buxom brunette Russell working in a dentist's office, making ten dollars a week. When he reached Jane at home, the loyal actress immediately agreed to do the picture then asked, "Do you think I could get fifty thousand?"

Hawks eyed Zanuck then replied into the phone, "Nope, try again."

"Seventy-five?" asked Russell.

"You're being unreasonable," replied Hawks.

The conversation continued for another few minutes, then Howard put his hand over the receiver and said excitedly to Zanuck, "Great news. I got her down to two hundred thousand."

Darryl agreed to pay Russell's fee, and the comic pairing of Monroe and Russell onscreen proved to be priceless.

Extra: Jane Russell was the rare female who Marilyn Monroe (1926-1962) got along with. Their warm relationship came through in their performances onscreen. On many of her films, Marilyn would often refuse to come to the set when she was needed. Assistant directors dreaded fetching her; they'd get an earful of obscenities from Monroe if she wan't ready. But on *Gentlemen Prefer Blondes*, the brunette was not intimidated. She walked right up to the younger actress's trailer and knocked on the door. "C'mon, Blondie, time to work."

Marilyn came right out. "OK, Janie."

Other times, Monroe would be terrified to do musical scenes and Russell would give her pep talks. It didn't even seem to bother contract-player Marilyn that her free-agent co-star was making ten times the salary. When told she was not the lead in the movie, Marilyn smiled, "That's OK, I'm the blonde."

Till the end of her life, Monroe talked about how wonderfully Russell treated her.

Extra: Years after *Gentlemen Prefer Blondes* was made, director Howard Hawks (1896-1977) marveled that the public saw his two leading ladies as sex symbols. The pair were nothing at all like the on-the-make, glamorous showgirls that they played. Jane Russell was often very lonely with her husband Bob Waterfield (1920-1983), who played quarterback for professional football's Los Angeles

Rams, constantly on the road. She'd regularly show up at Hawks' house and offer to cook him dinner. As for Monroe, she'd sit around on the set in between shots like a bump on a log. Hawks' film crew, which was mainly composed of young guys who liked to hit on actresses, would walk by and ignore the blonde bombshell who never got asked out on a date during the entire production.

Extra: Marilyn Monroe was thrilled to be immortalized alongside Jane Russell in front of a large crowd at Grauman's Chinese Theater in 1953. As a little girl, raised in Los Angeles' foster homes, Marilyn had visited the famed cinema often and dreamed of becoming a movie star. And now at the Hollywood premiere of *Gentleman Prefer Blondes,* it was coming true. Like other movie legends, Monroe's hands and feet would be enshrined in wet cement. Hey, wait a minute — she had a great idea. The proceedings were held up as the blonde conferred with one of the 20th Century Fox executives. What if the two women left imprints of the body parts that people associated them with? How about if Jane leaned over the wet cement and Marilyn sat in it? Her suggestion was rejected, much to the disappointment of some photographers in attendance.

The Passion of Jim Cavaziel

While portraying Jesus in director Mel Gibson's *The Passion of the Christ,* former college basketball player Jim Cavaziel kept his humor in the face of separating his shoulder, suffering from hypothermia and literally being whipped. "I am not Jesus, I am an actor playing Jesus," he kept telling the Italian extras bowing before him.

For the more violent scenes of the crucifixion, a dummy was used in the actor's stead, but Cavaziel was needed for close-ups. At one point, when he was on the cross he was actually struck by lightning. The people on the ground scattered for cover while Jim Cavaziel looked up to the sky and asked, "What, you didn't like that take?"

Extra: Jim Cavaziel was not the first man to maintain his humor while playing Jesus. In 1927, H.B. Warner (1875-1958) starred in director Cecil B. DeMille's (1881-1959) *The King of Kings.* One day on the set, DeMille witnessed a newspaper photographer taking an unflattering shot of his leading man. The make-believe Messiah was slouching back in his chair, smoking a cigarette and reading the race results. DeMille chased off the unwanted visitor and then tore into Warner. They were already getting criticized by various religious organizations for making this picture. The last thing the famed filmmaker needed was some bad publicity about the Son of God behaving frivolously. The foul-mouthed tirade continued until finally Warner rose from his chair. Looking impressive in a long flowing white robe, the six-foot tall actor said solemnly, "Do you realize to whom you are speaking, Mr. DeMille?"

The Unlikely Sex Symbol

When Humphrey Bogart was cast opposite the beautiful Ingrid Bergman in the 1942 classic *Casablanca*, he fretted the audience would not believe that she could be attracted to him. The forty-two-year-old five-foot-eight-inch actor had come up through the ranks mostly playing thugs and had openly been called ugly by his employer Jack Warner. Humphrey was constantly troubled by battles at home with his third wife Mayo. The domestic stress had caused the harried performer's hair to abruptly to fall out one morning at the studio during a make-up session; the girl who was attending to him had gone into a screaming fit. Just before *Casablanca* started production, the unconfident Bogart sought counsel from his drinking buddies, actor Peter Lorre and director Raoul Walsh. How should he handle the romantic scenes with Bergman? Stand still and let her do all the work, they told him. By following their advice, the star who talked with a permanent lisp etched his place in cinema history as a sex symbol.

Extra: In *Casablanca*, Humphrey Bogart as nightclub owner Rick Blaine faces off with the villainous Major Strasser, played by the German-born Conrad Veidt (1893-1943). Unlike most actors, Conrad loved bad-guy roles and tried to make his characterizations as decadent as possible. An outspoken anti-Nazi, Veidt had been forced out of his homeland in 1933 when Hitler sent a death squad to assassinate him. Four years earlier, Veidt had starred in an adaptation of *The Man Who Laughed* by French writer Victor Hugo (1802-1885). Conrad's performance as a sad English nobleman whose face is disfigured by an angry king into a permanent grin later helped inspire the creation of Batman's arch nemesis The Joker.

Gangster Etiquette

Twenty-seven-year-old Howard Hughes resented accusations that he promoted crime as an attractive lifestyle when he produced *Scarface: The Shame of the Nation* in 1932. Loosely based on mobster Al Capone who was disfigured as a young man, *Scarface* upset the Hollywood censors with its onscreen bloodletting. For the shootout scenes, Hughes insisted that his cast use real machine guns, and then had to pay out a fortune in hospital bills after an on-set visitor was injured by a ricocheting bullet. The young millionaire, who served champagne at his dinner parties, felt that the film didn't get enough credit for its powerful statement against alcohol consumption, which was then illegal in the United States. Helped by the real Capone making headlines with his legal woes, the critically acclaimed picture became a huge hit at the box office. Actual gangsters went to the film in order to learn how to dress and behave.

Extra: Some people who played gangsters started to believe their own press clippings. One example was popular actor George Bancroft (1882-1956). In the 1928 film *The Dragnet,* the make-believe thug was given careful instructions by director Joseph von Sternberg (1894-1969). "Bancroft, start walking up the stairs, I will say bang, you clutch your chest and fall. Got it? OK, action."

Bancroft took three steps up the stairs. "Bang!" said von Sternberg.

No reaction. "Bancroft, didn't you hear me? Bang!"

Bancroft continued up the stairs. "Bancroft, you are ruining the shot. Bang!"

Bancroft reached the top of the stairs and turned. "Remember this, pal! It takes more than one bullet to kill Bancroft!"

Joseph proceeded to "execute" his star in the editing room.

Extra: In the 1930s, the Chicago mob was able to bring a semblance of order to the Wild West mentality of Hollywood. Los Angeles, in those times, was a city known for fixed elections, police corruption and the settling of disputes with gunfire. Some of the movie moguls, hit hard by the Great Depression, were willing to pay huge sums of protection money to Mafia types. The thugs were men of their word when it came to shakedowns. The gangsters made sure that film productions were no longer held up by strikes or Communist agitators. Organized crime bosses sometimes financed risky pictures that struggling banks were often unwilling to support. The federal government and legitimate unions teamed up to bring down what was, for a brief time, a very efficient business arrangement between tycoons and criminals.

Burt Reynolds' Wild Ride

In his humorous 1994 autobiography *My Life,* Burt Reynolds made light of risking his life to give a realistic portrayal in the 1972 movie *Deliverance.* On location at the Chattooga River in Georgia, his character had to go over a twenty-five-foot waterfall in a capsized canoe. The scene was too dangerous for the stuntman so a mannequin was used in his stead. It looked like a dummy going over a waterfall. Burt stunned director John Boorman by volunteering to do it himself. At age thirty-six, Reynolds felt this film had to be a success if he was going to reach his dream of movie stardom. The audience had to believe it. Burt didn't care what the insurance company said. After Boorman reluctantly acquiesced, the terrified actor got in the canoe and plunged over the falls. The impact left him completely naked and with a broken tailbone. It was three days before Burt returned to the set. "Well John, how did it look?"

"Like a dummy going over the waterfall."

Return of a War Hero

War hero Jimmy Stewart was unsure about his profession when he starred in the 1946 Christmas classic *It's a Wonderful Life*. The thirty-eight-year-old, who had been absent from the screen for five years, was a changed man after serving in the Army Air Corps. In 1943, a Madrid hotel refused lodging to Stewart because he was an actor; they had relented after he returned dressed in his military uniform. Maybe working in films wasn't for decent folk. After a few days of moping around the *Wonderful Life* set, James got a lecture from his wheelchair-bound co-star, Lionel Barrymore. The sixty-eight-year-old, who played the film's villainous Mr. Potter, told Jimmy that making pictures gave people more happiness than shooting at them from planes. The pep talk helped restore Stewart's pride in his craft; he delivered his most famed performance in *Wonderful Life* and went on to have a long post-war movie career.

Extra: Amadeo Pietro Giannini (1870-1949), was the founder of the Bank of Italy in 1904, renamed the Bank of America in 1928. He earned a reputation for lending money to people other financial institutions considered bad risks. A. P. only required a handshake and was proud to say later that he was always paid back. Giannini believed strongly in the hopes and dreams of some of the street merchants who gravitated into the film industry, and put his bank's money behind their ventures. Director Frank Capra (1897-1991) thought his fellow American of Italian descent would be a great subject for a movie. The idea involved a banker who made lending decisions based more on character than collateral. The financier would be hated by his competitors, who would celebrate when it looked like he was going to be ruined. When the hero's plight seemed darkest, the not so well-to-do people who had benefited from the moneyman's past generosity would come to bail him out. Capra came back to this plot more than once onscreen with the most famous version being *It's a Wonderful Life* in 1946, starring James Stewart in the Giannini role.

A Visit from Denzel

Retired high school football coach Herman Boone questioned whether Denzel Washington was qualified to play him in the 2000 family film *Remember the Titans*. The sixty-five-year-old Boone thought it was a gag when a man claiming to be Denzel called up and asked to meet him. But the nineteen-years-younger movie star turned out to be a very down-to-earth guy. He'd show up at Herman's Alexandria, Virginia, home without an entourage and spend hours listening to the ex-field general's tall tales. The completed picture about Boone's 1971 racially integrated, undefeated squad had been a real crowd pleaser despite its exaggerations. Boone was taken aback by Washington's harsh depiction of him. Sure, he yelled at his players a lot, but they could have shown his softer side too. Overall, the hard-to-please gridiron man, took pride in the movie and stated that Denzel was the greatest actor on Earth, even if he wasn't good looking enough for the lead role.

A Happier, Prettier Woman

A dark screenplay called *3000*, which referred to a prostitute's fee, evolved into the 1990 romantic comedy *Pretty Woman*. Twenty-one-year-old Julia Roberts had lobbied heavily for the lead role, which originally ended with her being brutally rejected by her billionaire client. As the story went into a happier direction, her co-star Richard Gere, twenty years her senior, had misgivings; he insisted that Julia should be the one who chased him. Once shooting began, the script was constantly re-written, forcing the actors to learn new lines on the spot. Roberts was not always informed of the changes; she often burst out laughing when her co-stars would do something unexpected. The producers found her reactions so charming they remained in the film. The title change made a difference at the box office; before the movie came out, some cinemagoers thought that *3000* was set in the future and was about a hooker from outer space.

Extra: In one *Pretty Woman* scene, Julia Roberts took a bath in Richard Gere's penthouse hotel suite. The actress was very nervous about being nude in front of a lot of burly men behind the camera. Director Gary Marshall told Julia to submerge then hold her breath for as long as she could. While she was under water, Marshall ordered the set cleared. When Roberts came up for air she saw that except for the cameraman, there was no one there and burst out laughing; her reaction was left in the completed movie.

Extra: Boulmıche, on Rodeo Drive and Santa Monica Blvd. in Beverly Hills, was the ladies clothing store where Julia Roberts' call-girl character was treated shabbily by a snobby saleswoman in *Pretty Woman*. The boutique's owners became concerned about their image after the film became an incredible box-office success. They put ads in Los Angeles newspapers that stated, "We were mean to Julia, but we will be nice to you!"

Lassie's Perks and Trappings

A rambunctious, motorcycle-chasing male collie named Pal beat out three hundred dogs to earn the title role in the 1943 family film *Lassie Come Home*. Trainer Rudd Weatherwax got him to lick his co-star's faces by covering them with ice cream and to open doors by enticing him with biscuits. Careful editing was used to hide any evidence of Lassie's true sexual identity onscreen. The novice actor was totally believable as a brave, loyal lady and became a major star with all the perks and trappings. Lassie flew first class on planes where the staff specially prepared his steaks and dined at the White House with President Roosevelt. On the downside, he could only work twenty minutes without sleeping, was often resented by human actors for scene stealing, and barely escaped some young fans who tried to shave off part of his beautiful coat to sell on the black market.

Who Was That Masked Man?

When twenty-four-year-old Eric Stoltz played the disfigured Rocky Dennis in the 1985 drama *Mask,* he found it was not a star-making turn. The actor endured daily four-hour make-up sessions learning how to perform only with his eyes. Eric walked around the filming locations feeling like his head was buried under ten wool ski masks. After sixty-two days of wearing his costume, he was prevented from entering the *Mask* wrap party by a security guard till he showed an ID. Once inside, Stoltz had to reintroduce himself to his castmates. He traveled around the world with his screen mother Cher to promote the film and good-naturedly smiled when she was mobbed while no one recognized him. One day the two co-stars visited the Tokyo Zoo. For once, it was Eric who was surrounded by picture-taking locals. It had nothing to do with the movie *Mask*; they had just never seen a man with red hair and blue eyes.

Extra: Unlike Eric Stoltz in *Mask,* some actors choose to wear disguises off camera. A case in point was John Barrymore (1882-1942) trying to buy his first house in Beverly Hills in 1926. Frustrated by rising real-estate prices, due to stars like Tom Mix (1880-1940) and Charlie Chaplin moving into the neighborhood, Barrymore went to look at a lot dressed up as his most famous movie character, Mr. Hyde. The realtor was taken aback by the long-haired, wild-eyed, fiendish-looking man who got out of the limo. Every time the broker would suggest a price, he was met by an intimidating growl. Finally, he made the sale to his hard-to-please client by lopping five thousand dollars off the initial number.

Extra: Being in disguise once helped Gregory Peck (1916-2003) make a quick choice regarding a major purchase. The very left-wing actor (1916-2003) was reluctant to take the title role in *MacArthur* (1977). As he did more research on the highly decorated military leader, Greg developed great admiration for the man and agreed to do the part. During production, Peck's seventeen-years-younger wife Veronique wished to buy a new lot in the very plush neighborhood of Holmby Hills, and wanted her husband's approval. Local residents were amazed to see what looked like Douglas MacArthur (1880-1964) chauffeured around in an open convertible wearing his full General's uniform, complete with the pipe and dark glasses that he was famous for. When Greg arrived, Veronique began telling him about the property. After two minutes, he interrupted her. "Buy it!"

He saluted, got back in the car, folded his arms and ordered the driver to move on. Later the former Berkeley student said, "How refreshing to have MacArthur's decision-making ability. Gregory Peck would have dithered around for days."

Extra: Sometimes it's a bigger surprise when you meet an actor out of costume. Kim Hunter (1922-2002) was shocked when she saw herself wearing chimp make-up for the first time, while playing Dr. Zira in *Planet of the Apes* (1968). She actually started crying in front of the mirror. "Oh my God, I'm not Kim anymore! I'm an ape!"

After Hunter calmed down, she turned in a great performance. The star of the film, forty-five-year-old Charlton Heston, attended the *Planet of the Apes* premiere with his same-aged wife Lydia. Rare for a Hollywood leading man,

Heston's marriage lasted sixty-four years without a hint of an extramarital affair. At the *Apes* after party, a strange woman came running up to him. "Chuck, how are you? Nice to see you."

She began hugging him and kissing him. "Hey, get off me, lady," said Heston, giving Lydia a bewildered look.

Of course, it was Kim Hunter who Charlton had never seen without her simian attire.

Extra: Heston and Hunter's *Planet of the Apes* co-star Roddy McDowall (1928-1998) kept his humor throughout the make-up ordeal. He loved driving down the 405 freeway in his full ape costume, waving at the other cars while stuck in traffic. Roddy also had fun at the expense of his old friend Julie Andrews, whom he'd co-starred with in the 1960 Broadway play *Camelot*. The recently divorced thirty-three-year-old actress was at that time filming the musical *Star!*, which told the story of British stage star Gertrude Lawrence (1898-1952). Late one afternoon, an exhausted Julie, who was then undergoing psychoanalysis, returned to her dressing room on the 20th Century Fox lot and shut the door. What looked like a giant talking chimp popped out from behind her cabinet, and gave Andrews the fright of her life.

The Equal-Opportunity Killer

After Frank Sinatra injured his hand so he couldn't hold a gun, and John Wayne refused the part, forty-one-year-old Clint Eastwood took the lead role in the 1971 police drama *Dirty Harry*. It was filmed in San Francisco and loosely based on the hunt for the real Bay Area Zodiac killer. Eastwood threw himself into the character of a vengeful cop not concerned with the rights of criminals. He performed his own dangerous stunts including jumping on top of a moving hijacked school bus. Audiences sick of bad guys ruling the streets mostly cheered, though not everyone who saw the film was happy. Some outraged critics called Harry a fascist who didn't care about the Bill of Rights. One time Clint was approached by an angry woman who accused him of killing too many minorities onscreen. After listening patiently, the six-foot-four actor put an arm around her and said in a comforting tone that she should not worry, he shot plenty of Anglos as well.

Steve McQueen's Need for Speed

Steve McQueen's addiction to fast driving earned him both trouble and more work while filming *The Great Escape* in Munich in 1963. The thirty-three-year-old actor got into a daily habit of racing to the set in his Mercedes, followed closely by German police who presented him with thirty-seven speeding tickets. His road antics frightened farm animals and kept studio lawyers busy. Once, Steve was almost thrown in jail for having forgotten his license back in Hollywood, and another time he wrapped his car around a tree. Herr McQueen ignored several warnings explaining he did his best thinking behind the wheel. The hard-to-deal-with star, who believed that writers ruined movies with too much dialogue, volunteered for double duty in *Escape's* climactic motorcycle chase scene. With careful editing, the audience didn't realize that one of the Nazis was actually a disguised McQueen pursuing himself.

Extra: Indiana-born Steve McQueen (1930-1980) only agreed to star in the World War II drama *The Great Escape* if he got to show off his motorbike skills. The film helped cement his place as an international star. Some European fans got hurt trying to mimic McQueen's Virgil Hilts character's daring sixty-foot jump for freedom. Later, the "King of Cool" admitted through gritted teeth that the stunt had been performed by a double. *Escape's* detractors were much more annoyed by other details. In the real 1942 breakout from the German prison camp Stalag Luft III, none of the prisoners used a motorcycle, the Triumph 650 model shown in the picture hadn't yet been invented and there were no Americans involved in the operation.

Extra: The production assistant on the 1976 low-budget action-thriller *Dixie Dynamite* blinked when he read the list of names. They had put out a call for some extras to do some dirt-biking shots. It was the end of the workday and he was handing out the checks for $120. "Oh my God, it says here, is that the Steve McQueen?"

An overweight, bearded man took off his helmet. Sure enough, it was the multi-millionaire movie star himself. Lately his enormous salary demands had kept Steve unemployed. What the hell, he figured he'd show up, do a job, have fun and get a little riding in.

National Velvet Memories

Twelve-year-old Elizabeth Taylor did her own riding when she played the gender-disguised jockey in the 1944 family classic *National Velvet*. Taylor was originally deemed too short for the part, but studio publicity people claimed she willed herself to grow three inches. The striking violet-eyed beauty both alarmed and impressed everyone on the set when she befriended King Charles, the temperamental horse used in the film. Elizabeth expressed such love and trust that MGM let her keep the animal after they completed their camerawork. Her adoring public believed that in real life she was just like the sweet girl on the screen. Years later, a much harsher Taylor would attribute her chronic back pains to a nasty spill she took in one of the riding scenes. She bitterly complained about still having to care for and feed the horse. But when asked what her favorite picture was, the actress always answered *National Velvet*.

Extra: Many actors have testy relationships with horses. One example was thirty-one-year-old Michael Caine, whose first movie *Zulu* (1964) required him to ride a steed after a hunting expedition. After several embarrassing takes, his career almost came to a premature end. "I thought you said you had riding lessons!" said the angry director.

"I did!" said the beleaguered newcomer. "And the first thing I learned was I never wanted to ride one of these bloody things again!"

Extra: Thirty-nine-year-old Jack Nicholson took a hard fall off his horse in *The Missouri Breaks* (1976). The actor shrugged it off saying, "It would have hurt if I was a real person instead of a movie star."

Extra: Most actors minimize their risks before riding. David Niven (1910-1983) bribed a trainer fifty dollars to use a gentle nag while filming *The Prisoner of Zenda* (1937). He brought his animal next to his co-star Raymond Massey (1896-1983) who was seated upon a stallion, and the two reluctant horsemen waited for the director to call action. Suddenly, Niven noticed a shadow above him; Massey's horse had risen on its hind legs. Niven realized his nag was in heat and dived out-of-the-way as Massey's stallion came down on David's mare. He watched stunned as the helpless Massey bounced on top of what now looked like a giant rocking horse!

The Vainer Sex

George Cukor, known as a women's director, put up with all kinds of prima donna behavior from the stars of the 1939 drama *The Women*. Norma Shearer complained that her lead character was too straight and that her more colorful co-stars were upstaging her. Joan Crawford, who had envied Shearer's career success for years, banged knitting needles during one of Norma's line readings causing Cukor to angrily throw Crawford off the set. Rosalind Russell pretended to be sick and missed work until she got equal billing to her co-stars and was miraculously cured. The off-screen antics may have helped provide some of the needed cattiness on screen; the film was a huge hit and Cukor stated he would rather direct ten actresses than one actor because females have less vanity!

Extra: During the filming of *The Women* (1939), longtime rivals at MGM Studios, Joan Crawford (1905-1977) and Norma Shearer (1902-1983), were summoned to the lot for publicity shots. Shearer had been married to the late vice president of production at MGM, Irving Thalberg (1899-1936). The hard-working Crawford was resentful of Shearer's queen-like position at Metro, and had made several catty remarks about Norma sleeping with the producer to advance her career. When the two women arrived for their photos, both refused to leave their limos first and ordered their drivers to circle around the building. George Cukor finally came outside and ordered them both to come in. In front of the cameras, the two divas acted like best friends.

Extra: Crawford had another classic encounter with an old rival on the set of *What Ever Happened To Baby Jane?* (1962). Her co-star Bette Davis, knowing that Joan was the widow of Alfred Steele (1901-1959), the former head of the Pepsi Corporation, had a Coke dispenser brought in for the cast and crew. When Joan was late for work, Bette would proclaim loudly, "Is the Widow Steele ready yet?"

Joan retaliated by lining her dress pockets with weights so in a scene when Bette Davis had to drag Crawford's nearly dead character across the floor, she almost broke her back.

The World of Spider-men

The worldwide success of the 2002 blockbuster *Spider-Man* inspired less powerful humans to don his costume. With the help of the local fire department, a sickly three-year-old British boy watched his favorite masked hero pretend to rescue his mother from the balcony of a smoke-filled building. In Hong Kong, another wannabe web spinner climbed on top of a thirty-foot crane to mark the anniversary of the 1989 Tiananmen Square protests against the authoritarian polices of the Chinese Government. On an entrepreneurial note, a cooking gas seller in Bangkok clothed her delivery people in the wall crawler's famous red and blue garb; orders for her canisters went up 50 percent. Some of the impersonators were greeted with cheers, while others faced threats of incarceration by the authorities, and nearly all felt uncomfortable wearing their skin-tight spandex outfits. After a long day one of them said, "I don't know how the real Spider-Man does it."

WESTERN VIGNETTES

"Anybody that doesn't want to get killed best clear on out the back."
— Clint Eastwood, from the movie *Unforgiven*

"Screw ambiguity. Perversion and corruption masquerade as
ambiguity. I don't like ambiguity. I don't trust ambiguity."
— John Wayne

Ideals at High Noon

Philosophically, John Wayne hated the classic 1952 western *High Noon* starring his good friend Gary Cooper. Imagine a sheriff, a lawman going to the local civilian population for help against outlaws. It was ridiculous; in real life, they would probably shoot Cooper's Will Kane character by mistake. He would place himself in more danger by being forced to watch out for his inexperienced helpers. What happened to rugged individualism? Seven years after *High Noon* was released, Wayne starred as a small-town sheriff facing a similar plight in *Rio Bravo*. The latter film allowed The Duke to rebut what he perceived *as High Noon's* un-American viewpoint on screen. But in Hollywood, career advancement can trump idealism. At the 1952 Oscar ceremonies, Wayne accepted *High Noon's* Best Actor Academy Award on behalf of the absent Cooper, and lamented that he had not been offered the role himself.

Extra: The initial test screenings of *High Noon* went badly. Leading man Gary Cooper (1901-1961) suffered from an ulcer throughout the shoot. He looked pained when his beautiful blonde co-star Grace Kelly (1929-1982) told him that she loved him. Audiences practically laughed the serious western drama out of distribution. After the negative feedback, many of Kelly's close-ups were cut (when a leading lady gets several favorable head shots in a movie that sometimes means she is having a relationship with the director). Cooper's uncomfortable reactions were placed after the scenes where the bad guys threatened to kill him. The new screenings with the edited version of *High Noon* did great and later Cooper claimed it was the only time an ulcer won an Oscar!

Extra: John Wayne's real name was Marion Michael Morrison. At age eleven, he was living in Glendale, California, and would walk around town followed by the family dog, an Airedale named Duke. They would often pass by some local firemen who would greet them by saying, "Hey, here comes Big Duke and Little Duke," a name the future rugged western hero preferred over Marion. By most accounts a very nice man, the six-foot-four actor would ignore strangers who called him by his studio-given name of John Wayne, but would warmly chat with fans who referred to him as Duke.

Extra: Gary Cooper turned down the lead roles in *The Big Trail* (1929), *Stagecoach* (1939) and *Red River* (1948). All three parts went to John Wayne and were crucial in advancing his career.

John Ford's Weatherman

In 1948, director John Ford went with John Wayne to their regular spot, Monument Valley at the Arizona/Utah border, to make the powerful western *Fort Apache*. Location shooting allowed the two old friends to relax by camping out, playing cards and avoiding contact with the bean-counting studio executives that Ford despised. The only drawback was that the unpredictable climate at the Arizona/Utah border could delay filming. Ford found a local Navajo medicine man and offered to pay him one hundred dollars if he could predict the weather. The Shaman shut his eyes, went into a trance and said, "Rain."

Sure enough, it did rain. The grateful director asked him to repeat his efforts the next day. "Mmm, cloudy."

Again, success! But on the third day when asked, the seer shook his head sadly and said, "Cannot tell weather today. Transistor radio broke."

Extra: Westerns made in Navajo country often provided a welcome boon to a depressed economy. One time a director hired two locals to create smoke signals. It took several hours but then finally the technicians finished the task. As the smoke arose from the ground, the assembled cast and crew watched in awe. The silence was broken when one of the Navajo extras stated, "Wow, I wish I'd said that!"

Extra: In the early days of Hollywood, for directors like John Ford (1894-1973) westerns were the easiest pictures to make. They required very few props and made use of the wide-open spaces available in the undeveloped area. Even the smallest studio, sometimes an empty space between two buildings known as a lot, could serve as a location for a cowboy movie. Because horses that had a taste for cereal grains were featured prominently in such films, westerns were nicknamed "oaters". Audiences were thrilled by wild chase scenes involving pure heroes like the white-clad Tom Mix going after dastardly villains. One time a theater was showing a western when the film suddenly broke right at the climactic scene. An emotional patron yelled out, "Hurry up and fix it before they get away!"

Quit Acting like a Pig

On location in Pineville, Missouri, in 1939, director Henry King was facing production problems on *Jesse James* starring Tyrone Power and Henry Fonda. The 20th Century Fox team had rented out a farmhouse from a grateful local, who made far more money from the movie people than she ever had raising pigs. It had come time to film the fateful scene where the James brothers would shoot it out with Pinkerton detectives, explaining why the persecuted small farmers became heroic bank-robbing outlaws. When the fake bullets started flying, the pigs started squealing in protest, sort of like the historians who later watched the movie. Several shots were ruined by the noisy animals and King felt that drastic action was needed. And so for the next few weeks, the cast and crew dined on bacon and sausages.

Extra: Jesse James (1847-1882) and his older brother Frank (1843-1915) were established outlaws when Pinkerton detectives firebombed their family farm in 1875. The resulting attacks blew off the James boys' mother's arm, killed their half-brother and helped turn the two murdering bandits into sympathetic figures.

Extra: During the Civil War (1861-1865), Jesse James, son of a prosperous slave-owning farmer, fought for the Confederacy as a bushwhacker. He would wait in the brush, and then would use brutal guerrilla tactics against Union soldiers. When such fighters were captured, it was demanded that they show that they weren't trying to commit an ambush. Jesse James' native Missouri became known as the "Show Me" state.

Extra: Jesse James never drank and carried a Bible with him, which he quoted from frequently. He survived brutal treatment during the American Civil War. The future outlaw was physically tortured by Jayhawkers, the northern equivalent to the bushwhackers, who were searching for his brother Frank. At the end of the conflict, Jesse tried to surrender and was shot in the chest. But most former Confederates never turned to crime. The James boys admitted that robbing banks and trains was easier than farming.

The Man Who Killed Jesse

Thirty-four-year-old John Carradine enjoyed his fame after he played Bob Ford, the cowardly assassin in the 1939 western *Jesse James*. Unlike many stars, the colorful Carradine would not pass up chances to meet fans and sign autographs. After all, just a few years ago he had been unemployed, running around Hollywood Boulevard yelling out lines from Shakespeare at the top of his lungs. So what if a crazy cinemagoer fired bullets at his image on the screen or the occasional kid kicked him in the shin? To try to convince a few lunatics that the man he killed in the movie was a murderous racist was folly. A few months after the hit film came out, Carradine was among the celebrities who rode in an open convertible in the Hollywood Christmas Parade. Someone shouted, "There's the snake that shot Jesse James!"

The happy thespian smiled and waved at the crowd, all the while dodging flying popcorn and paper cups.

Taking the Good with the Bad

Fifty-one-year-old Eli Wallach faced real-life perils playing Tuco the Mexican bandit, in director Sergio Leone's 1966 classic spaghetti western *The Good, the Bad and the Ugly*. On location in Spain, the New York-trained actor was perched on his horse with tied hands waiting to be hanged, when a perfect shot from co-star Clint Eastwood's character Blondie saved him. Unfortunately, the loud report frightened the animal into running at top speed, with the helpless Wallach unable to stop it for a mile. Other dangers Eli faced included being nearly crushed by an exploding bridge, almost getting decapitated by an oncoming train and accidentally swallowing some acid, which he mistook for lemon soda. After his job was finished, Wallach received a phone call from Henry Fonda. Leone wanted Hank for a western — should he do it? "Yes, you'll enjoy the challenge."

Fonda starred in *Once Upon a Time in the West* for Leone and later Henry called Eli to thank him.

Extra: After Eli Wallach was almost killed by an oncoming locomotive, he was shocked and refused when Sergio Leone (1929-1989) asked him to do it again. Other than that, both the director and his actor both shared the same wild sense of humor and got along great.

Wild Sam

Forty-four-year-old director Sam Peckinpah struggled to find the correct motivation for Pike Bishop, the main character in the violent 1969 western, *The Wild Bunch*. The hard-drinking, womanizing Sam wondered why a selfish outlaw would choose to ride into certain death for another man. Peckinpah decided the events of the film would force Pike to acknowledge that his past behavior lacked integrity. He had to sacrifice himself to reclaim his honor. After Lee Marvin turned him down, the director chose William Holden to play the part. At age fifty-one, the actor knew something about personal demons. After studying the script, William grew a thin mustache, projected a powerful air of authority on the set and delivered a performance that made Sam cry. The filmmaker angrily disagreed when the *Wild Bunch* crew members pointed out that Holden as Bishop was doing a near-perfect imitation of Peckinpah.

Extra: Utah-born Robert LeRoy Parker (1866-1908) took the alias Butch Cassidy so as not to bring shame on his parents. After a long string of successful train and bank robberies, he reputedly met a violent end in a shootout with some soldiers in Bolivia. His defenders argued that the handsome, charming Butch was a Robin Hood-like figure. Why shouldn't he steal from rich ranchers who were putting their smaller competitors out of business? Butch's boosters were quick to point out that Cassidy never killed anyone himself. A big hole in the outlaw-with-a-heart-of-gold theory lay in the actions of his accomplices. Known as The Wild Bunch, Butch's gang gunned down several victims on their leader's behalf.

Extra: In 1969, two movies came out based on the life of Butch Cassidy. The first was *The Wild Bunch* directed by Sam Peckinpah (1928-1984). Butch became Pike Bishop, a world-weary man who finally is forced to acknowledge he's lived a life without honor, and willingly rides to a violent end. Peckinpah's determination to show what really happens when a bullet hits a body turned off many shocked cinemagoers. Despite gaining some ardent supporters, *The Wild Bunch* received many negative reviews and did lukewarm business. In contrast, the comic romp *Butch Cassidy and the Sundance Kid* was one of the biggest hits of the year. In time, some films became so brutally graphic that *The Wild Bunch* seemed tame. Years after Peckinpah died, his revisionist western was generally accepted to be a groundbreaking classic.

Extra: Sam Peckinpah claimed that *The Wild Bunch* was an anti-violence movie. He hoped the onscreen bloodshed would be cathartic for audiences. The director was shocked to hear that the Nigerian army screened his film to inspire their soldiers before battles.

Extra: Sam Peckinpah directed fourteen movies many of them about men who found it difficult to live up to their professed ideals. In real life, the twice-married, boozing father of four, would sometimes apologize for his bad behavior even though drinking made Sam forget exactly what he had done. Many women, though knowing deep down he was probably wrong for them, were seduced by his charm, vision and talent. Once, Sam asked a lover/secretary to move his possessions into an apartment in Studio City. For three days, the attractive, would-be filmmaker worked her fingers to the bone to get everything unpacked and ready. She was shocked when Peckinpah called and told her to hurry up; he and another girlfriend were ready to move in. She yelled at him, cursed him, swore never to see him again and then accepted, a few weeks later, when Sam offered her a job on his new movie.

Thank Goodness She Was from Gary

If ever there was an ideal leading man to be in westerns it was the tall, quiet Montana-born Frank Cooper. Like many of the characters he played, in real life he was slow to anger and a man of very few words. His friends told stories of peacefully going fishing with him and staying gloriously silent for hours. Before becoming an actor, Cooper's earlier jobs had included shoveling manure on his father's ranch and trying to combine being a cowboy and cartoonist, which resulted in him often falling off his horse. In 1926, his agent told him there were already three Frank Coopers in Hollywood; she was from Gary, Indiana. "Why don't you change your name to Gary Cooper?"

The slow-to-react westerner stared at her for almost a minute and finally replied, "I'm sure glad you're not from Poughkeepsie."

Extra: Gary Cooper's intelligence or lack thereof was a widely discussed topic in Hollywood. Reporters lamented that the actor was eloquent only if the subject was guns or horses. Directors were often frustrated by Cooper's seemingly lackadaisical takes, then amazed later by his fine performances that showed up on film. One example was the 1929 western, *The Virginian*. In one scene, Gary caught a cattle rustler who turned out to be a good friend. The two men sat quietly discussing old times while they waited for the posse to come hang the thief. Cooper, who would go on to win two Oscars, received accolades for his perfect melancholy expression, which was largely caused by him not having memorized the script. Gary's eyes were downcast in order to read the lines taped to his captured buddy's back.

The Magnificent Scene Stealers

Yul Brynner tried to leave no doubt that he was the star of the 1960 western *The Magnificent Seven*. The young ambitious cast that included Steve McQueen, Charles Bronson, and James Coburn all seemed to accept that Yul would be getting the majority of the camera time. The Swiss-Mongolian actor showed up on the set dressed in black, with a huge trailer and entourage. He was the king and nobody could upstage him. The rehearsals went well and when it came time to begin shooting, everyone shook hands and wished each other luck. The first sequence called for Brynner to look impressive on horseback while leading his fellow gunfighters over a small stream. Yul didn't notice the scene-stealing antics going on behind him: McQueen, using his hat to scoop up water, Bronson with his shirt unbuttoned, flexing his chest muscles and Coburn reciting lines from Hamlet.

Extra: When Steve McQueen was offered the role of Vin in *The Magnificent Seven*, he was contractually tied into the TV show *Wanted: Dead or Alive* (1958-1961). The producers of the small-screen western refused to let their star out of his commitment. McQueen rented a car, crashed it and then leaked a phony story to the Hollywood trade papers that he was in a neck brace. The completely unhurt actor was excused from his main job, and promptly drove down to Mexico to do *Magnificent*.

Extra: During the filming of *The Magnificent Seven*, Yul Brynner (1920-1985) was fully aware that McQueen was engaged in scene stealing. At one point, Yul instructed his personal assistant to count how many times Steve touched his hat on camera.

Extra: The colorful, bigger-than-life Brynner was actually five foot nine, the same size as McQueen. For the first scene in *The Magnificent Seven* between Chris (Brynner) and Vin (McQueen), the lead actor built a mound of dirt that would allow him to tower over his co-star. But Steve kept blowing his lines. Before each new take, he would kick some dirt out from underneath Yul's hill. By the time McQueen got the scene right, Brynner was practically standing in a hole.

Shane Ran Into Trouble

When the 1953 western *Shane* was filmed on location in Jackson Hole, Wyoming, it ran into delays and budget problems. Jack Palance, playing one of the bad guys, couldn't ride a horse. After several failed attempts, it was decided that he would be far more menacing holding the reins and walking in front of his steed as he came into town. Another mishap involved the dog who refused to look at the coffin during a funeral sequence, until his trainer lay down in the grave. The cast was so into the moment that they forgot the animal instructor was in there and began shoveling dirt on him. Then there was the mischievous Jean Arthur, in her final film, urging her young co-star Brandon De Wilde to make funny faces at leading man Alan Ladd right before their scenes together to ruin his concentration. The finished *Shane* surprised its anxious backers with huge box-office success, and Oscar nominations for De Wilde and Palance.

Extra: Jean Arthur (1900-1991) was a nervous wreck on movie sets until the camera rolled, and then she would deliver a spectacular performance. On the set of *Shane*, the very shy actress typically stayed aloof. Her preferred company among her castmates was a litter of pigs, one of whom got sick after Arthur fed it. Jean refused to return to work until a vet was called in to care for her new friend. When the animal died, the producers feared that Arthur would be too distraught to complete the film, and quickly purchased a replacement before she could find out.

Extra: The one castmate Arthur got along with was Brandon De Wilde (1942-1972). The fifty-two-year-old actress, who once confessed that she herself was not an adult, encouraged her onscreen son to jump up and down in the mud or wander off to get a drink of water right before his scenes. Then when the camera rolled, Arthur would convincingly scold De Wilde for his character's bad behavior.

Extra: Jack Palance (1919-2006) was Marlon Brando's understudy for the role of the brutish Stanley Kowalski in the 1947 play *A Streetcar Named Desire*. One afternoon before the show, Marlon, who had taken an interest in boxing, asked a stagehand to spar with him. The man missed the intended target and hit Brando square on the nose. The bleeding, hospitalized star was unable to go on that evening. Palance made the most of his big break; his replacement performance got outstanding reviews and helped Jack land a movie contract.

Not a Calamity for Jean

Thirty-seven-year-old Jean Arthur plunged into her glamorous role as Calamity Jane in director Cecil B. DeMille's 1937 epic western *The Plainsman*.

The often difficult-to-work-with Arthur found Calamity to be an inspiring symbol of female independence. Just like her Old West character, the actress liked to defy feminine conventions of the day by smoking, drinking and wearing trousers. DeMille insisted his leading lady learn to use a bullwhip. Cecil refused to let Jean hit anyone but himself till she was fully trained, and personally suffered many lash marks on his wrists. As with most DeMille pictures, the audiences who flocked to see *The Plainsman* could not have cared less about historical inaccuracies. So what if the real Martha Jane Canary told many lies about herself, was generally not considered sexy and most likely never had an affair with Wild Bill Hickok? Arthur received fine reviews and her career soared into the stratosphere.

Extra: *The Plainsman* was a big break for Anthony Quinn (1915-2001). Trying out for a role as an Indian, the young actor, who claimed to be an authentic Native American, was brought in to meet DeMille and a technical adviser. "Say something in Cheyenne," ordered the famed director.

Feigning complete confidence, Quinn uttered some total gibberish. "Well?" Cecil asked his assistant.

"He speaks the language perfectly," replied the other fraud.

Quinn got the part and months later, DeMille found out that his new employee was born in Chihuahua, Mexico, and was raised in East LA. Eventually, the charming Anthony Quinn became Cecil's son-in-law.

Extra: It was hard to know what was true about Wild Bill Hickok (1837-1876) or Calamity Jane (1852-1903). The two Old West legends were experts at telling tall tales. Once in the Dakota Black Hills, Bill was spinning a yarn about him being totally surrounded by gun-toting enemies. There was no way he could escape. Abruptly, Hickok quit his story. There was silence for about a minute, and then somebody in the audience asked what happened next. "Well, they killed me, of course!"

Don't Mess With Sam

Thirty-nine-year-old Gary Cooper was upset that his old friend Walter Brennan had a better part in the 1940 film *The Westerner*. Playing an accused horse thief who talks his way out of being hanged, the cowboy star wondered why he was even in the picture. As the colorful Judge Roy Bean, Brennan, seven years Cooper's senior, would chew up the scenery and win his third Oscar. Cooper was thinking of dropping out when he received a shocking late-night call from his boss, Samuel Goldwyn. Using foul language, the legendary producer called Cooper a no-talent hack who better live up to his contract; otherwise, he'd be sued for every penny he had. The first day on the set, Brennan asked Gary, "What the hell is the matter with you? Why do you look so shaken up?"

Before Coop could answer, he was sent into hysterical laughter; Brennan started to repeat the earlier phone tirade in a perfect imitation of Goldwyn.

John Ford's Defense

Director John Ford faced tough questions from the critics regarding his 1939 western *Stagecoach*. The story about settlers in the 1860s traveling through hostile Apache territory revived the western as a genre and made a star out of thirty-two-year-old John Wayne. But now the press was grilling the filmmaker about the movie's authenticity. In the big chase scene, why didn't the Indians just shoot the horses? Ford sneered at them. Everyone knows Indians couldn't shoot worth a damn. The reporters were skeptical. Look, it's a known fact that the braves needed replacement horses. Nobody bought that either. All right, if they killed the horses the picture would be over! Is that what you want me to say? The journalists laughed and the interview ended. The questioners didn't notice that in the thrilling sequence they asked about, the thin wheels of the nineteenth-century stagecoach raced through wide tracks that were clearly made by modern truck tires.

Extra: *Stagecoach* (1939) was based on a short story called *Stage to Lordsburg*. John Ford gave it to John Wayne to read, and then asked him who should play the Ringo Kid. Wayne, who had toiled in B movies for ten years and doubted his own abilities as an actor, suggested Lloyd Nolan (1902-1985). "Hmm," replied Ford. Nolan was very good but not quite right for what would be a starring role in a major western. Didn't Duke know any young guys who could ride horses and act? Well, probably not with the type of second-rate movie Wayne usually starred in. Duke took the remark in stride; he was used to Ford's insults. Hell, the old man could have helped Wayne get better parts if he wanted to, but Duke would have never presumed to trade on their friendship. It was enough for the two men to play cards, go sailing and have a few drinks. The next evening, very casually Ford said that he wanted Wayne for The Ringo Kid. Duke was shocked then thrilled. This was the opportunity for stardom he'd dreamed of. Wayne's greatest fear over the next few weeks was that Ford would remember his initial suggestion and reconsider Nolan.

Extra: Many of the children who watched John Wayne's B movies were of college age when *Stagecoach* was released in 1939. The Duke was a loyal USC Trojan but it was UCLA students, who, at the premiere in Westwood, gave Wayne a loud ovation when he first appeared onscreen twirling his Winchester rifle and stopping the stagecoach. It was later considered one of the greatest entrances in the history of cinema, and John Wayne, who was in the theater that night, knew by the audience's reaction that after ten years of struggle, he'd finally become a star.

The Surprised New Star

Clint Eastwood felt his bosses on the 1964 low-budget film *The Mysterious Stranger* were disorganized and unprofessional. The thirty-four-year-old TV actor accepted a tiny salary to go to Spain, paid for his own wardrobe and argued that his character had too much dialogue. The blazing Mediterranean sun gave Clint a menacing squint, perfect for a nameless, cigar-smoking man who brutally shoots his enemies. The fighting on camera was nothing compared to the screaming in Italian when the crew wasn't paid. During a work shutdown, the frustrated Eastwood quit and boarded a plane headed home and was talked out of it just before takeoff. Weeks later, Clint returned to the States and did not hear anything about the completed picture for months; he assumed that with the high body count, it had to be a flop. The producers never bothered to tell Eastwood that the title of the spaghetti western had been changed to *A Fistful of Dollars* and he'd become an international superstar.

Extra: After his breakout role in *A Fistful of Dollars*, Clint Eastwood continued to succeed playing mysterious strangers who could shoot with uncanny accuracy in later westerns such as *High Plains Drifter* (1973) and *The Outlaw Josey Wales* (1976). Then in the early 1980s, the superstar acquired a script he wanted to direct and act in called *The William Munny Killings*. The plot was unlike anything Clint ever read before. *William Munny* blew up the myths of the Old West; it showed that no matter how good your aim was, if the other side had more firepower you were dead. In real life, nobody killed twenty men with twenty shots; instead, you needed to keep putting bullets into your enemy until you were sure they were never getting up again. Eastwood held onto the project for about a decade, figuring he needed to look older to play an aging reluctant mercenary who is transformed by events into an angry avenger. Several times during his self-imposed waiting period, Clint tinkered greatly with the screenplay and then remembered why he'd bought it in the first place. Eastwood ended up shooting the picture almost exactly as author David Webb Peoples originally wrote it; the epic western won the Academy Award for Best Picture in 1992. The sixty-two-year-old filmmaker's only major change involved the title; Clint didn't like *The William Munny Killings* and renamed the story *Unforgiven*.

Arguing About Liberty

Fifty-four-year-old John Wayne didn't get what his longtime mentor, director John Ford, expected of him when they made *The Man Who Shot Liberty Valance* in 1962. Jimmy Stewart was playing the greenhorn lawyer who falls in love with Vera Miles; Lee Marvin was the bad guy; and Wayne was supposed to...what? Kill Marvin so Jimmy could get the girl? Be a dying symbol of the Old West? It was unclear and the Duke disliked ambiguity. The sixty-eight-year-old Ford loved the big Republican, as he called Wayne, but he didn't like being questioned; in front of the crew he needled Wayne about staying home while Stewart fought in World War II. The cowboy star didn't take any of it personally; hell, if it wasn't for the old man he'd still be in B pictures. The arguments between Ford and Wayne continued till the end of the shoot, yet many fans considered *Liberty Valance* the finest of the thirteen films that they made together.

Sex Appeal in the Old West

Fifty-five-year-old James Stewart was surprised at the intensity of his co-star Carroll Baker during their love scene, in the 1963 epic *How the West Was Won*. The veteran actor had wondered if he'd be believable playing a grizzled independent mountain man who wins the heart of a blonde beauty twenty-three years his junior. After an awkward introduction, the two performers were driven out to the Kentucky location to be intimate. Stewart had tried to loosen her up in the car by playing a game called count the cows; the girl seemed to enjoy it. When they kissed each other on camera, the young lady shivered in his embrace. Well, it was nice to still have some sex appeal. Not bad for a fella who had considered getting plastic surgery seventeen years before. After the director called cut, Baker pointed behind him. The white-haired leading man turned to see that she had been reacting to a big snake in a tree.

PART SIX

WALT DISNEY STORIES

"Nothing in this world can take the place of persistence. Talent will not;
nothing is more common than unsuccessful people with talent. Genius will not;
unrewarded genius is almost a proverb."
— Calvin Coolidge

"When you're curious, you'll find a lot of interesting things to do."
— Walt Disney

Faint Praise from Walt

With the help of his loyal staff, Walt Disney won a record-setting twenty-six Academy Awards. He gave praise very grudgingly, and sometimes his employees wondered whether their moody boss appreciated them at all. After many years of toiling at the Disney factory, producer Ben Sharpsteen bought a ranch and retired. One day Walt came to visit him and immediately began barking orders about how the property should be improved. Sharpsteen gently pointed out that he didn't work for the cartoon maker anymore. After Disney left, Ben went back into the house wondering how he could have been so loyal to such a maddening man for so long, when a flash of gold caught his eye. Disney had left him a gift on the kitchen table, one of the Oscars they had earned together.

Extra: Walt Disney (1901-1966) felt that giving too much praise to his employees would create jealousy among the ranks. In 1941, 40 percent of his artists went on strike; one issue was that Walt, who actually was more idea man than animator, was getting the lion's share of the credit for features like *Snow White and the Seven Dwarfs* (1937). The angry producer pointed out that when he had box-office failures like *Fantasia* (1940), his cartoonists didn't get the blame either.

Extra: Walt Disney's staffers were never sure what to expect from their mercurial boss. Once, a pretty secretary encountered the cartoon maker walking down a studio hallway. "Hi Walt," she said, and was completely ignored by Disney, who was clearly occupied by a vexing problem.

A few hours later, she encountered him again. Walt was looking down on the ground and seemed deep in concentration. This time she decided not to disturb him. As she walked by him without a word, she heard her employer say in a playful tone, "How you doing, good-lookin'?"

Extra: Walt Disney, who often was harsh with those who worked for him, had no patience for anyone at Disneyland that was rude to the customers or as he put it, the guests. One time an unfriendly security guard didn't recognize Disney and prevented him from getting on a new, as yet unopened-to-the-public ride. Walt brooded about the matter for a day and then fired him, reasoning the man would also be unpleasant with others. But if someone was doing his or her job, they usually had nothing to fear from the boss. Once during a demonstration of a new Disneyland attraction, a young worker chided a man in the back of the room for lighting up a cigarette — it wasn't allowed. "Whose idea was that?"

"Walt Disney's."

The man stubbed out the cigarette. "That's good enough for me," said her employer.

The Thing at MGM

One day in 1928, MGM studio head Louis B. Mayer reluctantly agreed to a meeting with his creative staff. It was so damn annoying, these so-called artists wanting to bother him with their smutty ideas. The mogul felt that family films were what the public wanted; to stray from clean content was a mistake. His employees always wished to push the envelope with what they called more adult subjects, like rape and murder. Now they were all excited to show him a new comedy. The lights went down and Mayer was horrified by the images he saw on the screen. "Stop the projector! I ought to fire all of you! Imagine if that thing were ten feet tall in theaters. All the pregnant women would flee out into the street."

Mayer abruptly left, while his astonished personnel wondered who would tell the nervous young filmmaker in the next room that MGM would not distribute his Mickey Mouse cartoons.

Extra: Mickey Mouse's film debut was called *Plane Crazy* (1928), based on famed aviator Charles Lindbergh's transatlantic flight. The rodent was presented as a sometimes nasty character, who in midair tried to force himself on his girlfriend Minnie after she rejected his amorous advances; the angry female slapped him and then escaped by bailing out of the plane.

Extra: The man who gave Walt Disney his big break was a publicist named Harry Reichenbach (1882-1931). The manager of the Colony Theater in New York, Harry agreed to let *Steamboat Willie*, the first sound cartoon starring Mickey Mouse, show there for what turned out to be a successful two-week run. Before helping Walt in 1928, Reichenbach had pulled off some of the greatest publicity stunts in the history of Hollywood. MGM executives were uncertain if they wanted to re-sign silent film star Frances X. Bushman (1883-1966), until they saw a huge crowd trailing him through the streets from their office windows. It turned out that Reichenbach was following behind the actor dropping pennies. Harry was also assigned to sell the first *Tarzan* movie in 1918. The salesman arranged for a man named "Mr. Zann" to stay at a New York hotel. First, a huge crate was hoisted into his suite. Then fifteen pounds of beef were ordered from room service. The waiter fled in terror when he saw that seated next to "Mr. Zann" at the dinner table was a lion wearing a bib. When the press and police arrived at the scene, "Mr. Zann" explained he was simply a very enthusiastic *Tarzan* fan.

Dick Van Dyke's Senior Moment

Thirty-nine-year-old Dick Van Dyke fooled both audiences and co-stars, playing an old banker in the 1964 classic *Mary Poppins*. The TV sitcom star, who was already the leading man in the film, donated four thousand dollars to Walt Disney's newly formed Cal Arts University in exchange for getting the secondary role. With his cane, white hair and whiskers, the two child actors who had already worked with Van Dyke had no idea who he really was. One day in front of the Disney Studio, a bus full of tourists caught sight of the make-believe geezer just as he was about to cross the street. Leaning on his cane, he slowly walked to his destination, pausing sometimes to clutch his chest for dramatic effect till he made it. As the vehicle pulled forward, the passengers' sighs of relief turned to gasps of surprise when they saw the grinning senior citizen running full speed alongside them.

Extra: Critically and financially, *Mary Poppins* was by far the greatest success of Walt Disney's life. But the book's author, Pamela Travers (1899-1996), rejected the producer when he first approached her about acquiring the film rights to *Mary Poppins* in 1943. Her books were unsentimental, certainly not fit for some kind of Disney animated hogwash. But the dear man was so charming and persistent he wore her down. With her sales sagging, the writer finally gave in to Disney in 1960 on the condition she would get script approval. Twice she came to Hollywood to voice strong opinions about Walt's story changes. Mary Poppins was a harsh middle-aged taskmaster, not the caring young woman they were presenting onscreen. Yet somehow, every time Walt was able to charm her into thinking that his ideas were better. When Travers saw the finished product, she was aghast. Dick Van Dyke's English accent was ridiculous! And mixing cartoon characters with the live actors would never do. She was shocked to discover that contractually, her creative control only applied to the *Mary Poppins* screenplay, not what actually appeared on the big screen. For the rest of her life,

Pamela Travers badmouthed the hugely successful picture that delighted audiences and made her rich.

Extra: The 1964 premiere of *Mary Poppins* at Grauman's Chinese Theater was a crowning moment in Walt Disney's career as film producer. It had been forty-one years since he'd arrived in Los Angeles from Kansas City, a broke, unemployed twenty-one-year-old rube. Through all his struggles and failures, Walt felt he'd built up a special bond with the public. In the past, Walt had been mistaken about what people would buy, but he had a strong feeling moviegoers would take to the latest Disney offering. When *Mary Poppins* finished screening, the industry audience gave it a five-minute standing ovation, capping a nearly perfect evening. Hours earlier, Snow White, Mickey Mouse, Goofy and many other Disney staples entertained throngs of fans on Hollywood Boulevard. Then a black limo pulled up to the curb, a familiar figure emerged and his characters ran up to greet him. The crowd on the street erupted into a loud cheer when they saw Walt, as if they were watching a confident coach being mobbed by his players before a big game.

Snow White's Evil Queen

Walt Disney felt the evil queen/peddler woman was the key element that would make or break *Snow White and the Seven Dwarfs* in 1937. The princess was sympathetic, the little guys were humorous, but the villain had to be horrifying to keep the audience interested. The evil monarch's vocals were performed by a renowned stage professional named Lucille La Verne, whose haughty tone was perfect for the beautiful queen. The Disney staff was less satisfied by La Verne's interpretation of the villain after she magically transformed into the hag-like peddler woman. After several misfires, she held up her hand to stop the taping. "Wait, I have an idea!"

Lucille left the recording room for a few minutes then returned. "I'm ready."

The dialogue was now delivered in a way that chilled and thrilled her small audience at the studio. After the performance, there was applause and someone asked what La Verne did during the break. The actress smiled and said, "I took my teeth out!"

Extra: In the first three months of 1938, *Snow White and the Seven Dwarfs* made eight million dollars at a time when movie tickets cost twenty-five cents for adults and a dime for kids. The only downside to Walt Disney's triumph was that perhaps he made his peddler-woman villain too frightening. In England, children were barred from seeing *Snow White* without being accompanied by an adult. And Walt got some disturbing news from Radio City Music Hall in New York. Sure, the cartoon was breaking records, but every few days the kids got so scared that management had to keep replacing the wet seats.

Extra: *Snow White and the Seven Dwarfs* (1937) took three long years to complete and Walt suffered through many doubts about the film's marketing direction. He worried when the press called it "Disney's Folly," and then realized it was good to have people talk about it. Disney rejected a salesman's idea that he should eliminate the dwarfs from the advertising, pushing the love story between Snow White and the prince instead. But throughout the stressful production, his cartoonists stayed loyal and enthusiastic, often using their free time to run around Los Angeles and tack up advertising posters. *Snow White* was a worldwide success and after the money rolled in, Walt threw his animators a party in gratitude. He later regretted it when some of the more bohemian members of his staff chose to let their hair down, and the family event turned into a wild orgy.

Walt's New World

The very controlling Walt Disney felt that the immediate area surrounding Disneyland looked like a damn cheap Las Vegas. When he opened his Anaheim Park in 1955, he had only been able to purchase a few hundred acres. He couldn't prevent a slew of motels from popping up near it. Disneyland was a runaway success and by the 1960s, Walt hatched a scheme to build a new magic kingdom in Orange County, Florida. He sent proxies east to buy marshland secretly. The TV icon ignored warnings that if he were spotted in the vicinity, the real estate prices would shoot up; he had to get a close-up view of how things were going. While he was eating in an Orlando diner, a waitress asked him, "Pardon me, aren't you Walt Disney?"

"No, and if I ever see that blanket-blank Disney I'll give him a piece of my mind!"

By the time the sellers got wise, Walt's Florida land acquisitions were equal to twice the size of Manhattan.

Extra: Walt Disney was unique among Hollywood's moguls in not seeing television as a threat. In the late 1940s, if employees of major studios were found to own TV sets, it was sometimes grounds for dismissal. The tycoons blamed the little box for declining movie attendance, ignoring other factors such as couples who had been separated due to World War II, now had started families and preferred to spend their evenings at home. Walt saw the new medium as a way to tell the public about his projects and agreed to host the *Disneyland* anthology series in 1954. Many viewers were thrilled to see what the fifty-three-year-old cartoon maker they heard so much about looked like for the first time. They saw no sign of the temperamental longhaired, sometimes heavy-drinking artist who regularly cursed in front of his artists, and occasionally had not been allowed in fancy restaurants because of his casual attire. On television, Walt, who had dropped out of high school at age sixteen, stood in front of a bookcase wearing a suit and tie, often doing several retakes to make sure that he didn't mangle the English language. The charming Disney became a welcome weekly visitor in American households, and quickly became known as "Uncle Walt."

Extra: Walt Disney hated to repeat himself. For years, he sincerely stated that there would only be one Disneyland. By the early 1960s, he was much more interested in building what he called the Experimental Prototype Community of Tomorrow (EPCOT). If someone didn't do something about the deteriorating condition of cities, what kind of world would his grandchildren grow up in? The Disney board of directors had grave doubts about the viability of the new project. A city of the future where twenty thousand residents could not own property so Walt would maintain control? Citizens transported by the PeopleMover and monorail? All cars to be kept underground and to be used only for out-of-town trips? Residents not having to worry about the weather because the city would be climate controlled under a dome? Self-sufficient rented homes with underground trash removal? And then Walt wanted to build a second city to manage the first one. How would it ever be paid for? It wasn't their job as a company to inspire urban planners to make the best use of modern technology. They owed it to their investors to stick with what they knew, which was entertainment. Walt realized he'd have to go along with a Florida version of Disneyland in order to have a chance to finance his utopia.

Extra: In 1966, Walt Disney told a family member that he needed to live another fifteen years to complete his many plans. Sadly, it was not to be. Decades of heavy smoking caught up with the sixty-five-year-old cartoon maker. Walt went in for a routine operation and ended up having a lung removed. His family was told Disney was a goner; he only had a few months to live. No one told the patient himself, but he seemed to know. Studio employees were shocked to see how thin and gaunt their usually robust boss looked when he got out of the hospital. Walt told them that he had a scare, assured them that he'd be fine, but his expression said otherwise. At one point, he started crying in front of staff members, yet Disney never quit on his dreams. The night before he died, Walt lay in his hospital bed arguing fiercely with his board members that the new Disney Park in Florida could pay for EPCOT.

Extra: Walt Disney never wished to sell stock in his company. The initial box-office failures of *Pinocchio* (1940), *Fantasia* (1940) and *Bambi* (1942) forced him to make a public offering. Of the many challenges Walt faced in his life, the greatest one may have been convincing shareholders to go along with plans for a non-profitable city of the future. Disney died on December 15, 1966, before he had a chance to use his great powers of persuasion on the owners of the company to get behind EPCOT. Walt Disney World opened in 1971 with EPCOT deemed by the company's board of directors to be unfeasible. Instead, the World's Fair-like EPCOT Center was opened in 1982. The new theme park displayed cutting-edge technology, showcased a variety of cultures, entertained millions of paying guests and was very different from Walt Disney's original concept of an ideal place to live.

Extra: In 1994, the Walt Disney Company invested 2.5 billion to develop the city of Celebration, Florida. Home ownership was allowed in Celebration, which was modeled after a 1930s American small town, rather than a futuristic domed metropolis. The Disney brass decided that the underground trash removal was too expensive and prohibiting driving on the streets wasn't practical. But at least the car garages and garbage cans would be hidden from street view, strategically placed behind the new city's beautiful houses. Although the planned community was criticized by some for being artificial, creepy and overpriced, many residents found Celebration to be a wonderful place to live and a modified attempt at fulfilling the late Walt Disney's dreams.

Walt Disney Overcame Doubters

After World War II, the heavily in debt Walt Disney got tired of people telling him his ventures would fail. The frustrated entrepreneur had developed a half-hour featurette called *Seal Island.* He was told by distributors there was no market for it. Walt was also getting flack from bankers about his plans for a feature-length animated *Cinderella*; make less expensive projects, they said. Then there was the scoffing about his attempt to make a fully live action version of *Treasure Island,* a Disney movie without cartoons would never sell. Walt ignored the doubters and completed all three endeavors. *Seal Island* won the Oscar for best short subject, which led to many more highly profitable nature films, *Cinderella* became his biggest success in a decade and *Treasure Island* did fine at the box office. The positive results made it far easier for Walt to dismiss the negative voices who were making fun of his amusement-park idea.

Extra: In 1942, the financially teetering Walt Disney attended the premiere of *Bambi*. In the dramatic scene where Bambi's mother died, the young fawn was shown wandering through the meadow shouting, "Mother! Where are you, Mother?"

A teenage girl seated in the balcony shouted out, "Here I am Bambi!"

The audience broke into laughter, except for the red-faced producer who concluded correctly that war time was not the best time to release a film about the love life of a deer.

Extra: Disney's *Pinocchio* (1940), *Fantasia* (1940) and *Bambi* (1942) all failed in their first releases. World War II cut off international distribution. The national mood turned away from Walt's sentimental movies. Disney plunged four million dollars into debt and it looked like his line of credit would be cut off. In a dramatic meeting, A.P. Giannini, the founder of Bank of America, stood up and told the board members that Disney made timeless pictures and that the war would not last forever. They voted unanimously to keep Walt afloat after the old man's speech. Giannini was proven right years later when all three films became profitable classics.

Extra: Building an amusement park provided perfectionist Walt Disney with a creative outlet that in many ways was more satisfying to him than making motion pictures. Disney's most expensive animated film, *Sleeping Beauty*, (1959) lost money in its first release. After *Snow White* (1937) and *Cinderella* (1950), perhaps he'd gone to the fairy tale well once too often. Likewise, the live-action *Pollyanna* (1960) made Walt cry at the studio, but failed at the box office. The heart-warming tale of a young girl trying her best to bring happiness to the crabby residents of a small town may have turned off young boys with its title. Walt also second-guessed himself over the initial failure of *Alice in Wonderland* (1951). His brother Roy had accused him of adapting English scholar Lewis Carroll's (1832-1898) 1865 novel about a girl who falls down a rabbit hole, simply to impress highbrow critics who looked down their noses at cartoons. The dream-like characters in *Alice* lacked the usual Disney warmth and were probably too strange to go over big. With movies, either people liked them or they didn't; once they were in circulation, there wasn't much a producer could do. And even when Walt had a hit, like the submarine adventure *20,000 Leagues Under the Sea,* for the forward-looking entrepreneur the triumph was short-lived. After Disneyland opened in 1955, Walt was able to correct mistakes, and keep adding new rides and attractions, which gave him a joyful, never-ending project.

Extra: Had Disneyland been a movie, it may have been pulled out of theaters after a short run. On opening day, July 17, 1955, ten thousand invitation-only tickets were sent out. They were easy to forge and over three times as many people showed up. A man stood on the side of the park with a ladder and charged five dollars to climb over the fence until the police caught him. Just a few days before, there had been a plumbers' strike. Walt chose to sacrifice the drinking fountains so that the bathrooms worked; several of his guests passed out due to the heat, which went up at one point to 101 degrees. Pepsi Cola sponsored the event; many of the enraged thirsty patrons assumed the water shortage was a cynical attempt to sell soda. The asphalt on Main Street was not dry; women wearing high-heeled shoes got stuck and sank. The restaurants and concession stands ran out of food early. A gas leak shut down Fantasyland. Nearly half the rides broke down. As the afternoon wore on, fights broke out between the ride operators and customers. Disney himself had been busy running around his 160-acre Magic Kingdom filming a TV show and wasn't aware of all the mishaps until he read about them in the newspaper the next day. He immediately returned to Disneyland to fix things.

Extra: One of Walt's most loyal, yet challenging backers was his wife, Lillian Bounds Disney (1899-1997). She understood that her husband needed a sounding board; he was surrounded by yes men who were frightened of him. Walt listened in 1927 when she said, "I don't like the name Mortimer. Why don't you call your mouse Mickey?"

She agreed with his business partner and brother Roy Disney (1893-1971) in 1934 that making the first feature-length cartoon, *Snow White and the Seven Dwarfs,* would ruin them. When it turned out to be a smash hit, Walt took great pleasure in hearing Lillian admit she was wrong. But then he scared her again. "Why would you want to build an amusement park?" she asked him. "Amusement parks are dirty. They don't make any money."

Walt's reply didn't make her feel better. "That's the whole point. I want a clean one that will."

But in 1955, Mrs. Disney was at Disneyland the morning it opened with a broom, sweeping up the dust off the Mark Twain Steamer.

Extra: Lillian, a registered Democrat, didn't worry about her Republican husband cheating on her with another woman, but she would sometimes get jealous of Walt's real passion: his work. Often Disney spent nights at his studio prowling around the animators' desks, even going through their trash cans to pull out their best ideas. One time Walt came home late and drunk. Angrily, she locked him out. He made amends the next day by presenting her with a female puppy in a hat box. Lillian forgave him and the event became the creative launching point for the 1955 Disney-animated canine romance *Lady and the Tramp*.

Extra: The Disneys were world travelers. Lillian was thrilled to get the call from Walt to pack up for their next surprise vacation, and then she would marvel at how he would use their experiences to enhance Disneyland. On a trip to Switzerland, they were impressed by the breathtaking beauty of the most famous mountain in the Alps; it led to Walt developing the Matterhorn Bobsleds ride in 1959. The couple enjoyed buying antiques in the French Quarter, which inspired the 1966 creation of New Orleans Square (Walt had many great qualities but tact was not one of them. When the mayor of New Orleans came to visit the cartoon maker at Disneyland, he remarked that New Orleans Square looked just like the real thing. "Actually, it's cleaner," Disney replied.)

In the late 1950s, the Disneys heard a story from a tour guide about buccaneers hiding treasure near Cuba, which may have sparked the Pirates of the Caribbean ride in 1967, an attraction that took so long to create, Walt sadly didn't live to see it completed.

Extra: Lillian fell short of her own dream. She did not share Walt's love of classical music, preferring the easy-listening sounds of Lawrence Welk (1903-1992). But in 1987, twenty-one years after Walt's death, she donated fifty million dollars to build the Walt Disney Concert Hall, which would become the new home for the Los Angeles Philharmonic. What better legacy than to bring Beethoven and Tchaikovsky to the masses, just like her late husband had tried to do with the animated feature *Fantasia* in 1940? But Lillian became discouraged when her idea for a simple brick building became an elaborate stainless steel amphitheater, in the hands of architect Frank Gehry. Soon the fifty million was gone and Lillian wanted it back, fearing she had wasted her money on an incomplete boondoggle. Her daughter Diane convinced her that Gehry's design was wonderful, but Mrs. Disney passed away six years before the hall opened in 2004.

Extra: One great thing about Walt building Disneyland was that he and Lillian got to play tour guide to world leaders. Mrs. Disney was very disappointed when the head of Russia, Nikita S. Khrushchev, and his wife didn't come to the park in 1960. The Anaheim police said they could not provide enough security. The Soviet prime minister grumpily settled for a star-studded luncheon at 20th Century Fox Studios instead. During the meal, Frank Sinatra was informed of Mrs. Khrushchev's disappointment at missing out on the Magic Kingdom. Ol' Blue Eyes slammed his fist on the table. "Screw the cops. I'll take the old broad down there and watch her myself."

The singer grabbed her by the hand and was near the door when he was stopped by security. Back at Disneyland, Walt made Lillian smile by telling her he was just as disappointed as she was. Disney was dying to show the Communist ruler his new submarine fleet, the eighth largest in the world.

Extra: For *Treasure Island* (1950), Walt Disney hired British actor Robert Newton (1905-1956) to chew up the scenery as the one-legged pirate Long John Silver. A notorious alcoholic, Newton once got so inebriated he showed up at the wrong movie set. The happy producer put the big star in four scenes until people from the film he was actually supposed to be in arrived and hauled him away.

Walt Disney's Nurse

After Walt Disney took a bad spill from one of his polo horses in 1936, his greatest confidant became his no-nonsense studio nurse Hazel. Late at night, after most of the employees had gone home, she applied therapeutic treatments to his neck while Disney would talk to her about his hopes and dreams. They had a similar sense of humor and would often share a good laugh over the latest workplace gossip. Like Walt, she held parent-like affection and impatience for his zany, childlike animators. Once, Hazel was called to help one of the cartoonists who had gotten sick after having lunch in the commissary. The concerned caregiver raced to the rescue and found the poor man lying on the floor clutching his stomach. "What happened?" She was told that he had taken a bet that he could drink ten chocolate sodas. "Oh for Pete's sake!"

Her boss later approved of her remedy; Hazel kicked the already suffering artist in the rear.

Extra: Hazel George (1904-1996) contributed to Walt's well-being in other ways besides her healthcare treatments. In 1952, Disney confided to his nurse that he was having trouble convincing his partner and brother Roy Disney (1893-1971) that building Disneyland (at first called Mickey Mouse Park) was a good idea. Hazel lent her boss money for the ambitious endeavor and convinced other studio employees to do the same. When Roy heard about Hazel's new group, "the Backers and the Boosters," he was impressed and became much more supportive of the amusement-park project. George also moonlighted as a songwriter and quietly provided several numbers for Disney television shows and movies.

Good Neighbor Zorro

While playing Zorro on television for Walt Disney in 1957, actor Guy Williams found he could not always please his fans. As Grand Marshal of the Portland Rose Parade, he was jeered for riding in a car instead of a horse. When the former male model cited safety concerns, a local newspaper printed a picture of a five-year-old girl looking very comfortable on horseback. Despite the embarrassment, *Zorro* remained highly rated for two years then was abruptly cancelled due to legal wrangling between Disney and ABC. Williams' acting career continued in the 1960s with sometimes unsatisfactory roles on TV shows like *Bonanza* and *Lost in Space*. Finally, the discouraged Italian thespian left Hollywood and moved to Argentina, where he found great happiness. Guy became a rancher and his neighbors were thrilled to have Zorro living among them.

Extra: The inspiration for writer Johnston McCulley (1883-1958) to create the dashing Hispanic hero Zorro in 1919 may have been a redheaded Irishman. As a young man, William Lamport (1615-1659) left his British-ruled homeland and embarked on a series of adventures. After a scandalous affair with a Spanish noblewoman, William moved to the Spanish colony of Mexico. Once there he became sympathetic to the plight of both the native Indians and black slaves. Mexico must be independent of Spain, he said, which made him an enemy of the Crown. Lamport was arrested, held in a dungeon for ten years and then made a miraculous escape. The fugitive then hid in Mexico City, only sneaking out at night. For two consecutive mornings, some locals were thrilled to see the anti-Spanish graffiti that mysteriously appeared on government buildings. Lamport was then re-captured and strangled himself before he could be burned at the stake. As the years passed, William's skill with a sword and wild womanizing ways were exaggerated to the point of legend.

Extra: Armand Joseph Catalano or Guy Williams (1915-1989) was not happy being the leading man on the TV sci-fi classic *Lost in Space* (1965-1968). Other characters on the show eclipsed him in viewer popularity and he found his dialogue greatly diminished. "I must be the highest paid actor per line since Laurence Olivier," he said bitterly.

Extra: Walt Disney, who was a strong political conservative, sometimes used *Zorro* episodes to rail against the evils of big government. When Guy Williams was auditioning for the part, the cartoon maker suggested the actor grow a mustache similar to Walt's.

Extra: Disney's TV show *Zorro* (1957-1959) started a wave of children brandishing toy swords and getting in trouble for writing graffiti. Once, after a long day of shooting, Guy Williams found an unwelcome Z scratched into his car door. He was placated by Walt Disney rewarding him with 2.5 percent of the massive *Zorro* merchandising sales.

Reactions to Walt

Walt Disney was often amused by critical reactions to his more famous cartoons. *The Three Little Pigs,* made in 1933, was seen by many as a symbol of the Great Depression; the happy swine danced like the carefree people in the 1920s until the big bad wolf wiped them out with the force of the 1929 stock market crash. The usually Republican Walt never intended that the hard-working pig that lived in the brick house be seen as an endorsement of President Roosevelt's New Deal policies. Seven years later, a columnist fumed over *Fantasia.* In her mind, the film's climactic scene, where the devil damned human souls into a volcano, meant Disney was saying we were all helpless against Nazi demons. How funny that now he was seen as an appeaser. Back in 1937, a left-wing newspaper had praised *Snow White*; when the seven dwarfs had taken down the wicked queen, it was a clear triumph for a miniature communist society.

Extra: With *The Three Little Pigs,* Walt Disney injected personality into a cartoon for the first time. The pigs looked alike but acted differently. The eight-minute film was rejected by some distributors in 1933 because it only had four characters. The common wisdom was that animated shorts should have as many figures on the screen as possible. Walt finally pushed his bold new product out onto the marketplace, but the producer was hugely disappointed when it received a lukewarm reception at Radio City Music Hall. Disney later speculated that the Hall's huge screen muffled the pigs' individuality; when *Pigs* moved into smaller, neighborhood theaters it was a smash hit. The picture's original song, "Who's Afraid of the Big Bad Wolf," became an anthem for the Great Depression. (Disney had initially not bothered to get the publishing rights and hastily hired musicians to go into darkened cinemas with flashlights, pencils and paper to copy down "Big Bad Wolf's" lyrics). At some venues, *The Three Little Pigs* played for so many years that the posters outside the buildings featured the animated hog stars drawn with long white beards.

Extra: Donald Duck made his first appearance in 1934 after Walt Disney heard vocal artist Clarence Nash (1904-1985) recite the poem "Mary Had a Little Lamb" in a duck voice. The animated angry waterfowl went over big with audiences and immediately was compared to a famous public figure. Harold Ickes (1874-1952) served as United States Secretary of the Interior from 1933 to 1946 and helped to implement many of Franklin Roosevelt's New Deal government relief policies. Ickes also waddled when he walked, spoke with a high-squawking voice and sometimes blew his top; his boss gave Harold the nickname Donald Duck. In the 1930s, moviegoers recognized similarities between the personalities of Disney's temperamental big-screen mallard and the president's irascible cabinet official. Walt himself admitted that it was difficult to tell whether the cartoon duck was imitating Ickes or vice-versa.

Extra: In 1938, the conductor of the Philadelphia Orchestra, the longhaired flamboyant Leopold Stokowski (1882-1977), had a chance encounter with Walt Disney in a Los Angeles restaurant. The cartoon maker and the maestro were surprised that each was a fan of the other. As always, Walt regarded meetings with talent as an opportunity to push the creative envelope. In fifteen years of running his studio, Disney had used music to supplement gags and stories, now he wanted to reverse the formula. While recently attending a symphony at the Hollywood Bowl, Walt had been enthralled listening to *The Sorcerer's Apprentice* by the French composer Paul Dukas (1865-1935). What if the ballad, about a not fully trained pupil whose magic backfires on him, was combined with a state-of-the-art, twenty-minute animated cartoon? It could raise animation to a higher art form and introduce new audiences to classical music who had never appreciated it before. Stokowski loved the idea so much he volunteered to conduct it for free. But even with Leopold's generous offer, the twenty-minute *Apprentice* was too expensive to stand on its own. Stokowski later suggested to

Walt that several other pieces could be presented in a similar way; Disney's short project was transformed into the unique feature film *Fantasia* (1940).

Extra: Disney's other reason to make *The Sorcerer's Apprentice* was to save the career of Mickey Mouse. A superstitious man, who like many in Hollywood consulted fortunetellers, Walt felt that if Mickey died his whole organization would go down with him. The problem was that Mickey, like many other stars, was now typecast. The mouse was no longer the brave Douglas Fairbanks-like swashbuckler his fans had fallen in love with in 1928. In ten years, Mickey had gone from being mischievous to bland; he had been surpassed in popularity by the mean-spirited but more versatile Donald Duck. The mouse was such a nice role model that Walt got letters of complaint every time the little guy misbehaved on the screen. Disney also felt that the high-pitched voice that he himself provided for the mouse was not exciting for audiences to hear; Mickey's role in *Fantasia* would be silent. Disney remained Mickey's strongest advocate, despite his artist's suggestions that the four-foot rodent was a dumb character who should be replaced in *Fantasia* by Dopey, the silent dwarf from *Snow White*. It galled Walt that "Mickey Mouse" eventually became an accepted slang term to describe something that was second rate, as in, "This is such a Mickey Mouse outfit."

Extra: *Fantasia* was a crushing disappointment for Walt when it was released in 1940. Many movie theater owners refused to pay for the installation of Disney's at-the-time new stereophonic acoustic system called Fantasound, giving the film very limited distribution. The exhibitors who did show *Fantasia* charged much higher admission prices than normal, which kept audiences away. Some patrons were put off by *Fantasia's* lack of a story while others felt that the *Night on Bald Mountain* sequence, which featured a huge devil damning souls, was not fit to be shown in front of children. Disney's masterpiece was cut in length and went on to be the second half of a double bill with a western. Unlike some of his other initial money losers, such as *Pinocchio* and *Bambi*, Walt never lived to see *Fantasia* become profitable. Shortly before Disney died in 1966, he said, "*Fantasia*? Well I don't regret it but if I had to do it over again, I wouldn't."

In 1968, the Beatles cartoon *Yellow Submarine* did very well with the psychedelic crowd. Sensing a new market, the Disney studio re-released *Fantasia*, and the amazing cartoon concert was finally made into a box-office success. Some of the drug-tripping hippies who saw *Fantasia* speculated that Walt must have been on something when he produced it. (Walt only drank Scotch and smoked cigarettes as far as I know.)

Walt Disney's Daughters

Walt Disney's two daughters, Sharon and Diane, grew up sheltered from the limelight. The children had no images of Mickey Mouse around their home. Their father didn't go to many parties, preferring to stay in after a long day of work. Sometimes he would playfully chase the youngsters upstairs, cackling like the evil peddler woman in *Snow White*. When they behaved badly, Walt would admonish them with a raised eyebrow; his stern demeanor inspired the character of the wise old owl, in the 1942 animated feature *Bambi*. As toddlers, the brainy Diane and beautiful Sharon stayed blissfully unaware that their parents worried about them being kidnapped and allowed no pictures of the sisters to be publicly circulated. Once in 1939, a curious classmate questioned six-year-old Diane about her family. She went home and said, "Daddy, you never told me you were that Walt Disney," and asked him for an autograph.

Extra: Disney came up with Mickey Mouse in 1927 to replace Oswald the Lucky Rabbit, one of Walt's earlier characters, which he hadn't copyrighted and lost to Universal Studios. The young filmmaker made sure that from then on, he owned everything he created. Some on Disney's staff thought that he was like an overprotective father when it came to his favorite rodent. Never one to hold grudges, Walt had given Woody Woodpecker artist Walter Lantz (1899-1994) his blessing to draw the Oswald shorts, but it still killed Disney to see the cartoon bunny at another studio. In 2006, forty years after Walt passed on, Universal now merged with NBC, began showing NFL football on Sunday nights. To obtain the services of sixty-two-year-old broadcaster Al Michaels, still under contract to Disney-owned ABC, Universal transferred ownership of the Lucky Rabbit back to its original company. The trade thrilled Walt's seventy-three-year-old daughter Diane to no end.

MOGULS AND DIRECTORS

"If I wasn't the head of a studio, who would talk to me?"
— Harry Cohn, head of Columbia Pictures

"Give me a smart idiot over a stupid genius any day."
— Samuel Goldwyn

Goldwyn's Conclusion

After a bad preview for the 1947 Christmas film *The Bishop's Wife*, producer Sam Goldwyn hired writers Billy Wilder and Charles Brackett to fix it up. The movie, about an angel who rescues the marriage of a neglectful man of the cloth, had left Goldwyn feeling frustrated by his actors. Cary Grant was giving a lackluster performance as the spirit, leading lady Loretta Young was complaining about her dowdy costumes and David Niven, playing the bishop, wanted Grant's role. Over one weekend, the two script doctors worked their magic and saved the picture. Due to potential tax problems, the two scribes decided not to accept any payment for their work. At a lunch meeting with the grateful Goldwyn, Wilder and Brackett told him that they had come to the conclusion there should be no fee. "That's amazing!" said the smiling mogul. "I have come to the same conclusion."

Who Won the Race?

Writer/director Billy Wilder liked to mess with producer Samuel Goldwyn's head. The Austrian-born Wilder, who had fled Europe when Hitler rose to power, respected how the former glove salesman from Poland had good taste in stories, even though Sam hardly ever read anything. One time Wilder pitched the mogul a screen idea about Nijinsky, the famous Russian ballet dancer. Goldwyn was dubious, Wilder persisted; the story had great cinematic possibilities. As a young man, Nijinsky danced for the Bolshoi and received international acclaim. Then he met the great love of his life, was rejected, ended up in an insane asylum and thought he was a horse. Goldwyn stared daggers at him. Sam didn't just fall off the turnip truck. The public would never pay to see something so negative.

"Don't worry, Sam, it has a happy ending."

Goldwyn asked what could possibly be happy about a man who believes he's a horse.

"He wins the Kentucky Derby!"

Harry Cohn's Maladies

From 1923 till his death in 1958, Harry Cohn ruled Columbia Pictures with an iron hand. The foul-mouthed mogul had fought his way up from the streets, and continued to battle in the boardroom. His harangues could reduce other Hollywood power players to tears. "I don't get ulcers, I give them," he proclaimed. But sometimes Cohn's bravado was peeled off and revealed vulnerability. Studio employees would snicker when their tough-guy boss came down with an illness. The slightest ailment and an army of attendants would be summoned to Cohn's bedside, including a nose and throat specialist, a chiropractor, a heart expert, a surgeon, an osteopath, and for good measure, a rabbi, a priest and a Christian Science practitioner. "You never know," explained Harry. "One of 'em might know something."

Extra: Writing screenplays for Hollywood moguls was usually far more lucrative than penning novels. Yet the highly paid scribes in Tinseltown sometimes could not resist biting the hands that fed them. The shrewd studio tycoons, who hired outstanding talent to make many excellent motion pictures, were often portrayed in Hollywood lore as illiterate, tyrannical buffoons. One such anecdote about Harry Cohn (1891-1958) had him chewing out some of his more educated employees. "This script is garbage! Four hundred years ago people didn't run around saying yes siree and no siree!"
The screenplay actually said, "Yes, Sire. No, Sire."

Extra: Harry Cohn protected his reputation fiercely. Once two producers at Columbia were arguing about the mogul's overbearing personality; one of the men said Cohn was within his rights to boss the staff around. The loyal employee stated Harry's favorite quote, "He who eats my bread sings my song."
Later, Cohn, who had electronic listening devices placed throughout the studio, summoned his defender to the office. "I want to thank you for the nice statements about me. If you ever need a good reference, I will speak highly of you as well. But I can't have someone here that I feel indebted to, so you're fired."

Extra: Columbia Pictures was full of secret passageways allowing Harry Cohn to sneak into starlets' dressing rooms for private liaisons. Once, the mogul made a wrong turn in a dim tunnel and accidentally came out of Bette Davis' closet. The actress, who had been loaned out from Warner Bros., was sitting in front of the dressing-room mirror, her face covered with cold cream. Bette stared at Cohn's reflection with burning eyes. "What the hell do you want?"

For once Harry was intimidated. He tipped his hat and backed up into the darkness.

That Barrymore Temper

The great Lionel Barrymore prided himself on keeping his terrible temper in check. In 1930, the fifty-two-year-old stage veteran was hired to direct a picture at MGM Studios. His innovative ideas included the invention of the boom microphone that could be held over actors' heads while they spoke. One day everyone was blowing their lines, which caused several retakes and Barrymore felt an explosion coming on. Still smiling, the enraged filmmaker excused himself, went upstairs to the sound control room and let loose a barrage of foul language; none of the cast members were spared his wrath. When he finished he felt better and calmly returned to the set. To Lionel's delighted surprise, his performers excelled for the rest of the day. Later a jubilant Barrymore told a crew member that patience always wins. The man replied, "That little broadcast from behind the glass booth didn't hurt any either."

Extra: Lionel Barrymore was not the only star to be eavesdropped on while working. One day during production of the TV show *The Pride of the Family* (1953-1955), fourteen-year-old Natalie Wood was engaged in an animated conversation with one of her young male co-stars. Her Russian-born mother Maria watched nervously from a distance as the teenage actress seemed to get more excited while she talked. Finally, the English-challenged stage mom couldn't take it anymore; she asked a soundman to lower a microphone over her daughter, and then was shocked to hear Natalie's probing queries about her fellow actor's private parts. The Van Nuys High School student was quickly hauled off to her dressing room; from then on, Wood and her *Family* castmate spoke in code whenever they discussed adult-only matters.

Woody Gains Control

Thirty-year-old television writer Woody Allen was thrilled when he was hired to script the 1965 comedy *What's New Pussycat?* Woody's idol Warren Beatty was perfect to play the lead role of a wild womanizer who tries to stay faithful. Fittingly, the film's title came from a pickup line Beatty used to great success in real life. But both the star and the scribe felt the movie was compromised when

Producer Charles Feldman insisted that a role be created for his French girlfriend Capucine. As her character grew, Beatty saw his own part lessen, and chose to walk off the picture, leaving Woody to fend for himself. Allen despaired as the actors and executives regularly changed his dialogue. After the completed *Pussycat* received very weak notices, Woody vowed to retain creative control of his stories on film by personally directing them.

Extra: Although he had great luck with the "What's New Pussycat?" line, the womanizing Beatty admitted that it earned him an occasional slap in the face. Warren also made the observation that if you get married in Hollywood, always do it by noon; that way if it doesn't work out you don't kill your evening.

Extra: Twenty-four-year-old Warren Beatty thought he found a kindred spirit when he met talent agent Charles Feldman (1904-1968) in 1961. Both men were Hollywood pleasure seekers who preferred being behind the camera. The plot line of *Pussycat*, about an out-of-control Don Juan, appealed greatly to both the young and older womanizers. But Feldman was even more enamored with Capucine (1928-1990). After meeting the Swiss model at a party in New York, Charlie brought her to California to learn English. They eventually moved in together, and Feldman put her career ahead of his surrogate son Beatty. The most valuable lesson Warren learned from Feldman was never to sign a contract so that you couldn't be sued if you quit a movie.

Extra: Charles Feldman and Warren Beatty were impressed when they caught Woody Allen's stand-up act at the Bitter End club in Greenwich Village. They offered the talented TV scribe thirty thousand dollars to pen the *What's New, Pussycat* script. Allen wanted more money and agreed to do the job on the condition that he got to be in the movie. As the production went forward, Warren Beatty noticed that Woody's character was getting to say all the good jokes, and decided to leave the project. Warren's replacement, Peter Sellers, was a much bigger star and demanded the funny lines for himself, much to Allen's chagrin. After *Pussycat*, Woody realized that he needed more creative control over his work. He embarked on a prolific career where he wrote and directed a slew of relatively low-budget pictures ranging from pure comedies like *Take the Money and Run* (1969) to heavy dramas such as *September* (1987). The films Woody chose to put himself in were typically lighter fare; his usual womanizing, nerdy and cowardly alter ego was based on the screen persona of Bob Hope. Woody also claimed the main reason he stepped in front of the camera was because he couldn't afford to hire major stars like Dustin Hoffman. The bespectacled Allen, who in actuality was a very athletic and popular kid, once said that his movies had no relationship to his own life and another time stated that almost all of his films were autobiographical.

The Biggest Man in Town

From 1924 to 1951, the paternalistic Louis B. Mayer was arguably the most powerful tycoon in Los Angeles. As leader of MGM Studios, Mayer was willing to defend his throne with either fists or histrionics. When stars asked for a raise or turned down a role, Louis would sometimes break down in tears, which caused many of his famous employees to back off their demands. Hollywood's greatest actors never got to see their boss flash a Cheshire Cat-like grin as soon they left his office. Mayer once decked Charlie Chaplin during an argument and forcefully tossed Erich von Stroheim off the studio lot when the Austrian director made a derogatory remark about women. Another time Louis had to be restrained from choking a story man for being dull. People were often surprised at the mogul's diminutive stature. Once, Mayer was working behind his desk when he received a glaring female visitor. "Can I help you, Madam?"

"Sir, in my country when a lady enters a room a gentleman stands up."

"Madam, I am standing."

What Hitch Really Thought About Actors

When director Alfred Hitchcock came from England to America in 1939, he had difficulty finding major Hollywood stars willing to work with him. The "thriller" type movies Hitch specialized in were looked down upon in the States. But with war breaking out in Europe, Alfred's fellow Britisher Cary Grant was anxious to get away from frivolous romantic comedies and agreed to star in Hitchcock's *Suspicion*. The movie's plot had Grant killing his wife, played by Joan Fontaine. Preview audiences, especially female ones, were unwilling to accept Cary as a murderer; the ending was changed to where it was all imagined by Fontaine, who went on to win an Oscar. Hitchcock was happy about the film's success but was disappointed by the compromises involved in working with movie stars. He later said that Walt Disney's animated characters were the best actors because you could just rip them to pieces at the end of filming.

Extra: While directing the 1954 suspense thriller *Rear Window*, Alfred Hitchcock was confronted by his leading man James Stewart. Did Hitchcock really think all actors were cattle? Alfred cried foul; what he really said was that all actors should be treated like cattle! After the angry star calmed down, Hitchcock showed him some footage of Stewart looking out the window at a beautiful woman with a leering expression. It was followed by another view of James, this time tenderly spying on a dog. The Master then revealed that both times he used the same shot of Stewart, proving that if movie stars weren't exactly heifers, their performances could certainly be led into the editing slaughterhouse.

Alfred Hitchcock Versus David O. Selznick

It was David O. Selznick, the famed producer known for his controlling ways, that lured Alfred Hitchcock from England to America. Hitch assumed that the independent Selznick would allow him more creative freedom than the major studios, and then became frustrated by the bespectacled mogul's constant interference and suggestions. At one time Hitch referred to a Selznick memo as "The Longest Story Ever Told." The producer responded with his own complaints about Hitchcock's economical shooting of films, which left David very little to cut in the editing room. Hitchcock got his revenge years later with the 1954 thriller *Rear Window*. The film starred Jimmy Stewart as the broken-legged hero, a man confined to his chair, kind of like the overweight Hitchcock fighting the villainous Raymond Burr, who was cast because of his physical resemblance to The Master's former boss.

Hitchcock's Fear of Policemen

London-born Alfred Hitchcock explained his fear of policemen by relating an anecdote from his child. As a small boy, Hitch had acted naughty and his father's punishment had been to send him to a local constable who locked him up in a cell. The incident traumatized the great director for life. Hitch became the rare Los Angeles resident who didn't drive due to his worry that a cop would pull him over. His phobia manifested itself in the 1960 horror classic *Psycho*, when an intimidating patrolman with sinister dark glasses (provided to the actor by Hitchcock) peers through a car window at a startled Janet Leigh. As the years passed, Sir Alfred told the press his childhood in jail tale so many times that the details varied wildly; in one version he was four and another time he was eleven. One associate cracked, "Hitch told that story so many times he came to believe it himself."

Extra: After David O. Selznick hired Vivien Leigh to play Scarlett O'Hara, for what would be her Academy Award-winning performance in *Gone with the Wind* (1939), he became concerned about her endowments or lack thereof. The producer requested that the twenty-five-year-old British actress put on some falsies. Vivian went into the dressing room, did as she was asked, examined herself in the mirror and said, "Oh Fiddle-dee-dee. I'm not going to wear these things."

Leigh straightened out her posture and left the unwanted undergarment in the cubicle. The bespectacled O. Selznick rubbed his chin while examining her for several moments, then said, "You see what a difference that makes!"

The same story was told fifteen years later about Alfred Hitchcock and Grace Kelly during the making of *Rear Window* (1954).

Robin Hood's Greatest Foe

Errol Flynn was furious when the Warner Bros. assigned Michael Curtiz to direct him in *The Adventures of Robin Hood* in 1938. The twenty-nine-year-old Tasmanian actor had clashed with the English-challenged Hungarian on two previous movies and couldn't stand him. Curtiz caused instant fireworks by ordering one of the extras dueling with Flynn to keep the safety tip off his sword. It would be more exciting if Robin Hood was really threatened. When Errol found out he took the filmmaker by the neck, throttled him and said, "How's this for exciting!"

Undaunted, Curtiz moved things along at a fast pace and the angry swashbuckler delivered a lively, high-spirited performance. *Robin Hood* became the Warner's biggest hit up until that time and the signature role of Errol's career. The studio front-office staff knew when they had a good thing going; Curtiz was assigned to make seven more movies with Flynn.

Extra: Errol Flynn (1909-1959) was not the only actor Michael Curtiz (1886-1962) tangled with. In 1940, Curtiz directed *Santa Fe Trail*, which featured Flynn as Colonel Jeb Stewart (1833-1864) going up against famed American abolitionist John Brown (1800-1859), played by Raymond Massey. The very inaccurate film hinted that Brown (who in real life killed five pro-slavery Southerners and was hanged for treason) was responsible for the Civil War. Massey and Curtiz did not get along and argued ferociously throughout the entire production. A rumor spread on the set that the director was furious he had to fake John Brown's hanging.

All Is Not Welles

The box-office failures of *Citizen Kane* and *The Magnificent Ambersons* did not humble twenty-nine-year-old director Orson Welles. The cash poor but high-living genius, newly married to beautiful Rita Hayworth, accepted a lucrative offer to play the mysterious Mr. Rochester in the 1944 version of *Jane Eyre*. Orson immediately alienated the company by showing up late the first day, bossing everyone around and crudely bragging about his sex life. The gentle director Robert Stevenson put up with his leading man's forceful suggestions on casting and camera angles, and then later denied claims that Orson had made the movie. For Welles, *Jane Eyre* was a mild and fleeting success, his salary was soon spent, the marriage to Hayworth ended after a few years, and filmmakers ridiculed him at Hollywood parties, even as they continued to copy his techniques.

Extra: Despite his many box-office failures, director Orson Welles (1915-1985) never lost his appetite for extravagance. After coming to Hollywood in 1938, Welles, who was nicknamed the boy wonder, ran up huge debts on limos, mansions and fancy restaurants. Once, the financially struggling filmmaker was visited at his expensive digs by a bill collector. "I'm afraid I can't pay you now, I have a severe cash flow problem," said Orson.

"How am I supposed to survive in the meantime?" asked the upset creditor.

The director paused, took a puff of his cigar and advised the man to live simply.

Extra: After it opened in 1939, Pink's Hot Dog Stand on La Brea Avenue in Los Angeles became one of the city's most popular eating spots. Many celebrities through the years waited in long lines to scarf down Pink's world-famous chili dogs. Once, Orson Welles went there, ordered eighteen and ended up in the hospital. The doctor advised him if he ever again bought dinner for four, make sure there were three other people around.

My Fair Dubbee

Producer Jack Warner caused a huge controversy when he chose not to use Audrey Hepburn's singing voice in the 1964 musical *My Fair Lady*. Many fans were upset that Julie Andrews, who played Eliza Doolittle on the Broadway stage, had not been picked for the movie. Hepburn trained hard to prove she had the necessary vocal chops and was deeply disappointed by her employer's decision. It hurt when critics stated she only gave half a performance. When Andrews won the Oscar for *Mary Poppins*, the not-nominated Audrey privately told friends that *My Fair Lady* was a miserable experience. Jack Warner didn't get how a broad could get paid a million dollars and still be unhappy; editing was just part of the business. He longed for the old days when his top star, the German Shepherd Rin Tin Tin, never complained when another actor dubbed his bark.

Extra: A lifelong gambler, seventy-two-year-old Jack Warner spent seventeen million on *My Fair Lady*, more than any other film in his career. The wisecracking tycoon had fallen in love with the story of a cockney flower girl who tries to better herself by taking lessons from a snobbish English professor. Warner insisted that the musical be a first-class production all the way. The cream of New York society was invited to the premiere, the picture was well received and it went on to be extremely profitable. But at the after party at the Sherry Netherland Hotel, there was a great deal of talk about Warner's companion. Who was this stunningly dressed, quiet twenty-something beauty that looked like *My Fair Lady's* fictional Eliza Doolittle at the ball? The mogul referred to her as Lady Cavendish, but no one there had ever heard of her. At the end of the night, Warner instructed his limo driver to return his date home. The mysterious girl, whom Jack had met earlier that night in the lobby, told the chauffeur, "You know, I had such a fun time; I'm not even going to charge him!"

The Winning Signal

One time in the late 1950s, director John Huston was sitting in the stands at the Santa Anita Park racetrack when he got a surprise tip from a trusted friend. As the horses paraded around before post time, jockey Bill Pearson, who was riding a long shot, caught the filmmaker's eye and gave him a meaningful nod. Ten years earlier, Billy had improbably ridden a filly that Huston owned to victory, and the two had been drinking buddies ever since. Although Billy loved telling tall tales and playing practical jokes, he had amazing knowledge on many subjects and had once been a big winner on the TV quiz show *The $64,000 Question*. Huston hurriedly went to the ticket window and placed a huge wager on his pal's steed, which just as the oddsmakers predicted finished in dead last. Later he demanded to know why Pearson had signaled him to bet on a dog. The little man looked surprised. "Hell, John, I was just saying good morning!"

How Many Do You Need?

Forty-two-year-old Cecil B. DeMille convinced his reluctant Paramount Studio bosses to let him direct an expensive silent version of *The Ten Commandments* in 1923. The executives questioned if anyone could make entertainment of a story where old men wore tablecloths. DeMille's obstacles included nightmares transporting his sphinxes to sand dunes up California highways in open trucks; low tunnels caused many of them to be decapitated. Another mishap occurred when the Orthodox Jewish extras refused the ham they were served by a thoughtless caterer. As Cecil soldiered on, the studio brass screamed about the bloated budget, prompting the filmmaker to ask them if they wanted "The Five Commandments". Though he was mocked for using the Bible as a cover for putting sex and titillation onscreen, the often-pious showman was vindicated when his completed spectacle became a runaway hit with the public.

Extra: The 1923 version of *The Ten Commandments* started off by telling the Exodus story of Moses parting the Red Sea. Then the movie changed direction with a modern tale about two brothers who live in San Francisco, with one choosing not to live by the Commandments. One critic cracked, "It's easy to see where God left off and DeMille began."

Extra: Cecil B. DeMille's final film was the remake of his own *The Ten Commandments* in 1956, which was the subject of many legendary, on-set anecdotes. The 220-minute epic's behind-the-scenes lore included Cecil changing the Queen of Egypt's name from Nefertiti to Nefretiri to avoid breast jokes (not true, Ramses the II was the Pharaoh of Egypt from 1279 to 1203 BC; his queen was named Nefratiri; Nefertiti lived sixty years prior). The director also required Charlton Heston as Moses to carry actual stone tablets carved out of the real Mount Sinai. On the first take, former high school football player Heston's knees buckled and he was injured, unable to film for several days. Later he completed the scene with lighter wooden tablets. Undaunted, the determined DeMille, who suffered and recovered from a heart attack during filming, decided to focus on the children of Israel frolicking at the base of Mount Sinai after giving up hope that Moses would ever return to them. The young, virile, scantily clad cast tackled their assignment with great enthusiasm, but after a few days the orgy became tiring. One exhausted beauty asked an assistant director, "Who do I sleep with to get off this picture?"

Extra: Cecil B. DeMille was usually a cultivated, genteel man who often was unaware of his ferocious temper. On the set of *Sampson and Delilah* (1949), DeMille clashed with star Victor Mature (1913-1999) about Sampson wrestling lions. "They have no teeth," the director insisted.

"I don't want to get gummed to death," replied Mature.

Cecil allowed Victor to wrestle a lion skin, but still needed a shot of some real lions running up a ramp. When the docile animals refused to cooperate, the angry DeMille frightened the beasts into obeying with a stream of foul language and threatening waves of his riding crop. The next day when the film was developed, DeMille watched the rushes with his assistants and said seriously, "We'll have to do some editing. Can someone tell me who that foul-mouthed bald fellow is?"

Extra: DeMille was well aware that his expensive biblical spectacles were more popular with the public than the critics. When one of his writers suggested that *Sampson and Delilah* would actually get good reviews, the director acted like he was upset. "Don't say that, I have a lot of money tied up into this thing."

Extra: During the production of *Sampson and Delilah*, one of the production assistants became angry when he heard that the prop department required the jawbone of an ass for the biblical hero to slay an army with. "Listen, this is a DeMille picture. Sampson gets the whole ass!"

Harry Cohn's Fantasies

Columbia Pictures head Harry Cohn overcame internal opposition when he gave a green light to the fantasy film *Here Comes Mr. Jordan* in 1941. The-tough-as-nails mogul had gotten a kick out of the story of a prizefighter who dies fifty years before his time and gets to live again as a millionaire playboy. The company's board of directors complained that type of story never did well. Cohn argued that the movie business required following your gut. You couldn't just look at some past year's performance for future results. Starring Robert Montgomery in the lead role, *Mr. Jordan* was a huge success both critically and financially. Many years later, a screenwriter at Columbia pitched a fantastic tale to Cohn and was turned down because that type of picture never works. "But Harry, you produced *Here Comes Mr. Jordan* and that did a ton of business."

"I know, but think how much more we would have made if it hadn't been a fantasy."

Spielberg's Talent for Destruction

As a young boy, Steven Spielberg's greatest talent was causing destruction. Once, he cut off the head of one of his sister's dolls, and then served it up on a head of lettuce. Another time his pet lizard got out of his cage; it was three years before his family found it. A school counselor told Spielberg's mom that he was special; she didn't know how to interpret it. Steven was messy, a poor student and was constantly destroying his electric trains. Finally, his fed-up father told him another crash and the whole miniature locomotive set would get tossed. The innovative adolescent used an eight-millimeter camera to film one final wreck. By showing low angles and clever cuts, he made the staged accident look much worse than it was. As the youngster watched and relived the collision, he realized that making movies was a great way to get away with things without getting punished, and was steered toward his future career.

Extra: Steven Spielberg's innovative abilities served him well throughout his career. During the making of the 1981 adventure *Raiders of the Lost Ark*, the thirty-five-year-old director was preparing to film an intense sword fight that was scheduled to take about twelve hours. One of the participants, Harrison Ford who played the heroic lead Indiana Jones, showed up on the Tunisia set with a bad case of dysentery. Spielberg took one look at his thirty-nine-year-old leading man's anguished face and said, "Harrison, just shoot the guy and let's get out of here."

The make-believe archeologist quickly completed the assignment, which resulted in one of the most crowd-pleasing scenes in the movie, and made his way to the lavatory. (In another version, Harrison Ford came up with the idea to use the gun and convinced his director to go along with it.)

The Jewish President

Before he signed his first contract with Warner Bros., tough-guy actor John Garfield battled with his potential boss Jack Warner not to have his name changed. The son of Abraham Warner wanted all his stars to have all- American personas. The actor was informed that his current name, Jules Garfinkle, was not acceptable. It was way too ethnic-sounding to make cinemagoers feel comfortable. Undiplomatically, Warner told his new prospective employee that if he wanted to work there from now on he would be called James Garfield. The twenty-six-year-old street kid, from the Lower East Side of Manhattan, reacted fiercely. Did Mr. Warner realize that James Garfield was the name of a former president? It was ridiculous; people would laugh at him. Why not just rename him Abraham Lincoln? He was astonished when Warner told him quite seriously that Abraham sounded way too Jewish, and the studio would never allow it.

Extra: The four Warner Brothers, which included the wisecracking Jack, the conservative Harry (1881-1958), the quiet Albert (1884-1967) and the visionary Sam (1887-1927), had risen from obscurity with *The Jazz Singer* (1927), the first famous and financially successful talking movie ever made. Tragically, Sam Warner, the real brains behind the whole project, died of a brain tumor two days before *The Jazz Singer's* debut. The rebellious Jack was crushed by Sam's death; from then on, he fought constantly with his older brother Harry over money and the younger Warner's womanizing ways. One time Harry chased Jack through the studio with a two-by-four, threatening to kill him. The feud became so bitter that Jack opted to play tennis rather than attend Harry's funeral in 1958. One time Jack met Albert Einstein (1887-1959) and told him, "Mr. Einstein, I have my own theory of relativity. Don't hire them."

Extra: As a boy, Jack Warner wanted to be a singer and when it didn't happen, he seemed to resent similar ambitions in others. One day the tycoon was strolling through the studio lot when he heard some lovely sounds coming from a security guard shack. Curious, the mogul walked up to question his startled employee. "Young man, was that you singing?"

"W-why yes, Mr. Warner."

"Young man, you have a beautiful voice."

"Oh thank you, Mr. Warner."

"Hmmm. Tell me, young man, would you rather be a security guard or a singer?"

"Oh Mr. Warner, I always dreamed of being a singer."

"Ok young man. You're fired!"

Extra: Jack Warner's famed contract players gave their employer all he could handle. Jack was incensed when Humphrey Bogart called him a creep, but it was nothing compared to the icy fear the mogul felt after Errol Flynn actually threatened to kill him. James Cagney, after spotting Pat O'Brien's (1899-1983) name billed above his own on a movie marquee, sued Jack for breach of contract and won. Betty Davis, who constantly complained about her assigned roles, decided to give up Hollywood in 1937 for a new career in British film; Warner tracked her down in England and legally compelled her to return. But perhaps the toughest of all Jack's battles was with George Raft (1895-1980). Raft, who in real life hung out with underworld figures like Benjamin "Bugsy" Siegel (1906-1947), was loath to be cast as a thug in gangster movies and turned down virtually every part he was offered. Finally, Jack decided to buy George out of his contract. "Will $10,000 do it?" Warner asked Raft wearily.

To the tycoon's astonishment, George Raft pulled out his own checkbook, promptly paid his boss ten thousand dollars and stormed out of the office!

Extra: Jack Warner often treated his employees with derision, but none worse than the writers. Many of them, although better paid at the studio than they ever were penning novels, resented the nine-to-five routine they were forced to adhere to at the Warners' factory. Where the actors were free to leave the studio at lunch, the scribes had to be "chained" to their typewriters. One time Warner called a writer into the studio screening room for his suggestions on how to fix a weak script. "I'm sorry, Mr. Warner. I have no ideas after five."

Extra: Another time Jack summoned a writer to his office. "Look, pally, I got to fire you because I heard you were a communist."

"Mr. Warner, please! I'm not a Communist, I'm an anti-Communist!"

"I don't care what kind of Commie you are! You are out of here!"

The Secret of Longevity

At the end of his life, Paramount Studios founder Adolph Zukor was able to look back with pride at his accomplishments in the film industry. The Hungarian-born Zukor had been a success in the fur business by the age of thirty with several men working under him. Then in 1903, he discovered moving pictures and was captivated. Normally cautious, he changed his career direction, explaining later that movies were unlike cars or boats where one searched for a workable model and copied it. Each new film was a different entrepreneurial experience, one that could lead its financial backers to thrills or heartbreaks. From the silent films of Mary Pickford to the Hope/Crosby Road pictures to classics like *Sunset Boulevard* and *The Lost Weekend,* Zukor remained involved with the inner workings of Paramount. When he reached the age of 103, the feisty mogul was asked the secret of his longevity. "Well, I gave up smoking two years ago."

The Magic Man

Shortly after *Citizen Kane* was released in 1941, its twenty-five-year-old star Orson Welles was invited to a party at the home of studio-head George Schaeffer. The executive wondered if he had been correct to give *carte blanche* to this young man to make his film. Though Welles denied that *Kane* referred to any one person, the apparent biopic about seventy-eight-year-old William Randolph Hearst had infuriated the newspaper magnate. Hearst had pressured other Hollywood producers to buy the picture and burn it. When Schaeffer refused to sell *Kane*, the vindictive old man had ordered his periodicals not to review it. For all its merits, the movie was either too much or too cold for the public. Still, Schaeffer was glad he stuck by Welles who tonight was entertaining his guests with magic tricks. A friend remarked that Orson possessed great sleight of hand. The studio head grimaced. "You should see him make money disappear."

Goldwyn's Opinion of Children

Producer Sam Goldwyn argued with director William Wyler about a scene involving Humphrey Bogart's gangster character in the 1937 crime drama *Dead End*. After serving Bogart some alcohol, a suspicious innkeeper took a pen and marked the bottle. The furious Goldwyn stated that audiences wouldn't understand what was happening. At that moment, eight-year-old Samuel Goldwyn Jr. came into the projection room. His father asked him to watch the sequence in question. After they ran it again, Goldwyn said to Wyler, "Now if your shot makes sense a kid should be able to comprehend it. Sammy, do you know what's going on in the scene?"

"Sure, the bartender knows that Bogart is a rat and might try to swipe some liquor so he's marking the bottle so he can check if some booze is missing later."

Wyler could not help grinning at Goldwyn's open-mouthed reaction. The mogul paused then said, "Well, what do children know anyway?"

Extra: Writer Sidney Kingsley's (1906-1995) successful Broadway play *Dead End* was a gritty tale about New York youth raised in bad housing conditions, turning to crime. When Samuel Goldwyn (1879-1974) adapted the story two years later, he could not abide the grimy look created on his Hollywood back lot. "Why is it so dirty here?" he asked director William Wyler (1902-1981).

Wyler told him the story took place in a slum. "Why can't it be a clean slum?"

On some mornings, the very neat, fastidious producer would arrive at the studio and personally pick up the trash off the *Dead End* set. Wyler would then pretend to begin shooting the scene, while secretly instructing the cameraman not to roll. When the satisfied mogul left after a few minutes, the garbage would quickly be dumped into the make-believe ghetto, and the real moviemaking would begin.

Good Old Romeo

Legendary producer Irving Thalberg and his cast struggled with age and health issues when they made *Romeo and Juliet* in 1936. Thalberg convinced his thirty-four-year-old wife Norma Shearer, who had just given birth, that she was perfect for the teenage lover Juliet. He got more resistance from his Romeo, Leslie Howard, who thought that playing a man that does nothing but love would be a bore. The forty-three-year-old Howard decided to do the role only because his boss Jack Warner forbade it. Then there was fifty-four-year-old John Barrymore playing Romeo's doomed friend Mercutio. Off camera the heavy-drinking star stayed in a sanatorium where Thalberg could keep an eye on him. When the difficult production was completed, the box-office results were disappointing. But Thalberg, only thirty-seven, sickly with just a few months to live, was proud to add a well-reviewed version of Shakespeare to his cinematic accomplishments.

Extra: Irving Thalberg (1899-1936) once compared being a producer to building a road through a mountain. There might be six different routes, but once the decision was made the top man had to show absolute confidence, even if inwardly he was wracked with doubt. Thalberg also said that near the end of a picture, the hero should be down six points on their own two-yard line with time running out, and then run ninety-eight yards to score the winning touchdown.

Goldwyn Backed Winners

Samuel Goldwyn always preferred backing proven winners. The mercurial mogul would pass up chances to buy stories from unknown writers for cheap, and then turn around and pay big bucks for the same property when it became a bestselling book or a hit play. Likewise, Sam only hired established directors like John Ford or Howard Hawks. Newcomers who came to work for Goldwyn in the 1930s realized it was a dead-end job. He produced only two or three features a year, paid for them out of his own pocket and won every argument. One time staff writer Garson Kanin told Sam he wished to be a director. Could he try his hand making screen tests for some new actors at the studio? Goldwyn told him to forget it; Garson was a nobody. Kanin replied there was a time when someone gave John Ford and Howard Hawks chances; they were once nobodies too. Goldwyn paused and then replied, "Don't you believe it."

Success and the Repo Man

Born in 1901, movie-producer Sam Spiegel refused to allow heavy debts to stop his lavish lifestyle. The independent mogul created mixed emotions for his famed employees such as actor Humphrey Bogart and director David Lean. Spiegel's underfunded artists fumed when their Polish patron would somehow purchase fur coats and diamonds for beautiful women, while hotel managers threatened to put them out because of their boss's bounced checks. At the same time Sam's cheaply hired talents were thrilled to make classic films such as *The African Queen*, *The Bridge on the River Kwai* and *Lawrence of Arabia*. Till his death in 1985, the colorful Spiegel threw expensive parties in his Beverly Hills mansion, sailed happily on his yacht and continued to put out pictures. And when the repo man came round, Sam could always count on friends like Clark Gable to let him hide his Rolls Royce automobiles in their garages.

Extra: After the success of *Lawrence of Arabia* (1962), director David Lean (1908-1991) decided to end his partnership with Sam Spiegel (1901-1985). It was infuriating for Lean to have been out in the Jordan desert busting his rear to make the epic Oscar-winning movie, while Spiegel fleeced the budget by living onboard his lavish yacht. David didn't buy the Jewish producer's nonsense that he was too afraid of the Arabs in Jordan killing him to sleep in the hotels there. And the filmmaker had been promised a share of *Lawrence's* profits. When no money came to Lean, Spiegel had made excuses. "Baby, the budget was really big, you can't expect any profits. Be understanding, baby."

Understanding? So David was supposed to get nothing while Sam made eight million dollars and lived like a pasha? Sure he loved making their collaborations on both *Lawrence* and *Bridge on the River Kwai* (1957), but to hell with Sam. In the 1980s, Lean was still complaining about how Spiegel had cheated him when the director's lawyer discovered a huge pile of unopened mail. The letters contained not-yet-cashed *Lawrence of Arabia* residual checks adding up to millions of dollars.

Orson Welles Loved Hollywood

Twenty-four-year-old Orson Welles was gleeful about his lucrative contract with RKO Pictures in 1939. The New York-based boy genius, who usually spent more money than he had, fell in love with Hollywood. Who would not be enamored of a lifestyle that included mansions, limousines and servants? It was thrilling for Orson to meet eleven-year-old actress Shirley Temple; they were like a couple of kids playing together. And sometimes the Swedish beauty Greta Garbo came over to take a nude dip in his swimming pool. Welles admitted that his new status went to his head; his behavior to others was insufferable. He was taken down a peg when he and some fellow performers had their limo break down on the way to the airport and were forced to hitchhike in a trash truck. When they reached the gate the driver told the guard his cargo was actors and garbage; Orson was grateful that at least they got top billing.

Is There A Doctor In The House?

Writer Sylvia Fine once set up Samuel Goldwyn to deliver one of his famous malapropisms. The two of them had teamed up to manage the career of Sylvia's husband Danny Kaye. Beginning with Danny's 1944 movie debut *Up in Arms,* they had mostly agreed how to best present the thirty-two-year-old comedian to moviegoers. Sylvia didn't object when Goldwyn made Kaye dye his hair blonde; it improved his features onscreen, especially his long nose, which photographed like Pinocchio. In turn, the producer appreciated the job Sylvia had writing tongue-twisting songs, which Danny could deliver like nobody else. But the combination of being married to a nervous star and working for a temperamental mogul could be stressful. One morning Kaye told Goldwyn that Sylvia would be late for a story meeting because she had gone into therapy, which prompted the reply, "Anyone who goes to see a psychiatrist ought to have their head examined."

Extra: In 1775, Irish playwright Richard Brinsley Sheridan (1751-1816) wrote a comedy of manners called *The Rivals* about wealthy fashionable people who went to Bath, England, on holiday. One of the more comical characters was named Mrs. Malaprop who substituted incorrect words with similar sounds. A century and a half later, Samuel Goldwyn became legendary for his malapropisms (or Goldwynisms) and other incorrect uses of the language, even though very few of his friends could remember Sam actually making the quotes attributed to him. The producer enjoyed the sayings himself and always said his favorite was, "We've passed a lot of water since then."

Universal Justice

In the early days of Hollywood, German-born Carl Laemmle, the founder of Universal Studios, fought a furious battle against Thomas Edison over the right to make movies. After patenting the motion picture camera in 1890, the shrewd self-promoting Edison required all producers to pay him a fee before their pictures could be legally exhibited to the public. Laemmle became an outlaw guerilla filmmaker who outmaneuvered the inventor at every turn. Unlike Edison, who refused to reveal the names of the actors who worked for him, the tiny mogul created the movie star system, which grew his company enormously. The battle was decided in 1915, when the courts declared Edison was not entitled to a monopoly. Laemmle, who had gotten used to his unlawful and underdog status, misunderstood when his lawyer sent him a triumphant telegram: JUSTICE HAS BEEN SERVED!
Carl's reply? APPEAL IMMEDIATELY.

Extra: The early movies shown in famed inventor Thomas Edison's (1847-1931) time had no stories, no movie stars and no sound. Often, short films were called "chasers"; they were shown continuously at the end of a program until the patrons left the theater so a new paying crowd could come in. One such production, shown in the early 20th century, involved two girls getting undressed by a lake. Right before their last garments came off, a train came by and blocked the audience's view. In the next scene, they were swimming. The three-minute film was shown throughout the country. One old farmer became a big fan and kept paying to see it repeatedly. One day the theater manager came down and said, "Say old timer. Every day you sit and watch the same thing over and over."
"Well sonny, one of these days I'm hoping the train will be late!"

Extra: Many early film actors, fearful of being blacklisted by legitimate stage theater owners, were content to stay anonymous. The flickers were considered by serious performers to be an embarrassing novelty that probably would soon fade away. Those who joined the new industry were expected to work all day long, even when the cameras were not rolling. Their duties included hammering nails, painting scenery backgrounds, picking up trash and lifting heavy equipment. There were no on-set trailers, perks, glamour or big mansions. Casting directors met newspaper boys on the street and then hired them as a lead actor for five dollars a day. Ladies of the evening were often given jobs mainly because they provided their own wardrobes. More often the studios would hire teenage girls who needed no make-up, which in the pre-Max Factor days would melt under the hot lights. Not knowing their real names, the movie-going public gave their favorites appropriate monikers such as "the waif" or "the cowboy." The growing curiosity surrounding the cinema led to the birth of movie magazines, such as *Photoplay* in 1909. The new publication conducted a poll asking what kinds of screen stories people would like to see. Was it romance? Crime? The overwhelming answer was that fans were far more interested in learning about the mysterious, bigger-than-life figures they watched in the darkened movie theaters. But concerned that their players would demand huge salaries, the producers still refused to reveal who they were.

Extra: One of the most prominent movie-theater owners was a former clothing store manager who had been based in Oshkosh, Wisconsin, named Carl Laemmle (1867-1939), the eventual founder of Universal Studios. By 1909, the German-born Laemmle was sick of buying films from Thomas Edison (1847-1931) or European providers. He concluded it was easier and cheaper to make his own movies. Many nights, Carl would listen as his patrons left his theater as they would excitedly discuss the magical people on the screen. If Carl was going to pay for his own pictures, he would sell them by creating a star. He wasted no time in hiring a twenty-year-old actress named Florence Lawrence (1886-1938), known to the public as "The Biograph Girl" (she was named after the studio she worked for). One tale had the four-foot-ten Laemmle conducting a midnight raid of Biograph's offices, where he carried his new charge away over his shoulder. He revealed her name and two-hundred-and-fifty-dollar-a-week salary to the new fan magazines, and then arranged for Lawrence to mysteriously disappear. "My competitors will stop at nothing to ruin me. They've kidnapped poor Florence, perhaps even killed her!" he told the press.

For the next few weeks, Americans followed the saga in the newspapers; there were several false reports of foul play. One account stated Florence was killed by a streetcar. Then, as pre-arranged by Carl Laemmle, Florence "miraculously" resurfaced in St. Louis where she was mobbed, her clothes ripped off by fans (some of them hired). Florence Lawrence gained a huge following, her name on a cinema marquee guaranteed ticket sales and she arguably became the world's first movie star.

Extra: Carl Laemmle quickly became discouraged by the movie stars he created and the high-salary demands that predictably followed. Universal eventually become a horror factory, where actors playing the Mummy or the Invisible Man could easily be replaced if they asked for too much money. The mogul often tried to exit show business. One time vaudeville producer Florenz Ziegfeld (1867-1932) was desperately strapped for cash and sent a messenger to Universal with a proposal that Carl Laemmle buy some leftover wardrobe dresses for five thousand dollars. Not interested was the reply. Undeterred, Ziegfeld asked for a personal meeting. "Mr. Laemmle, how much to buy your studio?"

Eagerly, the tiny mogul named a price that was in the millions. "I see, well, let me talk it over with my lawyers. You should hear from me in a few weeks."

Ziegfeld got up to leave then paused at the door. "Oh by the way, I have some dresses left over from an earlier show. I'm trying to get rid of them for ten thousand dollars."

"Yes, of course," said Laemmle. Ziegfeld left the lot with his money, but the studio purchase was never consummated.

Extra: For Florence Lawrence, glory was fleeting. A few years after her public breakout, she was working on a film when a fire broke out on the set. The young woman courageously risked her life to save one of her fellow actors and the incident left her temporarily paralyzed. Unable to work, the actress painfully watched the rise of new silent film sirens such as Mary Pickford and Gloria Swanson. By the time Lawrence recovered, no one, including Carl Laemmle, would hire her. She ended up in obscurity and tragically committed suicide years later at the age of fifty-two. But during her appearance in Saint Louis in 1910, Florence Lawrence, the world's first movie star, drew a bigger crowd than President William Howard Taft (1857-1930), who came to town a week earlier.

The Final Word on *Citizen Kane*

In 1985, the last year of his life, seventy-year-old Orson Welles was approached by a young man who wanted to ask him yet another question about *Citizen Kane*. The Wisconsin-born writer and director, who was often annoyed by repeating the same answers about his classic 1941 film, decided to be gracious. Sure Welles had spent most of his Hollywood career hustling and had never become rich doing so, but it was gratifying to be recognized for creating a masterpiece. His admirer surprised Orson with a query about the film's famous opening scene. When Charles Foster Kane uttered the phrase "Rosebud," he was alone in his bedroom. A few moments later, his nurse came in and discovered him dead; how did the other characters in the movie know it was the newspaperman's final word? Welles hesitated then pulled the fan close and whispered, "Promise you'll never repeat what you just said to another living soul."

PART EIGHT

SILENTS TO "TALKIES"

"Supposing you have tried and failed again and again.
You may have a fresh start any moment you choose,
for this thing we call "failure" is not the falling down,
but the staying down."
— Mary Pickford

"If it's a good movie, the sound could go off and the audience
would still have a perfectly clear idea of what was going on."
— Alfred Hitchcock

Silent Film Causalities

The addition of sound to film in 1927 took lots of causalities. MGM Studios fired silent pictures star John Gilbert after his high-pitched voice did not go over well with movie audiences. The former screen lover became a bitter, unemployed boozing recluse. John always claimed his voice was fine and that Metro's engineers had deliberately sabotaged his efforts. Gilbert's fortunes temporarily turned when lowly Columbia Pictures hired him in 1934 to make *The Captain Hates the Sea*. Restoring Gilbert's stardom was a chance for the struggling studio to put itself on the map. But beach filming was delayed by a heavy fog, which caused the nervous Gilbert to drink heavily, and his fellow actors joined him. By the time the weather cleared, they were all too sloshed to shoot their scenes. The anxious bosses at Columbia sent a telegram to the film crew: HURRY UP AND FINISH! THE COST IS STAGGERING. They received their reply: WELL, SO IS THE CAST!

Extra: During the silent film days, audiences had often been loud and demonstrative, cheering for heroes and hissing at villains. With the birth of "talkies", cinemagoers quieted down and strained to hear every word. Movie houses had to be rewired for sound, costing major studios like Paramount and Fox millions of dollars. Movies now had to be filmed mostly at night; any passing truck noise could ruin a sound recording. Nervous stars began consulting astrologists and tarot card readers to foretell their futures. "How boring!" said silent film star Mary Pickford (1892-1979). "At first we moved! Now everyone is standing around talking!"

Extra: One ironic thing about talking motion pictures was that everyone had to be quiet on the set. Many of the silent film studios located in the sleepy town of Hollywood had been small buildings, some of them converted saloons. With no noise restrictions, generally good weather and wide-open spaces, it was simple for production companies to film outdoors. The change to sound required more land for indoor shooting on soundproof stages. By the 1930s, the movie factories were spread out in a fifty-mile radius in the Los Angeles area. Studio public relations people continued to promote Hollywood as a glamour town where you could expect to see stars walking down the street.

Somehow the phrase "Made in Hollywood" sounded more exciting than "Made in Culver City" or "Made in Burbank." The word "Hollywood", originally the name of a Dutch settlement in Ohio, came to denote both a suburb in Los Angeles and the cinema industry of the United States.

Extra: French director Robert Florey (1900-1979) thought working with The Marx Brothers on their first feature *The Coconuts* (1929) was a nightmare. Groucho, Chico, Harpo and Zeppo were always late to the set, running around, chasing girls, gambling or, in Groucho's case, on the phone with his stockbroker. It was almost impossible to get them all together in front of the camera, and then they refused to stay in the frame. The sophisticated Florey questioned whether four grown men running around a Florida resort hotel was amusing. Without the laughter of a stage audience, the Marxes lost their confidence; the comedians thought the completed film was so awful that they wanted to buy *The Coconuts* back and burn the negative. But the Paramount Studio executives rebuffed them and released the picture. With mainstream talking movies still only two years old, many cinemagoers were enthralled by Groucho's motor-mouthed insults and went back to see *The Coconuts* four or five times, just to catch his every word.

The Golden-Haired Negotiator

In 1909, struggling Broadway actress Charlotte Pickford told her reluctant daughter Mary that she would have to try to find employment in the movies, not then considered a respectable medium for performers. Dutifully, Mary set up an appointment at Biograph Studios with legendary director D.W. Griffith, who examined her critically. "You know you're a little fat. The camera adds weight. And you are a stage actress. I don't need talking."

Annoyed, the sixteen-year-old was about to leave when Griffith said, "Wait, I can use you. I'll pay $5.00 a day."

"Well, Mr. Griffith, because of that fat remark I'll have to charge you ten."

He laughed and agreed. Griffith later marveled that there were two sides to Mary's face: the empathetic little girl she played on screen and the hard businessperson, who during an era when women didn't have the right to vote, and without using an agent, negotiated with Hollywood's most powerful moguls to became the first millionaire movie star.

Extra: Mary Pickford was called the most famous and beloved woman in world history by a journalist who covered the silent film era. In 1916, the twenty-four-year-old superstar had a marathon negotiation session with Paramount Studios founder Adolph Zukor. The five-foot tall actress' determination to have complete creative control of all her pictures, plus an (at that time) unheard of ten-thousand-dollar-a-week salary, reduced the tough-minded mogul, who was nicknamed "The Killer," to tears. At one point, Zukor offered Pickford two million dollars to go away and leave him alone, before finally giving in to her persistent contractual demands.

Charlie's Disguise

Mack Sennett was annoyed when twenty-four-year-old Charlie Chaplin arrived at the Keystone Studios in 1913. The Charlie Chaplin that the producer had seen on stage in Montana was an old drunk; Sennett had been impressed enough to send the performer a telegram offering him a movie contract. It was hard to believe that this young man was that same person. Mack, whose roster of talent included the funny-looking Fatty Arbuckle and Ben Turpin, had no confidence that the seemingly ordinary Chaplin would be amusing to cinema audiences. With his job on the line, Charlie put together a makeshift costume, complete with a cap, a cane, a painted mustache and a walk borrowed from a London cabbie. The Tramp became a beloved, world-famous movie character and made Chaplin a millionaire, but didn't always help him get recognized. At the height of Charlie's fame, he once entered a Charlie Chaplin look-alike contest...and lost.

Extra: Charlie Chaplin wasn't the only actor who fooled people pretending to be a tramp. One time the great John Barrymore showed up to a Beverly Hills costume party dressed as a hobo. His disguise was so convincing he was turned away and went home.

The Unsuccessful General

After a string of comedy hits, Buster Keaton sold his financial backers on a pet project called *The General* in 1926. The thirty-one-year-old stone-faced comedian had fallen in love with the true Civil War story of a Confederate engineer who loses his train named "The General" to Union soldiers, and then fights to get it back. Keaton had *carte blanche* from his investors to improvise amazing, sometimes violent stunts; his dedication to realism for the sight gags caused several injuries on the Oregon set. The completed film was blasted for containing deadly battle scenes that were inappropriate for a chase comedy, and did poorly at the box office. Buster lost the trust of Hollywood's moneymen and never again achieved the same level of creative freedom. He had no regrets. For the rest of his life he was happy to talk up *The General* and always said it was favorite movie. Too late to help Keaton's fortunes, many fans and critics came to agree with him.

Extra: Six-month-old Joseph Francis Keaton the VI got his nickname when he took a nasty tumble down a flight of stairs in 1895. The great magician, Harry Houdini (1874-1926), who was a friend of the family, observed the unhurt crying toddler and said, "That was a real buster," meaning a fall that could injure you.

Three years later, young Buster joined his mother and father in vaudeville. The boy played a prankster child whose parents punished him by tossing him around. The future "Great Stone Face" was able to keep a deadpan expression no matter how hard he landed on the stage.

Douglas "Robin Hood" Fairbanks to the Rescue

Thirty-nine-year-old Douglas Fairbanks almost scared himself out of playing Robin Hood in 1922. Deciding to personally finance the picture, Fairbanks had traveled to New York while his Hollywood film crew recreated medieval England. Upon his return, the swashbuckling actor was stunned by the massive castle, the biggest set ever built. Good God! There was no way Fairbanks could do the part and not be lost among the scenery. After a few days, Doug calmed down enough to consider some of the wonderful stunts that could be done using stairs, balconies and trampolines. Maybe he could make this thing work. With his confidence restored, the agile star became like a bird in flight. Whether he was fighting the sheriff or saving Maid Marian, his humorous bravado dominated the screen. The slumping film industry received a welcome job-creating boon when Douglas Fairbanks' *Robin Hood* broke box-office records.

Extra: The 1921 recession was devastating to the US economy including the movie business, but it was also a mere blip on the historical radar screen. President Warren G. Harding (1865-1923) decided to cut taxes, spending and regulations; both America and its movie houses came out of the financial downturn very quickly (Vice President Calvin Coolidge, who succeeded Harding after his death in 1923, maintained similar policies – United States unemployment fell from 11.7 percent in 1921 to a peacetime record of 1.8 percent five years later). It was quite a contrast to the 1929 stock market crash.

Both the Hoover (1929-1932) and Roosevelt (1933-1945) administrations chose to interfere greatly with the free market. In 1933, almost one third of American movie theaters went dark and salaries were cut throughout the film industry. Patrons got two features for the price of one and some cinemas gave away free china with an admission ticket. One film lover upon receiving a teapot asked, "Do you have a good movie to go with this?"

Extra: One of Douglas Fairbanks' contemporaries, Harold Lloyd (1893-1971), had struggled to gain traction in silent films. Lloyd's friend and fellow actor Hal Roach (1892-1992) inherited some money in 1915 and produced some short comedies featuring Harold. After two years, Roach suggested that his pal needed a disguise; he was too handsome to be funny. Lloyd remembered seeing a film about a mild-mannered, bespectacled clergyman who became a he-man in dangerous situations. The young comedian purchased a pair of cheap glasses at a dime store and transformed himself into an all-American boy next door. Cinemagoers identified with this new, go-getting character who maintained his pluck in perilous situations. In 1938, Harold's onscreen persona became the inspiration for the comic book character Clark Kent; while Fairbanks' gravity defying Robin Hood helped bring forth the creation of Clark's alter-ego Superman.

Royal Wedding

When they married in 1920, Douglas Fairbanks and Mary Pickford were known as the king and queen of Hollywood. The thirty-seven-year-old Doug and his nine-years-younger Canadian-born wife took up the mantle of America's unofficial ambassadors to the world. When they weren't working, the famed couple made speeches, led parades and cut ribbons; big crowds greeted them everywhere. Prominent Americans, as well as European royalty, vied to get invitations to the Beverly Hills Pickfair mansion. The agile and athletic Fairbanks loved climbing trees, walking on his hands and instigating pool party contests to see who could keep their head underwater the longest. Mary, who pretended to be a little girl in silent films, enjoyed her husband's boyish antics. But with the coming of talking movies, Pickford's career declined and she began to drink heavily. Growing up in Denver, Fairbanks had been lectured by his father about the evils of alcoholism; he couldn't stand his wife being bombed out of her mind by noon. In 1936, their incompatible lifestyles drove them apart. The health-conscious Fairbanks died of a heart attack in 1939; Mary outlived him by forty years.

Extra: In 1920, Douglas Fairbanks and Mary Pickford went on their European honeymoon. The two international icons had divorced their previous spouses and were concerned about how they would be greeted. They needn't have worried; in London, their limousine was surrounded by admiring women who pulled Mary Pickford out of the car to shake her hand, still grateful after three years for her efforts selling war bonds. Doug and Mary went on to Paris where they found it difficult to sleep at night; large crowds gathered below their hotel room to serenade them. At a party in Amsterdam, the celebrity couple was mobbed by the other guests; when the aggressive fans threatened to get out of hand, the agile Douglas Fairbanks placed his wife on his shoulder and escaped through the window. Finally, the two stars found privacy in Hamburg; because of World War I, their movies were not shown there. For an hour, the newlyweds walked the streets unnoticed, until the bored Mary turned to her husband and said, "Doug, I'm sick of this. Let's go back to one of those countries were they mob us."

A Tramp of Paris

Charlie Chaplin, whose silent films were seen and understood throughout the world, did not always succeed in communicating without words. One evening in the 1920s at a Paris restaurant, Charlie enjoyed a shellfish dinner. Afterward, he went for a stroll and suddenly was summoned by an urgent call of nature. There was no bathroom in sight; in desperation, Chaplin grabbed the first man he saw. Now in such pain, he was unable to speak and the comedic actor used pantomime to explain his predicament. Slowly it dawned on the passerby who the stranger was. "Mon Dieu, Charlie!"

A crowd gathered, and thinking they were getting a free show cheered the Tramp as he continued his wild gestures. Finally, Charlie took off running with the mob following, ducked into a hotel, found a lavatory and, with his admirers pounding on the door, achieved blessed relief. When Chaplin came out, he walked away with quiet dignity, much to the disappointment of his fickle French fans who wanted more antics and began to boo him.

The Three Faces of Clara

In the 1927 movie *It*, twenty-two-year-old actress Clara Bow astounded the crew with her natural instincts. Playing a shop girl who has designs on her boss, the Brooklyn-born redhead used three different expressions when she first laid eyes on him. Director Clarence Badger yelled cut and demanded to know what she was doing. Clara patiently explained her first reaction was a look of longing so that the young women in the audience would identify with her. The second take was for the boys; they would be excited by her knowing sexuality. The final expression was for the old ladies to show she regretted her naughty ideas, so they would come see her next movie. The bewildered Badger gave her very few instructions after that and said she was a pleasure to work with. Clara became known as the "It" girl, meaning that she had ultimate sex appeal, and that year received more fan mail than any other movie star.

The Power Tradition

Stage actor Tyrone Power Sr. had difficulty adjusting to the early talking films. In the 1930 drama *Hell's Highway,* director Henry King shot a scene with Power on a boat out in the Pacific Ocean. There was no dialogue in the script; like most movies in those days, the director made up the whole thing as he went along. At one point, Tyrone reverted to what worked for him in theater. "Throw me the line," he hissed at King.

There was no response and afterward the angry thespian confronted the director, demanding to know why he was left high and dry, not knowing what to say. "Because your look of desperation was perfect for your character," King replied.

Sadly Power would die of a heart attack a year later. In 1936, King was approached by a twenty-two-year-old dashing young man looking for work. Still impressed by the father's performance, Henry immediately cast Tyrone Power Jr. in lead roles and helped to make him a superstar.

Fairbanks Spreads Happiness

The very positive Douglas Fairbanks sought to lighten up people's lives in the 1916 comedy *The Habit of Happiness.* His all-American character believed that any problem could be solved by laughter. Doug's method worked with a millionaire, but then he faced the challenge of cheering up residents of skid row. To make the thirty-three-year-old actor's onscreen interactions seem real, authentic residents of a slum were bussed into the studio. At first, none of the poor wretches were amused by Fairbanks's wit; they tried to sleep through his monologue. Doug changed tactics by telling dirty stories — why not? It was a silent picture. His raggedy audience slowly began to stir, then broke into hearty, sometimes toothless guffaws that were captured on film. The completed movie was a big hit, but only after a great deal of editing. Fairbanks' close-ups were re-shot after the filmmakers received several complaints from deaf lip readers.

Mary in Charge

Mary Pickford wasn't interested in making friends when she starred in and produced the 1926 drama *Sparrows*. The thirty-four-old, five-foot-tall actress played the eldest of a group of orphans trying to escape the clutches of an evil farmer. In those pre-union silent film days, America's sweetheart expected to work from six a.m. to midnight, took no coffee breaks, never rested in a trailer, cheerfully entertained visitors like President Calvin Coolidge between shots and demanded that resentful co-workers keep up. One scene required her to carry children on her back, as she ran on a narrow board over a swamp infested with real alligators. The director saw a chance to put his domineering little boss in her place. He ordered three terrifying retakes until it was pointed out by someone on the set that the sequence could be shot safely by using a double exposure. A furious Mary berated the filmmaker for putting the kids in harm's way. "If you had only wanted to get rid of me, then I would have understood it!"

Extra: The free-market-loving, government-shrinking Calvin Coolidge (1872-1933) got along great with the very politically conservative Mary Pickford. Silent Cal often surprised both friends and enemies with his sense of humor. Once, the president disappointed an inquisitive reporter who asked Coolidge questions about national security, prohibition, Congress, etc; each time the commander-in-chief responded with, "No comment."
The frustrated journalist turned to leave when Coolidge said, "Wait."
The hopeful scribe said, "Yes?"
"Whatever you do, don't quote me!"

Intolerant at the Box Office

Expensive scenery was the highlight of film pioneer D.W. Griffith's 1916 drama *Intolerance: Love's Struggle Through the Ages*. The son of a Confederate soldier, Griffith resented charges that his 1915 Civil War masterpiece *The Birth of a Nation* was racist. His follow-up feature, *Intolerance*, told four tales about man's inhumanity to man throughout the centuries. Los Angeles residents were amazed by his mammoth recreation of ancient Babylon, complete with fantastic statues of elephants standing upright on pillars. The impressive set remained up in Hollywood for three years before it began to crumble on its own.

In 2001, when the Kodak Theater was built to house the Oscars, its designers paid homage to *Intolerance*, and giant pachyderms soared over Tinseltown once more. The new mall's eye-catching structures overshadowed the very film production that inspired them; Griffith had lavished a fortune on extra sex scenes, but audiences stayed away, and *Intolerance* bankrupted him.

Extra: In 1915, frustrated by his boss's unwillingness to let him make a feature-length film, director David Llewelyn Wark Griffith (1875-1948) decided to invest his own money to turn Southern writer Thomas Dixon's (1864-1946) 1905 novel *The Clansman* (the book advised people in the north to maintain racial segregation) into a two-and-a-half hour, sixty-thousand-dollar epic: *Birth of a Nation*. During filming, some of the crew questioned D.W.'s creative choices. They felt that many scenes, such as the assassination of President Lincoln or a white woman leaping to her death to ward off the unwanted advances of a black man, were overstated and melodramatic. Griffith's hired hands were amazed at the powerful impact the assembled footage made, especially when accompanied by a full orchestra. One thrilling sequence that featured horses racing toward the camera caused sophisticated audiences to duck down in their seats, fearing that the giant animals would leap off the screen into their laps. President Woodrow Wilson (1856-1924) called the Civil War epic "History written with lightning."

Press reports exaggerated the stunning picture's costs at two million dollars, and for the first time movies were considered an art form. But because *Nation's* story featured clansmen as heroes and former black slaves as murderous thugs, the director was branded a racist and the film was banned from several major cities. Griffith resented the charges of bigotry and went broke trying to prove his detractors wrong by financing his expensive follow-up *Intolerance*. Historians later gave *Birth of a Nation* credit for increasing membership in the Ku Klux Klan.

Extra: While making *Intolerance* in 1916, D.W. Griffith desperately wanted fifty-foot statues of elephants as part of the scenery. It vexed the filmmaker when his research assistants could find no records of the land mammals living in ancient Mesopotamia. Finally, one of Griffith's staff members claimed to have found an obscure reference about pachyderms on the walls of Babylon; that was good enough for the budget-busting director to go forward. When the movie was completed, representatives from the Los Angeles fire department told Griffith that the *Intolerance* set had to be removed; the broke director replied that he couldn't afford to dismantle it. Even after the city tore it down in 1919, the memory of Griffith's superstructure lingered in people's minds as a symbol of the film capital's overspending and excess.

Extra: When the thirty-five-hundred-seat Kodak Theater became the home of the Oscars in 2002, some in the movie industry carped about having the famed ceremony in a shopping mall. The design of the new six-hundred-million-dollar Hollywood Highland retail center was inspired by the Babylonian set from the movie *Intolerance*. Although many visitors to Hollywood Boulevard took photos of the giant marble elephants, it's probable that after eighty-five years, most people had never seen or heard of the 1916 silent film the statues were based on. There was very little historical tie-in; the Academy Awards began in 1928 twelve years after *Intolerance* was released. And just like D.W. Griffith's expensive picture, Hollywood Highland went over with an initial thud. Some critics stated that the flamboyant building with its grand staircases was unorthodox, confusing and ugly. Tourism dropped worldwide after the New York terrorist attacks on September 11, 2001, the property was quickly devalued and its owners sold it for two hundred million dollars in 2007.

Extra: When Bette Davis won an Oscar for the 1935 drama *Dangerous,* D.W. Griffith was assigned to present the twenty-seven-year-old actress her award. The film pioneer, who had revolutionized modern cinema by being the first to extensively use techniques such as the close-up, montages, and crosscutting, had retired four years before due to too many box-office failures. He lived alone in Hollywood, shut out from participating in the industry like a ghostly observer. And now in a very poignant moment, D.W. shared the stage with an ascending star. Before he handed over the prize, Griffith thought he'd impart some wisdom about the fleeting nature of success. "Young lady, do you realize how lucky you are?"

"I do," replied the smiling Davis.

"No, I don't think you do. Success at your age is a rare thing. To be so young, rich and talented-"

"Look, I realize how lucky I am! Now give me my award!"

The Master Faced the Music

After the birth of talking pictures, modern movie techniques developed slowly, with even the most accomplished filmmakers questioning what cinemagoers would accept. When Alfred Hitchcock went to 20th Century Fox to direct *Lifeboat* in 1944, he was greeted by a studio musician. "Mr. Hitchcock, the boys were wondering what kind of score you wanted for the picture." The famed Master of Suspense, who sometimes referred to film audiences as the moronic masses, said with disdain, "My dear fellow, the whole story involves seven people on a lifeboat. The audience will wonder where the music is coming from."

The composer thought for a moment then replied, "Mr. Hitchcock, if you can tell me where the camera is coming from, I will tell you where the music is coming from."

Extra: When Alfred Hitchcock directed his first movie *The Lodger* (1927), a silent drama about a Jack the Ripper-style serial killer, he didn't have enough extras and added himself in a scene. After the film became a success, Hitchcock got superstitious and made a cameo in each of his pictures. The filmmaker's most challenging appearance was in *Lifeboat*; how could he show up in the middle of the ocean? The Master had just completed a strict diet and lost about one hundred pounds. Hitchcock made up a magazine ad for a phony weight loss product called Reduco, complete with before and after photos that displayed his new thin physique, and had it float by one of his adrift characters who snatched it up. Alfred was delighted when he received letters from people inquiring where they could purchase Reduco.

The Same Old Battle

Producer Hal Roach decided to spend lavishly on his new comedy team Stan Laurel and Oliver Hardy, for their 1927 silent comedy *The Battle of the Century*. Laurel had come up with an old-fashioned routine that had gone out of style years ago. Stan's sequence would be expensive, and would require lots of extras plus thousands of disposable props. But in his last few movies, the thin comic had transformed himself from an annoying jester to a much more appealing sad sack clown. And maybe Roach had been wrong to cast the overweight Hardy in villainous parts; Ollie was wonderful as a pompous, bossy man who was actually the dumber of the two. Hal figured that Laurel and Hardy were like children, so easy for audiences to identify with, that he could put them into cliché situations. *The Battle of the Century* did great at the box office, and years later Stan Laurel would still break into hysterics recalling the film's wild climactic pie fight.

Extra: There are different stories as to how the cinema pie fights got started. One tale had silent film actress Mabel Normand (1892-1930) throwing a pie at her sad-sack co-star Ben Turpin (1869-1940) in 1913, just to get him to cheer up. Keystone Studios producer Mack Sennett (1880-1960) witnessed the incident, laughed and incorporated it into his comedies. A much wilder anecdote involved Roscoe "Fatty" Arbuckle (1887-1933) and some fellow performers having a picnic that same year near the Rio Grande River. During the meal, they were approached by some men on horseback from the other side of the border. The lead rider said, "I am the bandit Pancho Villa, gringos, and you will surrender to me!"

SPLAT! Pancho Villa (1878-1923) was outraged to be hit in the face by a blueberry pie. The revolutionary glared, dismounted, walked over to the picnic table, picked up a pie and returned fire. For the next few minutes, there was a wild melee of pastries being thrown back and forth, until a laughing Villa told his men to stop. Then Pancho shook Arbuckle's hand and rode off leaving the nearly three-hundred-pound comedian with a great routine for his next film. (I am rooting for the second version!)

Garbo Talks

Twenty-four-year-old Greta Garbo was extremely nervous as she arrived on the set to film the 1930 drama *Anna Christie*. So many of her colleagues had failed attempting what she was about to do now; as a result, their careers were over. Sure, sometimes the very shy Swedish beauty hated being a star; it was madness when these foolish fans invaded her privacy and chased her through the streets. And yet, if Greta left the business, it must be on her own terms, not because she was not up to the task. When the camera rolled, Garbo uttered the line, "Give me whiskey--ginger ale on the side. And don't be stingy, baby!"

When Greta heard the recording played back, her co-stars saw her break into a rare happy smile. And so the siren of the silent screen adjusted to the biggest change in movie history; *Anna Christie* broke box-office records with the advertising campaign: Garbo Talks!

Spontaneous "Talkies"

Forty-one-year-old Al Jolson spontaneously ushered in talking pictures when he starred in the 1927 Warner Bros. musical *The Jazz Singer*. The irrepressible Jolson had won the movie role of a young Jewish tenor with a taste for show business, after being passed over for the same part on Broadway. The egomaniacal vaudevillian was famous for infuriating playwrights by coming out of character, telling the audience the end of the story, and then breaking into new numbers, which would send his frustrated co-stars home. Now, performing on a Warner Bros. sound stage, he ad-libbed the line, "Wait a minute, you ain't heard nothing yet!"

The Jazz Singer was a sensation and soon silent films were considered passé. Ironically, the Warners never wanted their leading man to talk and almost deleted his words; the brothers wanted the cost-saving audio technology to add music, so hired orchestras and organists would no longer be needed in their movie theaters.

Extra: A few years before Al Jolson (1886-1950) made talking film history with *The Jazz Singer* (1927), producer Jesse Lasky created headlines by hiring Enrico Caruso (1873-1921), the great Italian opera tenor. The singer was paid one hundred thousand dollars and was put into two silent movies.

Extra: In the early days of talking films, an enterprising actor was hired for one day's work. When the director wasn't looking, the performer let a bunch of crickets loose on the set. It was five days before the crew could round up the chirping, leaping insects; the hired hand had to be kept on hold, and received five times the paycheck.

Just When You Thought It Was Safe

Twenty-one-year-old Gloria Swanson lied about her aquatic abilities to land the lead role in the 1918 movie *You Can't Believe Everything*. Because she had worked for producer Mack Sennett, everyone mistook her for one of his bathing beauties. Now she was in for it, her character had to lose her dress and dive off a dock into sixty feet of water. In reality, Gloria couldn't swim a stroke. Before the shoot she went to the YWCA to practice, became terrified looking at other girls floating on their backs and ran out of the building. Well, if she died, she died but Swanson was not going to let anyone else do the part. When the camera rolled, Gloria found the courage to plunge into the harbor; she performed all her required water sequences without incident. After her work was complete, the proud and happy actress was invited to a pool party. She stood on the diving board at the shallow end, froze up and never went swimming again.

Extra: In the 1920s, there were terrible stories about girls arriving in Hollywood hoping for an unlikely film career. Many of the wannabes ended up in squalor or turned to prostitution to survive. Sometimes they were prey for female slave traders who pretended to be directors. There was great fear among big stars and studio heads that if something wasn't done about the situation, the government would regulate their industry. Worse yet, an angry public could respond by boycotting them at the box office. The YWCA (Young Woman's Christian Association) received huge contributions from movie titans to provide the aspiring actresses with low-priced safe and clean housing.

Rin Tin Tin Redeemed

Thirteen-year-old Rin Tin Tin restored his professional status when he starred in the 1931 serial *The Lightning Warrior*. Like many silent film icons, the German Shepherd had ended up unemployed due to the birth of talking pictures. Now the canine had a chance to prove his former employers wrong and show that he still had value at the box office. Sure, he could no longer leap twelve feet in the air, but he could still follow instructions and completed most of his scenes in one take. Let the young dogs do all the stunts; the important thing about acting was to understand the correct emotion that each scene called for. In his final onscreen bow, the performing pooch even donned a beard and boots as a disguise to fool his enemies. The *Lightning* series was a huge success and Rinty's cooperative behavior put to the rest ugly rumors that he was a temperamental prima donna who bit his co-stars.

Just Another Chaplin Fan

In 1917, a young soldier decided to change his appearance after watching a Charlie Chaplin movie. It fascinated him to see how others in the audience responded to the little tramp onscreen. This motion pictures medium was the greatest form of communication ever invented. Imagine being able to influence people around the world, regardless of their language, without ever making a sound. And the comedian was a true subversive; a down and outer who kicked authority figures in the rear. Chaplin attacked the established order and yet people still loved him. Hearing his fellow patrons titter, the youth had a sudden inspiration that would kill two birds with one stone. His superior officers had ordered the men in his unit to trim their mustaches so they fit into gas masks in case of a chemical attack. Why not imitate Charlie Chaplin's grease-paint look so he could seem non-threatening, thought Adolph Hitler.

TELEVISION TALES

"I find television very educating. Every time somebody turns
on the set, I go into the other room and read a book."
— Groucho Marx

"One of the advantages of being a captain is being able
to ask for advice without necessarily having to take it."
— William Shatner

The Mirror has Two Faces

When Tim Conway became a full-time cast member on *The Carol Burnett Show* in 1975, he and co-star Harvey Korman became fast friends. The two comedic actors were going through divorces and were miserable in their personal lives. Korman was particularly unhappy after eight years of being perceived as Burnett's second banana. Performing their weekly routines in front of the CBS Studio audience became therapeutic. A turning point came when both men were discussing their emotional distress backstage, looked in the mirror and saw Harvey was in a dress and Tim wore a chicken suit. From then on, Korman was unable to get through a sketch with Conway without breaking into howls of laughter, and television watchers joined him.

Extra: Harvey Korman (1927-2008) once stated that the key to the success of *The Carol Burnett Show* (1967-1978) was Carol's generosity to her fellow performers. The thirty-one-year-old Burnett's thoughtfulness toward others was put on display at the end of a taxi ride in 1964. After he collected his fare, the driver didn't notice that his passenger's coat was caught in the door and pulled away. The terrified comedian ran full speed alongside the moving vehicle to avoid being dragged through the New York City streets. Fortunately, a passerby noticed Burnett's plight and waved frantically for the cabbie to pull over. Horrified by what had nearly happened, he asked Carol if she was all right. "Yes," said the out-of-breath Burnett. "How much extra do I owe you?"

Perry's Courtroom Rival

In 1933, writer Erle Stanley Gardner wrote two novels, one about a detective, the other featuring a lawyer. When neither sold, his publisher suggested that he should merge the two characters into one protagonist, which became *Perry Mason*. The hugely successful books, which featured the super defense attorney proving his clients were innocent of murder charges, were adapted into radio plays and movies, but Gardner was never happy with the treatments; the author jumped at the chance to produce the TV version in 1957.

Several famous actors auditioned for the lead, but when Gardner saw Raymond Burr, he shouted, "That's him!"

Perry Mason was a huge success, lasting on the air for ten years, and Gardner thought Burr was wonderful. But his favorite actor was Bill Talman who played Perry Mason's courtroom nemesis, the long-suffering District Attorney Hamilton Burger. "He actually looks like he thinks he's going to win the case," said the writer admiringly.

Extra: Raymond Burr (1917-1993) and William Talman (1915-1968) initially auditioned for each other's roles until Erle Stanley Gardner (1889-1970) insisted that they switch parts. The two make-believe lawyers realized that the *Perry Mason* (1957-1966) courtroom set was a nerve-wracking place for the weekly guest stars put on trial. Often, Burr and Talman intentionally blew their lines, which helped their fellow actors to relax.

Mistaken Columbo

There are times when an actor can become overwhelmed by the fame of his character. After Bing Crosby chose not to come out of retirement in 1968, the TV role of Lieutenant Columbo went to forty-one-year-old Peter Falk, who made it impossible to imagine anyone else playing the part. On location in Boston, Falk was starring the 1978 crime comedy *The Brinks Job* when he was visited on the set by a kindly old man whose wife had made lasagna for "Mr. Columbo." When the actor had a free moment, he gratefully took the food and signed an autographed picture. "Who's Peter Falk?"

When the elderly fan found out that the Russian Polish Falk wasn't really Italian or named Columbo, he tore up the picture and left. Peter laughed every time a crew member brought up the incident.

Extra: Two other men took on the role of Columbo, prior to the four-time Emmy-winning Peter Falk. Character actor Bert Freed (1919-1984) appeared as a very straight-laced version of the rumpled detective in 1960. The vehicle was a live television program called *Enough Rope*, which established the pattern of revealing to the audience who the murderer was at the beginning of the program. Then the seemingly forgetful, ineffectual Columbo would lull killers into a false sense of security before catching them. Two years later, the story was adapted into a play entitled *Prescription Murder*. Despite poor reviews, audiences loved the third billed character of Lieutenant Columbo, this time played by the scene-stealing Oscar winner Thomas Mitchell (1892-1962).

Mitchell sadly died of cancer ending the show's run before it hit Broadway. Then, in 1968, the same tale was made into a TV movie starring the forty-one-year-old Falk. Peter personally provided Columbo with a shabby old raincoat he brought from home, an ugly Peugeot with a flat tire, and the famous mannerisms that endeared him to TV viewers.

With a Little Help from My Friends

Billy Dee Williams played legendary Chicago Bears running back Gale Sayers, alongside James Caan as his cancer-stricken teammate Brian Piccolo, in the highly dramatized *Brian's Song*. Insiders on the Bears claimed that the 1971 made-for-television film exaggerated the two players' friendship. Gale Sayers, who outweighed Dee Williams by sixty pounds and had wanted to play himself, complained that the usually smooth-talking actor was making him sound like a poor public speaker. During the workout sequence, the athletic thirty-one-year-old Caan had to slow down so his three-years-older co-star could outrun him. James also cracked jokes in between retakes of his death scene. The night before the film aired, the Chicago Bears were clobbered by the Miami Dolphins, which increased the sympathy factor. *Brian's Song* made grown men unashamed to cry, and drew the biggest audience ever up until that time for a TV movie.

Extra: Twenty-seven-year-old Gale Sayers wrote his autobiography *I Am Third* in 1970. The book was largely about the running back's knee injury; Sayers was hoping to inspire his readers to overcome adversity. A small section that was devoted to Sayer's backup on the Bears, Brian Piccolo (1943-1970), came to the attention of Hollywood producers, which led to the making of *Brian's Song*. Sayers became better known for his friendship with his teammate than his relatively brief Hall of Fame football career (1965-1971).

The Most Beautiful Munster in the World

Once known as "The Most Beautiful Woman in the World," Yvonne De Carlo accepted the role of a one-hundred-year-old vampire on the TV series *The Munsters* in 1964. As Dracula's daughter, the forty-two-year-old actress impressed her co-stars with her comic abilities. Once she got over her initial shyness, Yvonne found that she loved wandering around the studio in full Lily Munster costume, complete with bile-green skin, black fingernails and long black hair topped off with a silver streak. She smiled when people on the lot would tease her with lines like, "What's the matter, Yvonne, did you eat at the commissary today?"

Another time, the scary housewife frightened an unsuspecting Marlon Brando by sneaking up on him on a movie set. But did she mind the three-hour make-up sessions she endured each morning? Yvonne admitted it was tedious. "But back in the forties, it took them just as long to turn me into a glamour doll."

Extra: The beautiful Yvonne De Carlo (1922-2007) was a favorite pin-up girl for US Servicemen in World War II. Some of the GIs encountered her at Hollywood parties where she'd be dressed in a two-piece bathing suit, inviting them to join in the fun. It was a thrill for the troops to meet her, despite a studio contract that said Yvonne couldn't date soldiers. Morale was also helped by watching De Carlo's curvy figure up on the screen, even though her movies sometimes didn't make sense. The always witty actress joked about her starring role in the 1945 picture *Salome, Where She Danced*. "I came through these beaded curtains, wearing a Japanese kimono and a Japanese headpiece, and then performed a Siamese dance. Nobody seemed to know quite why."

Yvonne's campy character in *Salome* was loosely based on an Irish-born Spanish dancer named Lola Montez (1818-1861). In real life, Lola had fled Bavaria after a scandalous affair with the deposed King Ludwig I (1786-1868), during the Revolution of German States in 1848. The film was actually a western.

The Kirk Spock Feud

William Shatner and Leonard Nimoy did not always get along when they played Captain Kirk and Mister Spock in the 1966 TV series *Star Trek*. Producer Gene Roddenberry was continuously lobbied by Shatner to make Kirk equal to the Vulcan scientist as a problem solver, resulting in extra dialogue for the Captain. Nimoy responded by stealing scenes with his reactions. He would lift an eyebrow, give his superior officer a quizzical look and offer one-word replies such as, "Fascinating." At one point, the two actors cornered Roddenberry and demanded to know who the star was. Frustrated by their pettiness, Gene instructed the show's writers to make Spock and Kirk buddies, which helped ease the tension. Always linked together in the public's mind, Shatner and Nimoy enjoyed a long fruitful relationship and made lots of extra cash by parodying their feud.

Extra: *Star Trek* creator Gene Roddenberry (1921-1991) served as a Los Angeles Police Sergeant under Chief William Parker (1902-1966). Parker had taken over what was perceived to be a very corrupt force in 1950 and restored public confidence. William instructed his underlings to cooperate with the makers of the TV program *Dragnet* (1951-1959). Based on factual cases, the show put the hard-working Los Angeles officers in a heroic light. Parker also assigned his men the use of more patrol cars. He reasoned that not walking a beat would expose the troops to less temptation. It was William Parker who coined the phrase, "Thin Blue Line," meaning that only law enforcement stood in between civilization and anarchy. Respect for the LAPD greatly improved due to William's leadership, but some critics pointed out that there were incidents of police brutality under his watch. The taciturn head cop lamented that as long he was only able to hire human beings, there would be problems. Ten years after Sergeant Roddenberry left the force in 1956, the writer partially modeled the very logical, half-alien Mr. Spock on his quiet, efficient former boss.

Extra: In the 1934 comic mystery *The Thin Man*, William Powell (1892-1984) and Myrna Loy (1905-1993) starred as Nick and Nora Charles. The sophisticated couple delivered witty banter and drank heavily while catching killers. The retired detective and wife formula was hugely successful and led to five sequels. Audiences didn't mind that "The Thin Man" was actually the lead suspect in the first movie and not Nick. The two actors got along well, but Powell occasionally complained that the scripts favored Loy. The leading man was often required to recite long pieces of dialogue that explained the case. His onscreen wife stood eying him with a quizzical expression, as she stroked their pet terrier. Then Myrna would steal the scenes with one-word replies like, "Really!" Some who observed the Kirk Spock byplay on the *Star Trek* set thought that William Shatner could identify with Powell's plight.

Extra: Thirty-five-old William Shatner was told that he was going to be the star of *Star Trek* TV series (1966-1969), but the fans had other ideas. Leonard Nimoy as Mr. Spock, a character who the network executives originally wanted eliminated from the show due to his devil-like appearance, got more viewer mail. One day Shatner arrived in the make-up room to find a *Life Magazine* photographer there to record the application of Nimoy's ears. Shatner, who wanted no one outside the *Star Trek* family to see his cosmetic secrets, announced from then on his own make-up would be done in his trailer and left. The fictional captain's feelings were quickly made known; shortly afterward, someone from the front office ordered the picture taker to leave. A furious

Nimoy confronted a very defensive Shatner in what was the first of several arguments between the two of them.

Extra: When Gene Roddenberry was asked by his two main actors who was the star of the show, he chose Shatner. One of the reasons may have been that the producer resented Nimoy's demands for a raise at a time when *Star Trek*, a very expensive TV program to produce, was losing money.

Extra: Immediately after *Star Trek* was canceled in 1969, Leonard Nimoy was a hot commodity. He joined the cast of the TV espionage show *Mission Impossible* (1966-1973) and made a fortune in real estate. Meanwhile, broke, divorced and unemployed, the Canadian-born William Shatner ended up living in a mobile home with his Doberman.

The Unstoppable Voice

Fifty-three-year-old Mel Blanc became very productive after a near-fatal automobile accident on Sunset Boulevard in 1962. After coming out of a coma, the legendary vocal artist received phone calls from both Warner Bros. and Hanna-Barbera. Did all those broken bones affect his voice? Mel excitedly invited them to his house. For several weeks, Blanc's bedroom became a makeshift studio. While recovering in a full body cast, he enjoyed providing the voices for cartoon characters ranging from his trademark Bugs Bunny to Barney Rubble on the new *Flintstones* TV show. Eventually, Mel was able to walk again, lived to the age of eighty-one and never retired. His only bitter moment regarding the car crash came when Lloyds of London informed him that Mel could not collect on his huge insurance policy since he was still able to work.

Extra: Alan Reed (1907-1977), who played the voice of Fred Flintstone on the animated TV series *The Flintstones*, gained a newfound respect for his co-star. Reed had previously been a regular on Mel Blanc's (1908-1989) short-lived radio show in 1946. After his former boss's near-fatal injury, Alan confessed years ago he had thought Blanc was a stuck-up little jerk. But after seeing the gutsy Mel laid up in bed and still providing the voice of Fred's best pal, Barney Rubble, he'd completely changed his mind. Reed apologized for his earlier mistaken impression, and the two vocal artists became even better friends than the fictional Fred and Barney.

The Cleaned-Up Groucho

After four failures with scripted radio shows, Groucho Marx was asked if he wanted to host a quiz program in 1947. The clean-shaven movie star, who often went unrecognized in public, agreed to trade his trademark grease-paint mustache for a real one. Contestants with offbeat personalities would meet Groucho for the first time on taping day. The fifty-seven-year-old comedian was in his element conversing in front of the studio audience. He would waggle his eyebrows, savor a long pause with his cigar, and then deliver wise cracks, which were often laced with sexual innuendo. *You Bet Your Life* was a success, first on radio then on television, for fourteen years even though the people at home only got a watered-down version; Groucho's best ad-libs were considered too risqué by the censors of the day.

Extra: Some said that Julius Henry Marx (1890-1977) received the stage name Groucho because of his general disposition. But the wisecracking comedian displayed a sentimental side when he became a game-show host. Groucho became very fond of his *You Bet Your Life* guests and couldn't bear to see them go home empty-handed. He would insist that if all else failed, contestants be asked questions like "Who's buried in Grant's Tomb?" to guarantee them some winnings.

Rockford Soprano

TV writer David Chase saw Hollywood as a place where slimeballs committed awful acts and got away with them. The only time he saw justice in Tinseltown was when he worked on *The Rockford Files* in the 1970s. One night the scribe was dining in a restaurant with series star James Garner when they spotted a talent agent who had pilfered some original music that was supposed to be used on their show. David watched amazed as the usually amiable actor got up from the table, calmly strode over to where the offender was sitting and punched him in the face.

In 1999, Chase created his own program inhabited by horrible people who didn't care if they hurt someone in pursuit of their own desires. Murder, treachery and mayhem were everyday occurrences. In this world, if one of the characters got too far out of line, the writer could sic Tony Soprano on him.

Extra: Actor James Garner once said, "If you have pride in your work you don't go into television." But the forty-six-year-old actor accepted the title role on *The Rockford Files* (1974-1980) with his head held high. Jim Rockford's house trailer and answering machine were a far cry from the typical fictional gumshoe's plush office and sexy secretary. He charged high fees, was willing to participate in con jobs with his sleazy pals and often could not collect money from his clients for services rendered. Despite the initial good ratings, network executives wanted to make the detective a more traditional good guy. But Garner, a veteran who'd received a purple heart after being wounded in the Korean War, balked at the idea. The star insisted that he was not a hero, there was no way he'd play one and went on a one-man strike. Garner's bosses agreed to leave the creative people alone, and *Rockford* continued to delight TV viewers.

Extra: The TV crime series *The Sopranos* (1999-2007) was a difficult sell. The premise about stressed-out mob boss Tony Soprano, whose struggles with both his personal and professional families drive him to visit a psychiatrist, was so unique that no network wanted to touch it. The *Sopranos* was based on fifty-four-year-old writer David Chase's time spent in therapy (largely regarding the volatile relationship Chase had with his mother), combined with David's love of 1930s black and white Hollywood gangster movies. Chase theorized that the show was initially rejected because it was about Mafia types and nobody got killed; he set out to rectify his mistake in a big way. With the new ratcheted up body count and blue dialogue, *The Sopranos*, which was originally intended to be a feature film, became a breakout hit on adult-orientated cable television.

Extra: Thirty-eight-year-old James Gandolfini, hired to play the brutal-when-he-had-to-be Tony Soprano (his co-stars thought the 260-pound Gandolfini to be an absolute pussycat) was put off by his character's violence, and sometimes (despite becoming rich, famous and winning three Emmys) considered leaving the program. A few months after *The Sopranos* first aired, the New Jersey-born actor (before his latest gig, James had been in about twenty movies and never played the lead in any of them) had a brush with his new celebrity. One night, James heard some loud knocking outside his Manhattan apartment. When he opened the door, the noisy man on the other side seemed to recognize Gandolfini's small-screen alter ego, turned white with fear and took off in a hurry.

I Love Ethel

Insiders who worked on the fifties sitcom *I Love Lucy* said that in real life, Vivien Vance was the funniest of the cast members. One week guest star

Tallulah Bankhead came backstage to be greeted by Vivien and Lucille Ball. Lucy gave Bankhead a sisterly hug and told the famed theater actress how much she loved her sweater. Tallulah sniffed. "This little frock, darling? You want it, take it."

"Oh no, Tallulah, I'm just admiring it."

"Now Lucille, Tallulah can see the envy in your eyes."

"Tallulah, we have the number one show in the country, I can afford my own sweater."

The outspoken Bankhead kept pressing the point until the weary redhead took the outer garment and put it on. There was a pause and Vivian Vance, who had quietly watched the whole exchange said, "Tallulah, I love those pants."

Extra: Lucille Ball (1911-1989) thought Vivien Vance (1909-1979) was too attractive to play her overweight landlady Ethel Mertz on *I Love Lucy* in 1951. Although Lucille insisted publicly that she was not a glamorous movie star type, the former model was from the old school. You never let your co-star look better than you. The affable Vance, realizing that being Ball's second banana was her big break, agreed to do whatever her role required. Every summer during the TV show's successful six-year run, the ex-Broadway trouper Vivian would get reminder calls from her boss: "Viv, dear, we start shooting in a couple of weeks. Start eating!"

That Grinchy Old Seuss

La Jolla, California's Ted Geisel, better known as "Dr. Seuss," feared that his children's book *How the Grinch Stole Christmas* would be ruined by television in 1966. The sixty-two-year-old childless artist shared many of the Grinch's attitudes; he felt the holiday was too crass and commercial. He peppered animator Chuck Jones with questions. Why was the Grinch not grey as he was originally drawn? Why was horror actor Boris Karloff narrating? He was too scary. Why did the Grinch's expressions make him look like Chuck Jones? His collaborator convinced Ted that green would show up better on TV, that Karloff would set the right tone between comic and frightening and that Jones needed to put himself in his cartoons to make them work. The positive response to the show put the curmudgeonly author in a festive mood. A few days after *Grinch* aired, Seuss led a huge Yuletide celebration in La Jolla.

Extra: The famed children's writer and illustrator Theodor Seuss Geisel (1904-1991) never had any kids of his own. "You make them, and I'll entertain them," he told people.

Desi Talks

Thirty-four-year-old Desi Arnaz guarded the integrity of his character Ricky Ricardo on the 1951 TV sitcom *I Love Lucy*. Each week his ditzy spouse, played by his real-life wife Lucille Ball, would come up with a crazy scheme to break into show business. The Cuban-born band leader recognized that Lucy was the main draw and didn't mind being her second banana as long as he didn't look like a fool. He insisted to the writers that Ricky see through her plans; that he was always on equal footing with the audience. Another issue was his accent, which only Lucy was allowed to make fun of. One time Desi stopped a rehearsal. Why did the script say *splain* and *thin*, instead of *explain* and *thing*? When told that it was the way that he spoke, Arnaz angrily denied it and demanded that the scripts be written in proper English. As soon as the corrections were made, the mispronunciations continued.

Extra: Jess Oppenheimer (1913-1988) came up with the weekly concept for the TV series *I Love Lucy*: A hard-working bandleader (Desi Arnaz) wants to come home after a long day to his wife (Lucille Ball), who much to his chagrin, was dying to break into show business herself. Lucille Ball called Oppenheimer the brains behind the show, but sometimes Jess clashed with the program's other producer, Lucille's headstrong husband Desi Arnaz (1917-1986). Both men agreed Ball's comedic talent was the main reason for the show's enormous success, and in 1955, they decided to make a truce. Desi proposed that all decisions regarding *I Love Lucy* be made by majority rules. If Jess and Lucy disagreed with Desi, the party of two would get their way; likewise, if Oppenheimer was the odd man out, he'd be obligated to go along with Arnaz and Ball.

"Wait a minute," Jess asked Desi, "what happens if you and I are the ones who agree?"

"Like I told you, majority rules. If that's the case then Lucy decides."

Did He or Didn't He?

The 2006 movie *Hollywoodland* reopened the mystery surrounding the death of *The Adventures of Superman* lead actor George Reeves. The official ruling was that in 1959, the forty-five-year-old TV icon, depressed about dwindling career opportunities, shot himself. His mother hired investigators to prove that foul play was involved, which led to other theories. However Reeves' demise came about, his co-stars and fans always had nice things to say about George's charm and generosity. Playing the Man of Steel made Reeves feel that he should be a role model for children; he quit smoking and kept his love affairs private. The public didn't need to know that he often drank heavily before scenes. George, who in real life once talked a kid out of shooting him because the ricocheting bullets might hit an innocent person, displayed impressive survival instincts on *Superman*. Each week a thug would fire six bullets that bounced off the big guy's chest. Then the desperate criminal would hurl the empty gun, and Superman would duck.

Extra: Before *The Adventures of Superman* TV show (1952-1958), the Man of Steel appeared on the radio (1942-1951). In dual roles, voice artist Bud Collyer (1908-1969) used his training as a singer to differentiate the mild-mannered Clark Kent from the powerful flying hero. With no reruns, the writers invented Kryptonite to give the hard-working Collyer time off. The rock remains from the comic book icon's native planet would incapacitate him, and allow Batman and Robin, played by two other actors, to step in and save the day.

Blue Language Bonanza

The creators of the classic TV western *Bonanza* considered the four main characters to be the noble descendants of The Knights of the Round Table. The show's impressive opening was filmed in beautiful locations throughout California. What better way to put the heroism and integrity of the Cartwright family on display than to have the foursome ride out and greet the audience? There were actually lyrics accompanying the theme music but they were quickly discarded. Michael Landon who played youngest of the three Cartwright sons, Little Joe, was grateful for the silent-movie effect. "Thank God they didn't have microphones on us when we rode those horses or you would have heard the foulest language ever."

Discussing the man who played his father, he stated, "You know, the whole thirteen years I was on that show I honestly thought Lorne Greene's horse was named: "Whoa, I said whoa, you dirty son of a-!"

Extra: Lorne Greene (1915-1987) was so warm and convincing as the father on *Bonanza* that runaway children would sometimes show up at his door looking for a new home.

Castaways!

Partly based on *Robinson Crusoe* by Daniel Defoe, the 1964 TV series *Gilligan's Island* was challenging work for its cast. Method actress Tina Louise thought that the program should center around her glamorous movie star character, till she was informed it was not called "Ginger's Island." Veteran actress Natalie Schafer complained that her small-screen millionaire husband, Jim Backus, was upstaging her with his constant ad-libbing. Russell Johnson, as the level-headed Professor, and Dawn Wells, who played the sweet-natured farm girl Mary Ann, put up with being excluded from the show's opening credits for the entire first season. Star Bob Denver struggled to give his Stan Laurel-like Gilligan enough subtlety so the audience would see he wasn't always so dumb, while Alan Hale Jr. as the Oliver Hardy-like Skipper kept an upbeat attitude through bad scripts and personal injuries. The program lasted for three years and had enough impact that some viewers called the Coast Guard demanding that the castaways be rescued.

Extra: The *Gilligan's Island* lagoon set was actually a parking lot at CBS Studios, near the 101 freeway. Each morning the cast and crew would wait for the traffic noise to die down before shooting could commence. Once, Jim Backus (1913-1989) and Alan Hale Jr. (1921-1990) were killing time by hitting golf balls over the water and out of sight. The two actors were each insisting that they were the more skilled player, emphasizing their points with profanity-laden insults. A man in uniform interrupted the friendly match. "Excuse me, gentleman, the President of the network just called about the windshield of his Rolls Royce being shattered by a golf ball. You guys know anything about that?"
Both braggarts dropped their clubs and immediately accused the other of being the more powerful driver. It turned out their co-star, Bob Denver (1935-2005), bribed the security guard to ask the question.

Extra: After years of playing dingbat society types, Natalie Schafer (1900-1991) was perfectly cast as the spoiled but kind-hearted Lovey Howell on the *Gilligan's Island* pilot in 1963. For the veteran actress, it was all about getting a quick paycheck, plus a free vacation to Hawaii. The script about seven castaways, without a single luxury, was so stupid; there was no way that the network would pick it up. With this kind of material floating around Hollywood, she couldn't wait to move back to New York. The Red Bank, New Jersey, native did a professional job, and then quickly forgot about being marooned. A few weeks later, Schafer was vacationing in Puerto Vallarta with some friends when she received a phone call. "What! Oh my God, no!"

Her companions, assuming that it was bad news about her ailing mother, ran to comfort her. To their surprise, Natalie's tears were caused by CBS' decision to make *Gilligan* a weekly series, which the actress was now contractually obligated to be on. At that moment, Schafer was crushed to have the new, well-paying employment that would make her famous.

Spock's Ears

Leonard Nimoy suffered while playing Mr. Spock in the 1966 TV series *Star Trek*. The thirty-five-year-old former cab driver from Boston created the Vulcan's unique attributes, such as the neck pinch that could render his enemies unconscious and the split-finger greeting, based on an ancient Talmudic sign used by Hebrew Priests. Mr. Spock got tons of fan mail and became an unlikely extraterrestrial sex symbol. The dedicated performer would have enjoyed it more if it wasn't for the damn ears, so painful to unglue they were driving him crazy. Desperate for relief, Nimoy sought the advice of one of the show's producers who had a possible solution. There was a renowned Beverly Hills plastic surgeon that could make his real ears pointy for the duration of the series, then change them back. The excited actor asked for an immediate appointment as his boss wondered how to break the news that he was kidding.

Extra: On the old *George Burns and Gracie Allen Comedy Show*, Burns maintained the same expression while his zany wife Gracie would prattle on about whatever was on her mind. Leonard Nimoy, without Burns' trademark cigar, borrowed the comedian's technique when Spock was forced to listen to the emotional ramblings of Doctor McCoy.

Extra: Leonard Nimoy went through a roller coaster ride of emotions playing Mr. Spock. When he first wore the pointed ears, it had been embarrassing to stand there waiting to step in front of the camera. The make-believe alien maintained his dignity while being teased by the burly teamsters who worked behind the scenes about his strange appearance. During *Star Trek's* run, Nimoy had been nominated for three Emmys, yet his requests for more money and better working conditions had been met with resentment from his bosses. Why couldn't they acknowledge that he deserved some of the credit for the show's success? Also, as much as he enjoyed playing Spock, Leonard wanted people to know that he had more to offer. After all, he'd done other parts, and was also a painter, photographer and poet. In 1977, Nimoy wrote his autobiography, which many of his fans never bothered to read because they were offended by the title: *I'm Not Spock.*

Extra: When Leonard Nimoy heard that the executives at Paramount wanted to make a *Star Trek* movie in 1977, he wanted no part of it. He had filed a lawsuit against the studio regarding not getting paid for the merchandising of Spock. The whole *Star Trek* thing had left a bitter taste in his mouth. Nimoy hated that in the last few years, Gene Roddenberry had made money with film showing the *Star Trek* cast flubbing their lines. As far as the actor was concerned, the blooper reels violated the privacy of the shooting set. But the new guys at Paramount settled the court case and paid him off, telling him that there was no way they could make their movie without the original Spock.

Despite his reservations about the weak script, Leonard Nimoy reluctantly agreed to come back into the *Star Trek* fold, reasoning that if the project failed to go forward, the fans would blame him.

Extra: After *Star Trek: The Motion Picture* (1979) got poor reviews in spite of its good performance at the box office, Nimoy thought he was done with the alien for good. Then he was lured back in by *Star Trek II: The Wrath of Kahn* (1982). The script contained every performer's dream: a great death scene. One last go-round and then people would stop asking him about Spock. But he'd actually enjoyed making the sequel. Maybe he'd been premature in agreeing to have the Vulcan killed off. The Paramount brass, fearful about the fan's negative reaction to the end of the one of their favorite characters, agreed. One executive insisted that the movie needed a hopeful ending for Spock because you couldn't have a story about Easter without resurrection.

Extra: Figuring that the franchise would not go on without him, Nimoy asked to direct *Star Trek III: the Search for Spock* (1984). Many weeks passed and he received no reply. Leonard was disconcerted; the man who'd wanted nothing to do with *Star Trek* was now anxious to guide the franchise into the future. It turned out that the Paramount brass actually believed that Leonard hated Spock and had insisted on killing him in his contract. Nimoy challenged them to examine the document. It wasn't true! He loved the Vulcan and wanted to make the movie. Realizing that Nimoy being behind the camera on a *Star Trek* picture would be a terrific marketing tool, the suits gave in to Leonard's request.

Extra: Nimoy did well enough on his first outing to be hired again to direct *Star Trek IV: The Voyage Home* (1986). The fun, fish-out-of-water story, involving the Enterprise crew going back in time to save Earth, attracted cinemagoers who were not fans of the TV show, and was the biggest hit of the movie series starring the original cast.

Extra: The last movie featuring the original cast was *Star Trek VI: The Undiscovered Country* (1991). Leonard Nimoy accepted that he and his longtime co-stars were being put out to pasture. He turned down an offer to join William Shatner in *Star Trek: Generations* (1994), feeling that there wasn't enough in the story, about the next crew of the Starship Enterprise, for Spock to do. The very rich performer mostly retired from his craft to pursue other interests. Sometimes Leonard was wistful that *Star Trek* films were being made without him, but he'd had a good run. Then out of the blue, Nimoy was approached to reprise Spock alongside new young actors playing rebooted versions of the original characters. For the first time in his life, Leonard was told that a project absolutely could not be made without him. The seventy-eight-year-old, who never expected to put on the ears again, let alone be in another movie, was overcome by deep emotions. The 2009 version easily surpassed all the previous films in the series at the box office, and, after forty-three years, Leonard Nimoy was very excited to be part of *Star Trek* once more.

The Smart Don

Comic actor Don Adams faced a difficult financial choice when he played the bumbling Maxwell Smart in the 1965 television series *Get Smart*. The producers offered him two options: he could take home a healthy paycheck each week or get very little money in exchange for a one-third ownership stake in the show. The ex-Marine swallowed hard and gambled for the long term. *Get Smart* stayed on the air for five years and was shown constantly in reruns. Adams' made-up catch phrases like "Would you believe?" and "Missed me by that much" were repeated often by viewers. The now wealthy star, who claimed he hated performing, was able to spend the last years of his life playing cards at the Playboy Mansion and traveling the world with his seven children. When asked how he ended up with such a large brood, the three-times-married Don shrugged, "No big deal. It only took seven minutes."

Young Knew Best

Forty-seven-year-old Robert Young became a beloved figure when he played the wise patriarch of the Anderson family on radio and television in *Father Knows Best*. The former movie actor, who had been told by studio executives that he had no sex appeal, provided a contrast to the typical dumb dad in situation comedies. For eleven years beginning in 1949, the soft-spoken insurance man would return home from his job, take off his jacket and solve whatever crisis his family faced. No matter that in real life the star drank heavily, went through long periods of depression and considered living up to his public image to be an unrealistic burden. For many Americans, Jim Anderson's conservative values were their own. Young won four Emmys for *Father* and became a rich man, even though he personally thought that mothers were usually smarter. When the show moved to television in 1954, Robert originally wanted to copy the earlier radio version and have the title be a question, not a statement, as in *Father Knows Best?*

The MacMurray Method

Fred MacMurray created a new way of filming when he played the widower father on the 1960 television series *My Three Sons*. The fifty-year-old actor had accumulated a massive real estate empire, worth hundreds of millions, and only wanted to work on the show for twelve weeks a year. All of Fred's scenes were completed over sixty-five days; his castmates would finish the remainder of the thirty-nine episodes without him. The kid actors were required to get haircuts each week; very few viewers ever noticed. Shooting consecutive TV episodes out of sequence became known as the MacMurray method and worked fine for twelve years until *Sons'* final season. Fred's character remarried; the new wife had a little girl. In one episode, the child was talking to some of the cast members with a bright, happy smile. Later, on the same show, she did a sequence with MacMurray that was made months before and she had no teeth.

The Jolly Second Banana

From 1957 till 1992, announcer Ed McMahon was the perfect second banana for *Tonight Show* host Johnny Carson. With his trademark booming laugh, Ed walked a delicate tightrope; he had to be supportive while not stepping on his boss's jokes. Early on they became drinking buddies; Carson, a former Navy man, marveled at the ex-Marine fighter pilot's ability to put them away. McMahon was there to sell Carson; he guffawed whenever the comedian teased him about his boozing. But once in a while Ed would get him back. One night Carson was conducting a nightmarish interview with a very dull author. He glanced at the time: oh my God, another ten minutes of torture to go. Then to his surprise, the band started to play, which signaled that the show was finished. Johnny later realized he needed a new, more secure desk clock, so his jolly friend at the end of the couch could no longer turn back the minute hand.

Extra: It wasn't always easy for Ed McMahon (1923-2009) to know when to step in on his sometimes temperamental boss's material. More than once, early in their relationship, Johnny Carson (1925-2005) wanted McMahon fired and was talked out of it by people close to the show, who realized nobody could do as good a job. McMahon was able to smile through all the booze jokes, even though they sometimes pained both him and his family. Did people think he could maintain his busy schedule if he was the alcoholic Johnny said he was? Well, of course he was a big Irishman so it was easier for people to think that he was inebriated. Sometimes Carson, who was much less able to handle his liquor, would publicly ascribe drunken behavior to Ed that Johnny had committed himself.

Extra: The very shy Johnny Carson hated parties and was famously withdrawn from *The Tonight Show* staff. He couldn't stand to be asked for anything, yet could be extremely generous behind the scenes. One time Johnny called Ed McMahon backstage for a private meeting after the broadcast. The normally jolly sidekick was taken aback by his boss's unusual behavior. "Oh my God, this is it; he's going to fire me."

Smoking a cigarette, Johnny said with hesitation, "Look, I know what you are doing out there...you're such a supportive person, you are doing a wonderful job and I appreciate --"

Carson got no further as the tearful McMahon turned and ran.

"See," Johnny shouted after him. "You can't take a compliment any better than I can!"

The Wholesome Thug

Producer Gary Marshall fought with his bosses at ABC television over the Fonzie character's leather attire in the 1974 situation comedy *Happy Days*. The Fonz was based on a tough guy Marshall knew while growing up in the Bronx, but the network brass thought he looked too thuggish to be friends with the wholesome Cunningham family who lived in 1950s Milwaukee. The bigwigs insisted that the fictional former gang member wear a windbreaker. Gary asked if Fonzie could at least put on his dark leather jacket when he rode his motorcycle, otherwise he would freeze. The suits agreed, and from then on Marshall made sure Fonz never did a scene without his bike. Once he even rode his machine into the Cunningham's living room, claiming he was afraid of vandals. Arthur Fonzarelli became a cultural icon, the leather jacket ended up in the Smithsonian Institution in Washington DC, while the windbreaker lay forgotten in a dumpster.

Free Johnny Depp

Twenty-four-year-old Johnny Depp thought that his starring role in the 1987 TV series *21 Jump Street* would not last a whole season. After a few weeks of playing a young-looking cop who goes undercover at high schools to catch drug dealers, the Kentucky-born actor began to feel that the spying he performed in each episode was immoral. Worse yet, *Jump Street* was a breakout hit, and Depp's busy schedule kept him from accepting movie offers. The resentful teen idol tried to provoke his bosses into terminating him. His onset antics included lighting his underwear on fire, constantly changing dialogue and suggesting wild plot lines, such as having his character cover his entire nude body with peanut butter. The program's creators realized that their leading man was the main reason viewers tuned in and held him to his contract. Johnny did a professional job and appreciated *Jump Street* for making him a household name, but compared his being able to leave the show in 1990 to the freeing of imprisoned South African leader Nelson Mandela.

It's So Hard To Meet Someone

When Tyra Banks became more famous, she had difficulty hooking up with a normal guy. As the self-proclaimed ugly duckling transformed into a hard-working supermodel, Tyra found no shortages of men willing to go out with her. One time, Banks was set up on a date with a famous Hollywood actor. Dinner had gone well; the man seemed to be very attentive until she realized he was checking himself out in the mirror behind her. He proceeded to brag about past conquests; Banks nodded off before she could become the next one. Tyra, who once wore a hat, dark glasses and a false beard at a club to avoid being recognized, turned to her fans for help with her love life. "I want to meet a normal man," the TV talk show host told her audience.

Soon after she was approached by a potential suitor who insisted he was normal. How so? Well, he didn't have a job, his car was in the shop and he still lived at home with his mother.

Fit but not Rich

In 1951, thirty-seven-year-old Jack LaLanne began to blaze a trail as an exercise instructor on television. A former juvenile delinquent who blamed his past bad behavior on a sugar addiction, the five-foot-six Frenchman defied predictions that nobody would want to watch a guy work out. Sure, maybe his audience couldn't match his ability to swim the length of the Golden Gate Bridge while shackled to a half-ton boat, or do a thousand push-ups in twenty-three minutes, but if they ate right and kept active they could be happy. He was called a crackpot for stating that lifting weights would give women better figures. The inspiring morning program lasted thirty-four years, physical fitness became a multi-billion dollar industry, but Jack himself failed to become a millionaire. Never bitter, LaLanne laughed about the time he railed on his show against an unhealthy food item, and then found out later it was made by his network sponsors.

Who Cares How Much It Costs?

Forty-nine-year-old Bob Barker became a beloved national figure when he began as host of *The New Price is Right* in 1972. Many of *Price's* participants were more excited about meeting the friendly gray-haired man who greeted them on television than the actual contest in which they tried to guess how much items cost. People came from all across the USA, sometimes camping outside the CBS Los Angeles Studio for eighteen hours just to get one of the 315 free seats. Some *Price is Right* winners struggled to pay the income taxes on their prizes. In his own life, the gentlemanly Barker had his housekeeper do all his shopping and claimed not to know the price of anything. Bob laughed about the time he came out on stage and his adoring fans would not stop screaming. The appreciative MC tried to quiet them down so they could start taping, unaware that they were reacting to a cute female contestant that had accidentally lost her top.

The Legend of Bozo

A character created for a children's storytelling record in 1946, Bozo the Clown became both a franchised television star and part of an urban legend. Over two hundred actors played the redheaded jester in different markets around the world. The jolly circus performer would lead little tykes in contests where they could win prizes. The most notorious rumor about *The Bozo Show* started in the 1960s. An underprivileged boy wanted to win a toy from Bozo's treasure chest. All he had to do was throw three ping-pong balls in a barrel. Unfortunately, the third attempt fell short; the disappointed youngster ran off and buried his face in his hands. The white-skinned host followed him. "That's a Bozo no–no."

The angry kid raised his head. "Cram it, clown!"

The unproven, not filmed incident was repeated so often that after years of denials, some of the retired ex-Bozos began to flip flop and swear the story was true.

Blind as a Bat

Actors who played demons on the 1997 TV show *Buffy the Vampire Slayer* worried about seeing and being seen. Young, good-looking performers would sit for hours to have their features altered for the privilege of being dusted by the blonde heroine. The creatures of the night dealt with painfully removing their make-up at the end of fight scenes, wearing vision-impairing contact lenses and missing out on catered lunches because they couldn't eat with their fangs. Some of the disguised performers, who wondered if playing fiends was a good career move, were often pleasantly surprised when they were recognized. Once, an ex-vampire, who was staked by the slayer in his episode, attended the Posting Board party, an annual charity event for *Buffy* watchers. A well-wisher told him he did a great job on the show. The former bloodsucker smiled. "Thanks, it's always great to meet one of the fans," he told his startled castmate.

The Unwilling Kissers

William Shatner and Nichelle Nichols defied powerful forces in 1968 when they kissed each other on the final season of *Star Trek*. NBC executives worried that the famed TV series was going too far in showing an interracial coupling between the thirty-seven-year-old Shatner and his gorgeous black, one-year-younger co-star. So what if aliens were forcing Captain Kirk and Lieutenant Uhura to act against their will? The scene was re-filmed where the compelled lovers resisted, but after viewing the footage, the network bosses reluctantly chose to air the original version. Viewer reaction to the steamy sequence was overwhelmingly positive. Nichols, who like others in the show's cast sometimes resented Shatner for hogging the limelight, could not help but be amused at her captain's hammy antics. During the takes where they didn't embrace, he had shouted out inappropriate dialogue or made funny faces so the shots were unusable.

Extra: *Star Trek's* producers only got one letter of complaint regarding the Shatner/Nichols kiss. A white Southern fan stated that generally, he was against the mixing of the races, but if an all-American boy like Captain Kirk has a babe like Lieutenant Uhura in his arms, what else is he supposed to do?

SINGERS AND DANCERS

"You don't swing where you sleep."
— Sammy Davis Jr.

"There's no business like show business."
— Irving Berlin

The Graceful Klutz

Ever graceful on screen, Fred Astaire claimed to be a klutz in his personal life. In the 1951 musical *Royal Wedding,* the fifty-two-year-old performed his most amazing dance routine. Astaire appeared to defy gravity and climb walls while his feet never actually left the ground. It was accomplished with the help of a spinning square room called a squirrel cage, combined with a rotating camera. Unlike many special effects, the sequence never looked dated. Pop singer Lionel Ritchie used the same technology thirty years later to film the video for his hit song "Dancing on the Ceiling." Away from movies, Astaire had less luck with gadgets. Always sensitive about his baldness, Fred once purchased a hair restoration machine complete with a rubber cap and electronic coils. Unfortunately, he misread the directions, and the device removed the few locks he had left.

Extra: Fred Astaire's (1899-1987) smooth style of dancing was obtained by long hard months of practice. The Nebraska-born hoofer was not nearly as confident about displaying his moves away from either the camera or stage. Once, at a father-daughter dance, Fred embarrassed Ava Astaire by tripping all over her in front of her friends.

Desperately Seeking Madonna

Twenty-six-year-old Madonna beat out over two hundred girls to win the title role in the 1985 comedy *Desperately Seeking Susan.* Director Susan Seidelman thought the Material Girl was the perfect casting as a kooky free-spirited hustler who exchanges places with a bland housewife, played by Rosanna Arquette. Like Frank Sinatra and Barbra Streisand before her, Madonna had trouble giving up the complete control she exerted in the recording studio for the team atmosphere of a movie set. The singer complained about the long waiting period between shots, feuded openly with the more seasoned Arquette and at times suffered from camera fright and forgot her lines. But with the director's help and patience, Madonna was likable in the role and *Susan* was a hit. Later, the pop star called the fictional Susan a "conniving opportunist." Madonna paused, remembering she played someone like herself, then added, "But one who cares deeply about others."

Calculated Beatlemania

In the summer of 1963, the bosses at Capitol Records refused to release the Beatle's albums in the United States, mistakenly believing that the Fab Four's music would not go over well with young American audiences. This provided an opening for United Artists executives who conceived of a plan where they would put the lads in a throwaway film and make a fortune selling the soundtrack. A meeting was scheduled in London but the Beatles were nowhere to be found. The moviemakers discovered John, Paul, George and Ringo standing on the street near their pad, hopelessly trying to hail a cab. Their antics reminded the producers of the Marx Brothers and became the basis for the movie *A Hard Day's Night*, named after a twisted phrase of Ringo's describing a long bout of work. The smash hit film, which presented a day in the life in the four young superstars, minus their less innocent activities, made it easier for American parents to accept their teenagers catching the feverish fan frenzy that was known as Beatlemania.

Extra: To prepare for *A Hard Day's Night* (1964), British Screenwriter Alun Owen (1925-1994) hung out with the Beatles and put their actual conversations into the script. With their hectic schedules, John Lennon (1940-1980), twenty-two-year-old Paul McCartney, twenty-four-year-old Ringo Starr and George Harrison (1943-2001) struggled to learn their lines, and mostly winged it through the picture. The United Artists executives were thrilled when they saw the footage; the throwaway film made to sell a soundtrack was turned into something special because the young men were so natural and likable on camera.

Extra: Beatlemania, a term first used by British newspapers to describe fan reaction to a Beatles concert in 1963, was an unprecedented nightmare for law enforcement. It seemed no amount of manpower could prevent female teenagers from stopping traffic near airports where the band landed, charging the stage during Beatles' concerts, or breaching security at hotels where the Fab Four was staying. At one heavily fortified resort in Seattle, the famed musicians discovered several girls (who had somehow evaded police, the Coast Guard and a barricade made of plywood and razor wire) hiding in their closets, bathrooms and under their beds.

Extra: One afternoon, shortly after *A Hard Day's Night* came out, a phony rumor started at Disneyland that the Beatles were in the park disguised as the Three Little Pigs and the Big Bad Wolf. The four costumed characters were mobbed by young girls for the rest of the day.

Extra: After the success of *A Hard Day's Night,* a couple of clever Hollywood producers decided that the Beatle's big-screen antics should be turned into a TV show. Since the Fab Four were unavailable and unaffordable, a new band was put together. *The Monkees* (1966-1968) was a wildly successful series; the misspelling of the makeshift musical group's name was an intentional tribute to the incorrect "a" in Beatles.

The Not-So-Happy Musical

An embattled cast produced happy results in the 1952 musical *Singin' in the Rain.* Twenty-seven-year-old Donald O'Connor was hospitalized after weeks of crashing through walls, performing the slapstick number, "Make 'Em Laugh." When he recovered, the heavy-smoking hoofer found out that the footage was ruined and he had to do it again. Meanwhile, Donald's co-star Debbie Reynolds lived in constant fear of director and leading man Gene Kelly, who angrily criticized her dancing skills. At various points during production, the twenty-year-old ex-gymnast Reynolds became bedridden with the flu, hid behind a piano so no one could see her cry and had to be carried off the set after the blood vessels burst in her feet. The forty-four-year-old Kelly demanded no less from himself; he sang the movie's lighthearted title song on a sopping wet sound stage with a 103-degree fever. *Singin' in the Rain's* audience didn't feel the actors' pain; the romantic parody about the end of silent films was considered one of the most joyful pictures ever.

To Serve and Protect Sammy

While working for a limousine company, I once had the privilege of driving Sammy Davis Jr. who was warm and friendly to me. This was shortly before Davis' death in 1990 at age sixty-five, due to throat cancer. Just before the great entertainer came out of his Beverly Hills house, Sammy's security guard had told me that previously he worked as a freelancer and protected several celebrity clients before breaking his leg. After six weeks, the disabled employee got out of the hospital and approached his mailbox, dreading the prospect of unpaid bills. To his surprise, Sammy and only Sammy had never stopped sending him paychecks. He now worked for Davis exclusively, and his boss had never mentioned the very generous act. I noticed there was a plaque by Sammy's front door that read, "This house welcomes anyone with peace, love and brotherhood in their hearts." My new friend assured me if anyone came over the singer's fence with those traits, he would shoot them dead.

Jimmy Durante Loved New York

Born in New York City in 1893, Jimmy Durante quit school in the eighth grade to become a ragtime pianist. The big-hearted, big-nosed comedian, who christened himself "Schnozzola", appeared anywhere he could get a gig including bars, cabarets and whorehouses. Jimmy's ability to talk to audiences helped him stand out from other musicians. By the late 1920s, he was a bandleader and a Vaudeville sensation. One night Durante impressed an MGM Studios talent scout with his charismatic onstage presence. Surely, there was a place in the new world of talking movies for this unique personality. The Hollywood man visited the headliner's dressing room after the show, introduced himself and remarked that Jimmy had enough skills to play Hamlet. The sensitive performer eyed him with suspicion. "Forgot da small towns, pal. New York's da place for me."

Extra: Jimmy Durante (1893-1980) tried to ensure that his generous nature didn't take time away from his true love. As a small boy, he'd been driven to tears when other children made fun of his looks. When he became a successful entertainer, Jimmy was passionate about raising money for abused children. The extra shows were a joy for both the warm-hearted performer and his adoring young fans. But if the workload got too big, Jimmy would implore other famous luminaries to join his benefits. "Ya got da help the kids," he'd say.

When they'd agree to assist, Durante would massage their egos with gushing introductions. Then he'd leave them on stage to fend for themselves, sneak out the back door and head to the racetrack.

Marlene's Wartime Regret

Marlene Dietrich found her true calling entertaining the Allied troops in 1943. The forty-two-year-old actress, who never enjoyed making movies, got a crash course in how to talk to audiences. Nothing could be tougher or more fulfilling than performing in front of young men who might die in battle the next day. The Berlin-born American citizen overcame suspicions that she was actually an Axis spy, and was proud of spurning Hitler's request to return to Germany. After World War II ended, she enjoyed being a lusty cabaret singer for many years and tried never to take herself too seriously. Marlene, whose long list of romances ranged from John Wayne to General Patton, once mentioned to her husband that she should have married Hitler back in the thirties, and then there would have been no war. She laughed when he agreed and stated that the Fuhrer would have killed himself much sooner.

Extra: In 1923, actress and singer Marlene Dietrich (1901-1992) married casting director Rudolph Sieber (1897-1976). They lived together for five years, had one daughter and never divorced. Rudolph took a mistress, while Marlene embarked on several notorious affairs. Dietrich stayed friends with the Roman Catholic Sieber until his death, and referred to him as the perfect husband.

Sammy's Sign

One time Sammy Davis Jr. and Frank Sinatra were asked to perform at the MGM Grand hotel in Las Vegas with Leo the famous lion who roared at the beginning of movies. They were assured it would be safe; the very old, very tame animal would be handled by a trainer with a choke chain. In the middle of the number, the lion looked at Sammy and licked its lips. The "King of the Beasts" hunched back like it was going to leap for Sammy, and the 110-pound scared-to-death entertainer made the sign of the cross. The trainer yanked the chain and nothing happened. After the show, the two shaken singers went into the casino and had drinks and cigarettes at the blackjack table. Sinatra couldn't keep his hands from shaking. He wondered why Davis, who years before had converted to Judaism, had made the Catholic religious gesture on stage. "Well babe, when that cat came at me, I didn't think I'd have time to make the Star of David!"

Extra: In 1944, foreign journalists, who lived in Los Angeles, were frustrated that many movie stars wouldn't talk to them. From the actors' point of view it was a waste of time; World War II had cut off the overseas market for their films. The European reporters were desperate to give the people back home something more fun to read about than bloody battles. They concluded that the best way to gain access to egomaniacal celebrities was to present them with annual awards. The Golden Globes ceremony was a formal affair until 1958 when Frank Sinatra, Sammy Davis Jr. and Dean Martin got bored by the slow pace of the presentation. The trio of singers came charging out of the audience and onto the stage, brandishing martini swords. They quickly hijacked the show and the statues were passed out within five minutes. Frank, Sammy and Dean's antics were a hit and they were asked to repeat their hosting duties the next year. The Golden Globes became known as an event where luminaries could let their hair down, compared to the much more formal Academy Awards. The more ribald moments included Jack Nicholson mooning the audience from the stage, and both Joan Crawford and Bette Midler coming to the podium with low-cut dresses and saying, "I'll show you my golden globes!"

It Doesn't Matter Who You Are

When Elvis Presley began his Hollywood career in 1956, the image did not always match up to the human being. The ducktail haircut he wore was imitated by young men throughout the country. Black slacks and opened-necked shirts went flying off the shelves. Although sometimes bitter about being accused of lewd behavior, Elvis embraced his lofty position. Jaded film community residents were amazed by his willingness to spend hours signing autographs. If he ever got too full of himself, the singer could recall staying at his first Hollywood lodging, the famous Roosevelt Hotel. An elevator operator refused to take him to the tenth floor, telling Elvis that it was reserved for Elvis. Presley confirmed his identity, causing the workman to stare and declare, "I don't care who you are, and you're not going to the tenth floor."

The good-natured star then simply got off on the ninth floor, and climbed the fire escape to the floor above.

A Gift from the Rolling Stones

One evening in the late 1960s, a feverish group of female fans gathered below the New York studios of *The Ed Sullivan Show*, hoping to catch a glimpse of The Rolling Stones. Suddenly, several floors above the screaming teenagers, a window opened and out came a long-stemmed rose, which caused bedlam in the street. The girls broke down barriers to retrieve the gift from their rock idols. After the police had regained control of the near riot, they entered the building and went upstairs to investigate. Mick Jagger, Keith Richards and the band, who had just finished trashing their dressing room, claimed innocence. Next door was Joan Rivers, Ed Sullivan's other guest that night. The young comic was truly frightened by the chaos she had witnessed and stated how disgusting the whole thing was. The officers left without examining her vase, which contained only eleven of the dozen flowers Sullivan had sent Rivers before the show.

Extra: In 1983, forty-year-old Keith Richards got married and shortly afterward started a family, but it was hard for him to shake his wild-man image. One night in New York at a prestigious movie premiere, some industry gossips were spreading rumors as to why the famed rocker was not in the theater. It was no secret that Richards had been arrested five times for drug-related charges. His limo had been surrounded that night by federal marshals; poor Keith was back on the smack again. The Rolling Stones guitarist had turned into a frothing-at-the-mouth animal when they put him in handcuffs and took him away; what an embarrassment for his poor wife. It turned out that their speculation wasn't true; the feds had mistakenly thought the car was stolen. The scandalmongers were put in their place when Keith Richards, who was sitting with his spouse in the row right in front of them, turned around and said," I'm right here you idiots; now be quiet so we can enjoy the show!"

Talk to the Animals

Doris Day's love of animals exceeded her affection for both Hollywood and husbands. At the height of her fame, the Cincinnati-born actress/singer invited her fans to leave abandoned pets on her Beverly Hills property. She could often be found in her kitchen cooking up formulas for sickly creatures, laid up in tiny beds around her mansion. Day turned down the role of Mrs. Robinson in the 1967 film *The Graduate;* the forty-three-year-old felt that movies were getting disgusting. Then Doris found out that her late husband's bad investments left her broke. Reluctantly, the wholesome blonde agreed to star in *The Doris Day Show* on TV for five years, and made enough money to quietly quit the business. The retired star purchased a hotel in Carmel, California, and gave marriage a fourth try. After five years, her new spouse gave up saying, "She's a wonderful woman but I couldn't get any sleep with all the dogs in our bed."

Extra: Doris Day's love of homeless animals brought unexpected baggage for the people that bought her Beverly Hills home. Several months after they moved in, the new owners posted a sign outside their front gate that said, "Please do not leave your small dogs and cats, Miss Day has moved!"

Judy Garland was a Natural

Director George Cukor was uncertain if thirty-one-year-old Judy Garland could convincingly convey her nervous breakdown in the 1954 musical *A Star is Born*. With her reputation for lateness and heavy drinking, Garland had fallen on hard times. The troubled actress had been fired two years earlier by MGM and was counting on the Warner Bros. vehicle to begin her big comeback. The show had been simple so far; Garland had not been required to stretch beyond her musical comedy comfort zone. But now it was time for Judy's dramatic reaction to the death of her screen lover, played by James Mason. After Cukor called "Action," the former vaudevillian went into such wild histrionics that the cast and crew were terrified. Her performance in the scene helped to land her an Oscar nomination. When the delighted Cukor congratulated her for giving him what he needed, Garland smiled. "It's nothing. I do it at home every day."

Generous Frank

Frank Sinatra's penchant for generosity was legendary among his friends. The singer would read stories in the paper about hard-luck cases, then anonymously send them a few c-notes. If Sinatra's buddies wanted Mexican food, he would order up a private plane and fly them to Acapulco. Waiters and waitresses in Las Vegas looked forward to Frank's arrival; it meant one-hundred-dollar tips and the high rollers spending all night in the casinos. And Sinatra could be counted on to show up at the bedsides of pals who were terminally ill. One time a very close associate of Frank's checked into the hospital and received a surprise visit from Sinatra. "Oh my gosh, the doctors told me it was trivial. I knew it was something worse! If you're here I'm a goner!"

Frank struggled to convince his friend that he was not the grim reaper; he just happened to be in town and their meeting was a coincidence.

Sold!

The unpredictably of the film industry can cause Hollywood home values to fluctuate wildly. Divorces, location shooting, work stoppages and career slowdowns often lead movie folk to unload unnecessary properties. A great example was Barbra Streisand, who found her acting services in less demand after starring in the 1996 drama *The Mirror Has Two Faces*. It would be eight years before she appeared in another film. Like many in her position, she kept two residences: one by the beach, the other closer to the studios. The idle superstar decided she no longer needed her inland mansion, located in the plush neighborhood of Holmby Hills. It was put on the market for ten million and Streisand waited for several months without an offer. Finally, the frustrated diva unhappily agreed to accept four million. The new owner wasted no time in tearing down the house, and then quickly sold the empty lot for seven million.

How not to Be a Director

Thirty-nine-year-old Clint Eastwood learned how not to make a movie when he starred in the 1969 musical *Paint Your Wagon*. Playing a prospector in 1849, who shares his wife with partner Lee Marvin in a California Gold Rush town, Clint gamely did his own singing. His lack of vocal talents was a minor issue compared to other problems on the Oregon set. *Wagon's* mishaps included the drunken forty-five-year-old Marvin often disappearing for weeks at a time; having no choreographer, which led to some awkward movements on camera by some overweight dancing miners; and some incensed hippie extras who passed out poison ivy to their co-stars after they were ordered to shave. Eastwood admitted the picture was a disaster, but it didn't have to be such an expensive disaster. The *Wagon* experience inspired him to start his own production company; Clint later became known as one of the most efficient filmmakers around.

Unaffected Louis Armstrong

Louis Armstrong walked with kings but never lost the common touch. His rendition of "Hello Dolly" in 1964 made the sixty-three-year old singer, known as Satchmo, the oldest artist ever to top the music charts. Yet Louis remained living in a modest two-story house in Queens. Armstrong paid for the homeowners on his block to have brick façades just like his. Local kids were welcome to come to Louis' place for ice cream and to look at westerns on TV. If things got a little crowded, he'd go upstairs on the balcony and blow some notes on his trumpet. Whenever Armstrong worked in the movies he got along well with his co-stars, but that didn't mean he wanted them for neighbors. One time at a Hollywood party, some snooty type told Louis he needed to start playing folk music so he could stay relevant. Armstrong threw back his head and laughed. "Let me tell you something, Pops. All music is folk music. I never did see a horse that played an instrument."

Sammy's Diction

The precise diction of Sammy Davis Jr. was often compared to that of stage actor Laurence Oliver. The Harlem-born Davis, who lived from 1925 to 1990, often amazed his concert audiences with his ability to mimic movie stars. Speaking with a powerful voice that belied his diminutive five-foot-three, 110-pound stature, Sammy would break off near-perfect imitations of luminaries such as James Cagney, Marlon Brando and Cary Grant. Many a woman was seduced by his silver tongue; they were surprised to find out that Sammy could not read until adulthood. As a boy, his father, Sammy Davis Sr., taught him how to sing, tap dance and play instruments. The tiny vaudevillian was quickly whisked from town to town; there was no time for school. Whenever they got word that the child welfare people were coming around, Senior pasted a mustache on the kid and then claimed he was a midget.

Sounds Good in a Dress

Twenty-six-year-old Jeanette MacDonald had problems following director Ernst Lubitsch's instructions in her 1929 Hollywood debut *The Love Parade*. Things had been tough for the Broadway diva since she arrived on the set. She didn't get along with her co-star Maurice Chevalier whom Jeanette had nicknamed the fastest derriere pincher in the west. And now she couldn't complete her singing number because her dress was too uncomfortable. After eleven flubbed takes, MacDonald had enough of Lubitsch's criticisms. "Let's see you do it!"

She ripped off the cumbersome outfit and threw it on the ground. To Jeanette's astonishment, the tiny Hungarian filmmaker was wearing the gown twenty minutes later, gracefully singing the song, all the while never removing his trademark cigar. After his demonstration, a chastened MacDonald did the scene in one ladylike take and the completed film made her a major movie star.

Extra: Ernst Lubitsch (1892-1947) liked to pull practical jokes on his movie sets. While filming *The Merry Widow* (1934), he arranged an unpleasant sight for his singing star Jeanette MacDonald (1902-1965). As the leading lady finished her song, she saw a carefully placed issue of the *Hollywood Reporter* on a table. The trade paper's cover story stated that MGM Studios was considering having MacDonald replaced with another actress. Jeanette ran to her dressing room crying, while Lubitsch laughed his head off.

Unfortunately for the director, MacDonald was good friends with the vengeful Sid Grauman (1879-1950), the famed manager and partial owner of Grauman's Chinese Theater. The premiere of *The Merry Widow* was in Santa Barbara, which required Ernst, Jeanette and the rest of the company to fly there in a small plane, still a frightening prospect in the 1930s. Once they were airborne, Lubitsch lit a cigar to calm his nerves and tried not to look out the window. Suddenly, two men in pilot's uniforms came out of the cockpit in a panic. "We're out of gas, abandon ship!"

Shockingly, they jumped out of the cabin with parachutes. It turned out they were stuntmen hired by Sid Grauman. Everyone on the plane was in on the joke except Lubitsch, who swallowed his cigar, fainted and luckily recovered from a mild heart attack.

How Bob Dylan Became a Star

Singer and sometimes actor Bob Dylan enjoyed kidding an interviewer about his road to fame. In the early sixties, Bob had his heart broken and ended up sleeping on a pool table. A Mexican lady dragged him to her house in Philadelphia, left him alone and the house burned down. The young poet went to Dallas and moved in with an eighteen-year-old girl, until the Mexican lady found him and burned the house down. Next Bob moved to Phoenix and roomed with a delivery boy who was also a good cook, and then the eighteen-year-old girl tracked him down and set his new residence ablaze. There was no peace in Omaha; Dylan moved in with a pretty high school teacher but the delivery boy found him, turned into an arsonist and once again, Bob was alone on the road. The first man that picked him up offered him a record contract. "So that's how you became a star?" asked the journalist.

Bob grinned. "No man, that's how I got tuberculosis."

Fred Astaire's Last Dance

There were times when eighty-two-year-old Fred Astaire didn't look like he was going to complete his last film, *Ghost Story*, in 1981. The cast and crew felt sorry for him; the former hoofer had been stuck with them for months out on location in freezing Sarasota Springs, New York. Fred was missing his new thirty-eight-year-old wife Robyn, he had found out that Adele, his sister and vaudeville partner from his youth, had died and he had come down with the flu; for a second there they had all worried that it was something worse. Fred had insisted that in forty-eight years of making pictures, he'd never been sick, but the old guy needed assistance to walk out in front of the camera on the last day of the shoot. When they finished the final scene, Fred's fellow workers witnessed an amazing transformation; a joyous Astaire grinned and began to gracefully dance over the icy surface, not stopping till he reached his dressing room.

Ringo Played Dumb

Twenty-five-year-old Ringo Starr pretended to be a fool when he starred with his fellow Beatles in the 1965 musical comedy *Help*. The good-natured drummer, who was the oldest member of the Fab Four, had been deprived of a full formal education due to childhood illnesses. Always a movie lover, he projected endearing vulnerability on the screen. Despite its ridiculous plot involving a cult that performed human sacrifices, *Help* became a worldwide hit. Ringo, who in past years had gotten the least fan mail of the group, saw his popularity soar. The critics called the percussionist a natural talent, which helped him to land several more acting roles. Starr became known as the most lovable Beatle, always had the affection and respect of his band mates and knew that the less sophisticated he seemed, the more people rooted for him. He laughed when John Lennon said Ringo didn't understand the meaning of fear…or any word with more than three letters.

Paul Loved Beatlemania

After making two successful films, *A Hard Day's Night* and *Help*, the Beatles saw the full power of Beatlemania while on tour in 1965. Twenty-five-year-old drummer Ringo Starr was unable to join the lads due to a bout of tonsillitis. When he recovered, the tiniest Beatle had to be carried to his limo slung over the shoulder of his bodyguard to avoid having his clothes ripped off him by screaming fans. Meanwhile in Australia, Starr's slightly younger mates rode in an open convertible while thousands of admirers cheered. Always security conscious, John Lennon pointed out that they could easily be shot. Likewise, George Harrison compared their position to that of assassinated US President John Kennedy. Only the fame-loving Paul McCartney, the friendliest of the Fab Four, enjoyed himself. McCartney sat upright and gave the crowd the thumbs up sign. When the parade ended, Paul was informed that in "the land down under", his well-intended gesture was considered obscene.

How Bing Stayed Calm

People who knew Bing Crosby were mystified by his laid-back demeanor. His friends found it remarkable that Bing could show up unrehearsed on a chaotic movie set, or at a recording studio and then deliver a near-flawless performance. Or how, after playing a charming priest in the 1944 comedy *Going My Way*, the forty-year-old actor had nearly missed receiving his Oscar because it interfered with his golf time. Some observers were amazed that Crosby felt comfortable visiting public parks; Bing would light his pipe, sit and gaze at the sky, oblivious to staring fans. Then there was the time his fourteen-room Beverly Hills mansion burned down; after being informed his family was unharmed, the crooner refused to examine the damage till he finished his morning coffee. Late in life, the very private star was asked how he could stay so calm. Bing pulled out a thick wad of cash. "Well, I've got to tell you this really helps."

On a Clear Day

Twenty-eight-year-old Barbra Streisand caused a huge headache when she refused to do any interviews to promote the 1970 musical *On a Clear Day You Can See Forever*. Desperate to bring some attention to the film, a Paramount Studios PR man created a phony story about a Chinese piano tuner named Wong Keye. Keye's concocted background included jobs as a fortune-cookie stuffer in a Chinatown bakery and an exotic fish seller. Overcoming his tone deafness, Wong had found his true calling tuning all the pianos in the Streisand movie and now was in great demand in Hollywood. The fictional story ran in newspapers throughout the country complete with a photo of an actor dressed in appropriate costume. The publicity wasn't enough to save *Clear Day* from a critical and box-office drubbing but there were some laughs around the studio when the star called to complain that Wong was getting more attention than she was.

Extra: Eventually Streisand agreed to do publicity for the movie.

Moved By White Christmas

Acclaimed songwriter Irving Berlin's "White Christmas" always warmed the hearts of the toughest audiences. Written in one night, partly to poke fun at snow-deprived Southern Californians, the song was featured in the 1942 movie

Holiday Inn starring crooner Bing Crosby. Bing also sang it to hard-bitten American servicemen stationed overseas during World War II; sometimes their tearful reaction would make Crosby want to stop, but the GIs would insist he go on. For Irving Berlin, Christmas was a sad day where his baby son had tragically died in his crib. As the years passed and music changed, the Russian-born Jewish composer became a recluse. On Christmas Eve 1974, for the sixth year in a row, some carolers sang "White Christmas" outside Berlin's New York townhouse. When they finished, for the first and only time, the visibly moved eighty-six-year-old invited them in and warmly thanked each one of them.

DRINKING TALES

"'Twas a woman drove me to drink. I never had the courtesy to thank her."
— W.C. Fields

"I've had a hell of a lot of fun, and I loved it, every minute of it."
— Errol Flynn's supposed final statement on his deathbed.

The Unwelcome Musketeer

When Oliver Reed joined an all-star cast in Madrid to film the 1973 version of *The Three Musketeers*, the producers fretted about his hell-raising reputation. Yet, in spite of his all-night booze festivals, the British actor endeared himself to his co-workers by always being on time and knowing his lines inside and out. The biggest hurdle for Reed's bosses was keeping a roof over his head. One night, in the lobby of the posh resort the cast was residing at, Oliver reached into an aquarium, pulled out one of the tank's inhabitants and appeared to bite its head off, causing some old ladies standing nearby to faint dead away. It was revealed that Reed had gotten the hotel chef to mash some carrots together in the shape of a fish, and after some hasty bribes and apologies, he was allowed to continue staying there.

Extra: Playing the world-weary musketeer Athos in *The Three Musketeers* (1973), Oliver Reed (1938-1999) had no prior experience with sword fight scenes. Yet he refused to rehearse for them and insisted on performing his own stunts with great ferocity. The Spanish extras who fenced with Oliver were literally shaking with fear after their on-camera battles. Finally, one burly man stabbed Reed in the arm sending the British actor to the hospital, where his room, not surprisingly, became the scene of a wild, overnight booze binge for him and his pals.

The Inebriated Oscar

Acting is one of the few professions where alcohol can improve your performance. Hell-raising ex-Marine Lee Marvin drank heavily to relieve his tension while filming the 1965 comic western *Cat Ballou*. Driving out to one of the Colorado locations, the forty-one-year-old Marvin scared his co-stars by firing a loaded colt 45 out of a car window and bragged proudly after he shot a cow. One night Lee gave out marriage advice in a slurry voice though he himself was headed for divorce court. He called his leading lady Jane Fonda's husband/director Roger Vadim "that blankety-blank Frenchman" and made funny faces on camera for no reason. Despite his constant state of inebriation, Lee won the Oscar for Best Actor, purchased a new home in Beverly Hills then got so drunk he had to buy a movie star map to locate it.

Extra: Lee Marvin (1924-1987) was a genuine hero in World War II. As a private in the Marine Corps, he was wounded in the brutal 1944 Battle of Saipan (an island in the South Seas that was crucial for the Allied forces to secure; it was heavily booby trapped by the Japanese; almost three thousand of Lee's fellow American troops lost their lives in the campaign). Marvin received the Navy Cross, the highest award the Navy can bestow except for the Medal of Honor. Lee claimed he learned how to be an actor by pretending not to be frightened in combat.

The Proud Boozer

John Wayne's career was almost derailed early on by Harry Cohn, the vindictive boss of Columbia Pictures, who was jealous when the cowboy star hooked up with a pretty starlet that the mogul had his eye on. The studio publicity department spread rumors that Wayne was a drunk on the set. The Duke finally convinced other producers that yes, he was a boozer, but not while he was working and his professional reputation was saved. In later years, Wayne gleefully turned down huge money to work for Cohn again and remained a proud consumer of alcohol. A reporter did an article about how much Gene Autry and John Wayne imbibed when they were making B westerns at Republic Pictures. The six-foot-four former football player Wayne angrily confronted the journalist. "How dare you imply that Gene Autry drank as much as I did! Why that piker couldn't carry my ice!"

Don Juan On and Off the Screen

Errol Flynn worried that the people would think he was playing himself in the 1947 comic romp *The Adventures of Don Juan*. When filming began, the thirty-eight-year-old Tasmanian ignored his contract and went sailing on his yacht until his bosses at Warner Bros. gave him a raise. When Flynn returned to the set, he defied his doctor's advice to stay away from alcohol by lacing prescribed nasal drops with heavy doses of vodka. During one scene, Errol and fellow drinking buddy Alan Hale Sr. unsteadily sat on their horses, while several off-camera property men held their legs in place. In the movie's climactic sword fight, stuntman Jock Whitney stood in for the out-of-shape swashbuckler to perform an amazing leap down a flight of stairs. Although *Don Juan* was not a hit when first released Flynn's hardcore fans couldn't have cared less about the production problems; to them the brawling, boozing rascal was a charming screen hero once more.

Extra: Sometimes a director can use an actor's drunken behavior against him. When John Huston (1906-1987) was ready to shoot the first scene in *Heaven Knows, Mr. Allison* (1957), on location in the South Seas island of Tobago, he sent an assistant director to get star Robert Mitchum (1917-1987) out of his tent. Mitchum showed up four hours later, explaining that he and the AD had started drinking scotch and the poor man was unconscious back in the tent. Huston smiled. "That's OK, Bob. Now let's shoot the scene where your character, the Marine, floats into the island unconscious on the raft."

Mitchum spent the next four hours suffering in the blazing tropical sun as Huston, sitting comfortably in the shade, ordered retake after retake. The actor was on time from then on.

One Late Night in Ireland

One very late night in Ireland, Peter O'Toole and Peter Finch shocked a pub owner who wanted to close up. The two inebriated actors offered to buy his establishment for twice as much as it was worth, as long as the alcohol kept coming. A contract was written and signed on a napkin. The next afternoon, the hung-over stars woke up and after some blurry discussions, they recalled what they did the night before. Fearing their business managers would kill them, they raced back to the saloonkeeper and begged for mercy. The man gave them a stern look, then smiled and tore up the agreement. They were so grateful they drank there over the next twenty years, whenever their schedules allowed, till the pub owner died. After downing a few pints, the devastated twosome headed off to the memorial service. Finch and O'Toole delivered long moving eulogies, which drove the mourners to tears, until they realized they were at the wrong funeral.

The Fall of Gene Autry

Gene Autry's taste for alcohol helped him get over the pain of losing his beloved horse Champion. Paying customers at rodeos throughout the country would "ooh" and "ah" as the famous twosome would ride out and make a spectacular leap through a fifty-foot ring of fire. Gene's career outlasted the horse's, who was eventually put out to stud. The show would continue with a replacement. On opening night, his wranglers were quite nervous about the new steed's abilities, but Gene had been hitting the tequila early and waved off their concerns. Once again, an enthusiastic crowd cheered wildly as America's favorite cowboy shot out of the tunnel, only to have his rookie partner come to a dead halt inches before the hoop. The wide-eyed Autry went flying through the ring solo and landed on his back. Luckily, the booze numbed much of the impact. Ever the showman, Gene got up to take a bow like it was all part of the act.

Extra: Orvon Gene Autry (1907-1998) was one of the richest people in the history of show business. He was the rare performer that found success in movies, television, radio, live road performances and record sales. With his hectic schedule, the cowboy star admitted that he turned to alcohol for relaxation. After being arrested several times for driving under the influence, Autry's friends suggested that the wealthy celebrity hire a personal driver. Gene did as they asked, and a week later faced another DUI. When Autry was pulled over, the police found the new employee in the passenger's seat, asleep on his boss's shoulder.

Kind-Hearted Fields

Once in a great while, W. C. Fields would undermine his reputation as a mean old man. Fields claimed to hate his three-year-old co-star Baby LeRoy in the 1935 film *Tillie and Gus* so much that he spiked the infant's orange juice with whiskey. Yet, when the child had difficulty finding work, the comedian wrote a part for him in one of his movies. W. C. would rant that Cecil B. DeMille was a hypocrite because he filled his moralistic movies with sex and violence, but in quieter moments Fields would heap praise on the director's talents. The Great Man used malicious gossip to spread distrust among his servants, and then was touched when they threw him a surprise party. And when America entered World War II in 1941, the patriotic sixty-one-year-old juggler had a few drinks before showing up at a local military recruiting office. Fields volunteered to give up his Hollywood career to be a commando. "Did the enemy send you?" was the reply.

Extra: W.C. Fields pointed out to any who would listen that his neighbor Cecil B. DeMille's moralistic films always contained scenes with leggy women luxuriating in huge bathtubs. One night in 1943, DeMille knocked on Field's door and said, "Mr. Fields, we are having a blackout in the neighborhood. I'm telling everyone to fill up their bathtubs in case of a water shortage."

The comedian who had been drinking said, "Not another of your bathtub scenes, DeMille," and slammed the door in his face.

Extra: One co-star who would not put up with Field's drinking was Mae West (1893-1980). During the filming of *My Little Chickadee* (1940), she insisted that W.C. stay sober. "Don't worry, my dear. I'm on the wagon."

The comedian's idea of giving up booze was trading sherry for gin. Mae West found him out, and Fields, as he tipped his hat to Mae, was physically carried off the set by crew members and suspended from the film. Stuck at home, W. C. sat on the lawn drinking, became surlier and started shooting at imaginary prowlers with a BB gun, which caused extensive property damage for his neighbors. The local residents responded by tossing empty whiskey bottles on W. C.'s driveway. Fields was certain that director Cecil B. DeMille, who lived across the street from him, was responsible. One night he gathered the bottles in a bag, stood on DeMille's front lawn and hurled them through the filmmaker's bay glass windows. "Take that and that, you sanctimonious knave!"

Afterward, Fields had no more problems with unwanted garbage on his property.

Extra: Fields was famous for his drinking, and while he was never falling down drunk, alcohol did not help his disposition. W. C. was notorious for carrying a flask on movie sets, claiming to interested parties that it contained mere pineapple juice. One time a co-worker stole it, emptied the contents and poured real pineapple juice in it. Fields unwittingly took a swig and almost choked. "What scoundrel has been putting pineapple juice in my pineapple juice?"

Extra: W. C. Fields was a mostly self-educated man who loved the English language. Screenwriters respected the comic's ad-libbing skills and usually wouldn't bother to come up with any dialogue for him. One night Fields seemed off his game; with the camera running, he delivered incomprehensible phrases like "Charles Forbusher."

"Cut! Bill, what was that?" asked the bewildered director.

The cantankerous star insisted that his phrase was a tried and true way to get laughs. After being told to change it, Fields muttered under his breath, "The fellow doesn't know what he is doing."

The actor seemed to get back on track, then again ruined a scene with an equally ridiculous name. Again, he was rebuffed and retorted angrily. It was whispered on the set that Fields was drunk. It turned out that W. C. received a bonus if he filmed past midnight, which he accomplished after several more screw-ups.

The Swashbuckling Solicitor

One night in the early 1950s, a police officer made the mistake of introducing his attractive wife to Errol Flynn. It wasn't long before the famous swashbuckler kissed her on the lips, resulting in the jealous cop handcuffing him and hauling him off to the hoosegow. The desk sergeant at the station wanted to drop the whole thing, but the inebriated Flynn demanded his rights. In a slurring voice, he recited passages from the Constitution. The fact that there was no charge against him was immaterial; he was entitled to a fair trial. In a short time, the Australian-born actor found himself locked in the drunk tank, alongside some illegal Mexican farm workers who were waiting to be deported. Flynn considered his cellmates comrades in arms; they all began to sing together in Spanish. A few hours later, his lawyer got him released. While his new friends cheered, Errol walked out of the jail proudly, convinced that he had a future in litigation.

Idiot Cards

Legendary stage actor John Barrymore's sometimes hazy memory was full of Shakespeare and poetry and he refused to clutter it with bad movie writing. He read his screen dialogue off strategically placed boards, and then immediately forgot it. On one occasion, the heavy drinker only had to deliver one line: "Yes." John's personal assistant stood ready to hold up a cue card. One of the film techs informed the director that Barrymore's helper was in the way; they would not be able to light the scene properly. When the great man arrived on the set the director said, "Jack, can I talk to you?"

"Certainly."

"Would it be possible for you to do this one scene without your idiot card?"

"Absolutely not."

The director sighed. "Jack, you only have to say yes, that's it. What happens if I order your friend to leave?"

Barrymore looked at him coldly. "I might say no." In the end, new lighting arrangements were made.

Clever Product Placement

Paris Hilton's arrest for drunk driving in 2006 revealed a dark secret. At the time of the incident, the inebriated blonde heiress revealed she felt a craving for an In-N-Out Burger. Scandalous, because she'd previously done commercials for Carl's Jr., a rival fast food company. Paris continued a long tradition of celebrities being disloyal to the advertisers that pay their way. Back in the 1930s, comedian W.C. Fields once made an appearance on a radio show sponsored by Lucky Strike cigarettes. On the air, Fields amused the hosts with charming stories about his mythical son Chester, repeating his name with emphasis over and over. After two funny segments, one of the Lucky Strike executives came bursting into the studio and demanded that W.C. be removed at once. After twenty minutes, it had dawned on him that the old curmudgeon was dropping in plugs for the rival cigarette brand Chesterfields.

Get Up Ward

The usually fun-loving Ward Bond was shocked when tyrannical director John Ford summoned him to the set of the 1955 naval drama *Mr. Roberts*. On location in Midway Island, the fifty-two-year-old hung-over character actor had been awakened out of a deep slumber by his co-stars who told him that Ford was furious with him being late. Bond was terrified, he had made several movies for Ford; the old man was capable of anything when he was on the warpath.

"I don't even remember what the hell he wants me for! Boy, it's getting darker outside. You guys think it's going to rain?"

Bond put on a heavy jacket and was just about to run out the door when he noticed his bunkmates could no longer keep straight faces. A suddenly wise Ward said, "Oh that's beautiful!" and joined in the laughter.

It turned out that the day's shooting was over; it was just after sunset and Bond's loud snoring had been ruining their tranquility.

Extra: By the late 1920s, The University of Southern California Trojans became a national powerhouse in college football. Director John Ford decided to make a movie using their players and asked his property man, an ex-member of the USC squad named Marion "Duke" Morrison (John Wayne), to help recruit his cast. Ford wanted Duke to land him an ugly lineman named Wardell Edwin Bond (1903-1960), who Morrison couldn't stand. "I can get you a player twice as ugly as Bond."

The thirty-five-year old filmmaker was undeterred; Bond had to be in front of his camera. The fact that Ward was a carousing braggart who helped himself to cash advances out of Ford's wallet endeared him to the director even more. The gridiron film *Salute* (1929) was a huge critical and financial success, and Bond, Ford and Morrison became lifelong, hard-drinking buddies.

Extra: In 1944, Ward Bond was hit by a car in Hollywood and fractured his left shin. The unconscious actor was rushed to a hospital. Just before Ward's leg was to be amputated, one of the staff recognized him and for the sake of his career it was decided to do a repair of the leg instead. Thankfully, the incorrigible Bond recovered and after three days was cheerfully hitting on the nurses.

Extra: One time in the 1940s at John Ford's house, a drunken Ward Bond bet an equally inebriated John Wayne that they could stand on the opposite sides of a newspaper and Duke couldn't hit him in the mouth. After Wayne agreed, a smiling Bond grabbed the paper, found his standing place and then shut the door before the punch could be thrown. His laughter was cut short when Wayne's fist came smashing through the wood and connected with the intended target.

Extra: When John Ford gave John Wayne his breakthrough role in the 1939 western *Stagecoach*, he called his new star "a big oaf" who didn't know how to act. But over the years Wayne got better and earned his mentor's respect. In the 1956 western *The Searchers*, Wayne delivered a powerful scene where his character was torn up about family members being killed by Comanche Indians. Ford was so emotionally involved that he applauded after he yelled cut; perhaps the greatest compliment the Duke ever got from the often insulting and hard-to-please director. The moment was undermined when the cameraman said he failed to get the shot. Ford was furious, "Why the hell not? Hey what's that noise?"
He went into the adjoining room to find Ward Bond whistling and cheerfully shaving with his electric razor; to do so, he'd pulled the camera plug out of the wall outlet.

Extra: In one 1950s western, John Wayne was dreading doing a love scene with an actress who didn't brush her teeth and generally practiced bad hygiene. "I sure hope we get this damned thing right on the first take," Wayne told his buddies on his set.

It looked like the Duke was going to get his wish; the kissing scene was going smoothly when Ward Bond "accidentally" tripped and ended up in the camera shot. "Oops."

The furious Wayne chased his laughing buddy for a few hundred yards, before unhappily returning to do it again.

Anybody Would Be Yelled At

One day in the early 1940s at Warner Bros., studio head Jack Warner was having lunch with a young executive when his older brother Harry came charging into the dining room. Harry stood over the table and went off on a diatribe regarding actor Errol Flynn. "You take a guy from nothing, pay to train them, photograph them, they become a big movie star and how do they repay you? By being ungrateful and demanding more money, that's how! By turning down scripts! By boozing, being late to work and acting like a prima donna!"

Harry pointed at the young man at Jack's side. "We could make him a star! That would show Flynn. This young man could replace him!"

The much calmer Jack wiped his mouth with his napkin. "Yes Harry, but don't you see, then he would make similar demands."

Enraged, Harry turned on Jack's startled, silent lunch companion and gave him a foul-mouthed verbal tongue lashing.

Extra: Right before the shooting of the 1945 Errol Flynn western *San Antonio*, Jack Warner had a meeting with the star in the mogul's office. Warner knew that Flynn had fallen in love with a horse that the actor had ridden in several movies. The studio head had decided to present Errol with the animal as a gift. Flynn seemed genuinely touched by his boss's magnanimous gesture and the two men embraced. Word quickly spread through the lot that one of the biggest feuds in Hollywood had come to an end. Jack Warner was pleased with his employee for several days. The good will came to an end when Errol announced that if Warner wished to use Flynn's new horse in the movie, the tycoon would have to pay rent.

How Much Did Dean Martin Really Drink?

Although his license plate said "Drunky," how much alcohol Dean Martin actually imbibed was a widely discussed topic in Hollywood. When the former blackjack dealer acted like he was buzzed, it was often a put-on. Orson Welles was once a guest on Dean's television show; Martin offered Welles some booze before his skit and was shocked by the actor's refusal. "You're going out there alone?"

Many of Dean's co-workers claimed he sipped apple juice all the time and didn't take him seriously. But at times he drove erratically, which forced law enforcement to take action. Once Martin was pulled over by the police and asked to perform some sobriety tests. He had no difficulty touching his nose with both hands and was able to count backwards from thirty flawlessly.

"That's fine, Mr. Martin. Now just one more thing. Could you please walk a straight line for us?"

"Not without a safety net," Dean replied.

Extra: When Dean Martin (1917-1995) announced that he was divorcing his forty-six-year-old wife Jeannie in 1973, he joked, "She'll get the house. Doesn't matter; I could never find it anyway."

One sore point during their union was despite Dean's reputation for drinking, he was unwilling to have any company over. The singer's main concern was getting up early to play golf. One time Martin reluctantly acquiesced to his wife's request to have a social gathering at their house. At ten p.m., Dean politely excused himself and went upstairs to his room. A half hour later Jeannie knocked on his door, "Dean, come out! The police are here."

An apologetic officer explained that they had received several calls about another loud obnoxious party at the Martin household. "But we never have parties," said Jeannie.

"Never mind that, Jeannie; you heard the officer. OK, everybody out."

The next day after rising early and playing a nice round of golf, old Dino confessed to her that he had made the complaining phone calls, disguising his voice several times.

The Surprise Drop-Ins

For nearly thirty years and five films, John Wayne and Maureen O'Hara were best friends in real life, while being lovers only on the screen. The three-times-married, heavy-boozing cowboy actor felt the beautiful redhead was a great gal and the only woman who could keep up with him. She was a good sport when Wayne dragged her through dirty grass full of sheep dung, in the 1952 romance *The Quiet Man*. Then there was the 1963 comedy *McClintock* where the electric movie couple had volunteered to slide down into a deep mud hole, sneering at the stuntmen who said it was too dangerous. But even for the gutsy Irishwoman, her buddy could be a handful. Once after cocktails, Maureen was giving the sleepy Wayne a ride home when he demanded she pull over. She was stunned when he took her hand, rang the doorbell of a total stranger's house, asked for drinks and the party continued for hours inside.

A Good Reason to Drink

One evening in Las Vegas in the 1960s, Dean Martin surprised a curious friend by saying that he drank to forget. The buddy found the answer strange; everything in Dino's career seemed to be going so great. How many stars had succeeded like Dean had on stage, in movies, selling records and now even on television? Even his friend Frank Sinatra, who had been a disappointment on TV, couldn't say that. Surely Dean was pleased that he was no longer perceived as comic Jerry Lewis' second banana. Could Martin be getting tired of the show-business grind? But Dean always said that acting was a breeze compared to standing on your feet all day long, dealing cards at the blackjack table. How sad that a poor boy from Steubenville, Ohio, who had risen up to be so handsome, rich and famous would feel that way. "It could be sadder," said Dean.

"How? What was sadder than drinking to forget?"

"Forgetting to drink," Martin replied.

The Aborted Drinking Contest

Film observers wondered if the often-inebriated actors, Richard Burton and Peter O'Toole, could get through the 1964 historical drama *Beckett*. The thirty-two-year-old O'Toole shone as a sometime bombastic monarch while Burton, seven years his senior, showed thoughtful restraint playing a man who chooses to follow God's will over his king's. Both were nominated for Oscars and had great fun pretending to be drunk in front of visitors on the set. But it hurt O'Toole's Irish pride that the Welsh-born Burton had the bigger reputation as a boozer. After the shoot was completed, Peter asked Richard to meet him in a pub for an alcohol contest. Burton insisted his friend go first; O'Toole consumed an entire large bottle of very potent whiskey. "Your turn, dear Richard."

Before the challenge could be met, Peter collapsed unconscious on the floor. Burton then stepped over him, ordered a drink and celebrated another victory by default.

Sideways Casting

When director Alexander Payne asked Paul Giamatti to star as the angry epicurean who wins the heart of Virginia Madsen's waitress, in the 2004 film *Sideways*, the five-foot-seven balding character actor thought it was a practical joke. The son of the late former baseball commissioner Bart Giamatti knew nothing about wine and was not your typical romantic lead. But with the help of Payne's directing, the well-written script and the warmth of his lovely co-star Madsen, Paul was convincing pretending to be a prissy lover who would abruptly leave a dinner date, rather than drink merlot. After *Sideways* became a surprise hit, the thirty-seven-year-old Giamatti boldly stated he now wanted to star in an action movie. Meanwhile the Oscar-nominated, six years older Madsen hoped that some eligible man would see the film and take her out on a date.

Extra: Merlot had a sales boom after a 1991 news report that it could potentially ward off heart disease. Twenty-five thousand new acres of the grape were planted in California. With the rush to get the product out on the market, many connoisseurs complained the red wine was coming from immature vineyards, which led to a drop in quality. Perhaps consumers were looking for a reason to escape the fad; demand for the healthy drink went down significantly after Paul Giamatti's character railed against it in *Sideways*.

Mitchum's Resort Prison

Robert Mitchum preferred hanging out with Hollywood's working-class film crews, rather than snobby executives, and always acted like he never had a care in the world. A poet and saxophone player, Mitchum had risen to superstardom despite being self-deprecating about his acting skills. In 1948, the thirty-one-year-old Connecticut-born actor made headlines by being arrested for pot smoking. Robert worried he was ruined and claimed he was framed. Sentenced to two months in jail, Mitchum became a model citizen behind bars. The charges were later reversed and his career went on as strong as ever. In later years, he never gave any hint that the incident troubled him, continued to drink and carouse, and compared his incarceration to one of the Hollywood community's favorite getaway spots. "It was like Palm Springs without the riff-raff."

Extra: Beginning in the silent film days, the California desert city of Palm Springs gave the movie colony a place to dry out in more ways than one. Not only did it provide facilities for Hollywood's heavy drinkers to be cured, Palm Springs also offered a good alternative for filming compared to Los Angeles's often rainy winters.

Errol's Fencing Partner

The classy South African-born Basil Rathbone and the crude Errol Flynn made an odd couple. Throughout the 1930s, the good-natured Basil was well paid for playing villains who were killed by Flynn and other movie heroes, even though Rathbone could out-fence any of them. "Dear Basil," Flynn once said fondly, "we crossed swords but never words."

For his part, Rathbone was sometimes unnerved by Errol's reckless, often vulgar behavior; still the Tasmanian was an amusing fellow. Once Rathbone invited Flynn to a sophisticated get-together in Beverly Hills; Errol got drunk and left with a very young girl. At dawn, her father returned to the Rathbones' estate carrying the unconscious swashbuckler over his shoulder and dumped him on the property. Basil and his elegant wife, Ouida, were sitting down on the veranda about to enjoy breakfast when they were startled by a smiling familiar figure that popped out of the bushes to join them.

Extra: While making the 1938 classic *The Adventures of Robin Hood,* Errol Flynn (1909-1959) was in hot pursuit of his twenty-three-year-old leading lady Olivia de Havilland. One night during production, Errol pounded on Olivia's dressing room door. "Go away, Errol, you drunken fool!"

Another time he tried to get her attention by putting a dead snake in her tent. When asked by her girlfriends about the handsome Flynn, Olivia stated she preferred a more sophisticated type of man like director John Huston; Flynn was like a little boy. She did, however, admit to messing up kissing scenes with Errol so they could have several enjoyable retakes.

Extra: At one point in the 1940s, Jack Warner instituted a strict no-booze rule at his studio, primarily to thwart the drunken unprofessional behavior of Errol Flynn, who rarely was able to complete any scenes after two in the afternoon. Flynn responded to the edict by bringing a bag of oranges with him to work. His boss approved of the swashbuckler's healthy new diet, unaware that the Errol injected the citrus fruit with a hypodermic syringe full of vodka.

Extra: One night in the early 1950s, Olivia de Havilland was at a Hollywood party when she felt a tap on her shoulder. An old man who looked vaguely familiar was smiling at her. The two-time Oscar winner felt uncomfortable and moved away quickly. When de Havilland turned, she could see the stranger had a very hurt, bewildered expression on his face. Later that night Olivia cried her eyes out at home after realizing the person she rebuffed was Errol Flynn, who had destroyed his physical appearance by using drugs and alcohol.

Extra: *The Swarm* (1978), a disaster film about killer bees, featured Michael Caine, Henry Fonda, Slim Pickens and Fred MacMurray. One day they were joined for lunch at the Warner Bros. commissary by their quiet co-star Olivia de Havilland. There were complaints that no booze was being served. "That's because of Errol Flynn," said de Havilland. "He used to get so drunk he couldn't work so Mister Warner said no more booze."

The men wanted to hear more about the famous swashbuckler who had died nineteen years before. "Oh my God, that Errol Flynn was something. Do you know he once got so drunk he wagered a film crew $100 that he'd have his way with me."

Her fellow diners could see she was a lady and the incident must have been embarrassing for her. Olivia grinned mischievously. "Oh, it was. And you see those trees out the window up on that hill? That's where Errol won his bet!"

Extra: Despite their many battles, Jack Warner always had a soft spot for the hell-raising, yet gallant Errol Flynn; it broke the mogul's heart to see the once handsome star get old and die before his time. When Warner attended the fifty-year-old swashbuckler's funeral in 1959, he ran into one Flynn's attorneys. "I wish you could get Errol out of this one," Jack told him sadly.

William Frawley's Drinking Buddy

After sixty-four-year-old William Frawley became a huge star on the 1951 TV series *I Love Lucy*, he was sympathetic to folks down on their luck. The frugal-living character actor took pity on a panhandler, who would hit him up when William walked home from the studio to his modest apartment, near the intersection of Hollywood Boulevard and Vine Street. One day Frawley inquired what the man spent the money he gave him on; the beggar admitted it was all going to booze. Frawley, who had lost work due to his own bouts with alcoholism, admired his pal's honesty. "C'mon, I'll buy you a drink."

A few minutes later, patrons at the famous Brown Derby restaurant were astonished to see television's Fred Mertz being seated at a good table with his very poorly dressed companion. "Bring me two double Scotch and Sodas," Bill told the waiter grandly.

The friendship came to a quick end when the bum blinked then shouted, "I'll have the same!"

Extra: When casting began for the TV show *I Love Lucy* (1951-1957), star Lucille Ball was surprised to get a call from a character actor she knew named William Frawley (1887-1966). "I hear you need someone to play your landlord." Lucy was in a quandary. She was from the old school where you help your fellow actors out if they are down on their luck. But Frawley was a well-known drunk. She suggested he talk to her husband Desi Arnaz. Frawley promised Desi he'd never miss time due to drinking. But could Bill, who was an avid baseball fan, have time off if the New York Yankees went to the World Series? Although William kept his word and was always on time, Desi later regretted giving into Frawley's wishes; in the 1950s, the Bronx Bombers made it to the top of the baseball heap nearly every year.

The Eighty-Sixth Wizard

Richard Harris loudly complained about playing Professor Dumbledore in the 2001 fantasy film *Harry Potter and the Sorcerer's Stone*. The wealthy seventy-year-old actor didn't want to keep brutal hours and be around Hollywood phonies. There were plenty of dumb jerks to talk to right here in his favorite drinking establishment. But his eleven-year-old granddaughter was a big fan of the *Potter* books; she threatened to stop speaking to him unless he took the role. One Harris was on the set, he found he loved pretending to be the headmaster of the Hogwarts School for Wizards. Richard got along splendidly with the film's young cast who enjoyed hearing his tales of past hell-raising. The worldwide success of the movie combined with good reviews from his family left the Irishman feeling rejuvenated. Well, he supposed he'd have to keep working; now that his bar pals knew how he felt about them, Harris was no longer allowed in the pub.

PART TWELVE

356011

MISCELLANEOUS
HOLLYWOOD STORIES

"A perfection of means, and confusion of aims,
seems to be our main problem."
— Albert Einstein

"An unmarried man is incomplete,
but a married man is finished."
— Zsa Zsa Gabor

You Can Trust Mr. Moto

The Hungarian-born Peter Lorre overcame physical challenges to play the Japanese detective Mister Moto in 1938. The thirty-four-year-old character actor had so many health problems he could barely walk up a flight of stairs without assistance. Lorre used blackened hair, a tongue-in-cheek attitude, a very skilled stuntman and some well-placed "Ahsos" to be convincing as the oriental gumshoe in eight movies. Peter had found fame portraying a child murderer in the 1931 classic German horror Film *M*, causing Berliners to flee in terror when they saw him in the streets. It was a pleasant change when Los Angeles residents recognized Lorre as Moto, and greeted him warmly. His new popularity came in handy when a studio prankster stole Peter's driver's license and replaced it with a document that said, "Mr. Moto, Spy," on a day when Lorre was stopped for speeding. The police officer recognized both the star and the joke and let him go.

Extra: Peter Lorre (1904-1964) was relieved that the role of Mr. Moto required very little physical exertion. When he starred in the 1931 German crime drama *M,* the actor was required to do his own stunts. These included being thrown several times down a flight of stairs into a cellar.

Lemmon on the Run

In the sophisticated 1965 satire *How to Murder Your Wife*, Jack Lemmon was paired up with the gorgeous Italian actress Virna Lisi. To Lemmon's relief, his beautiful co-star was a total professional, so unlike another blonde he had worked with: the late Marilyn Monroe. But the shoot was halted when Lisi's jealous husband objected to their steamy love scenes. During the break, Jack accidentally stumbled into Virna's dressing room to find her stark naked. The always well-mannered star awkwardly tried to apologize, but her enraged spouse came lunging at him from the couch, with his wife screaming in Italian for him to stop. Lemmon turned and ran around the MGM lot till he found a covered garbage dumpster. The actor stayed inside his smelly hiding place until some security guards told him it was safe to come out. After a few hours, Virna had calmed her man down enough so they could resume filming. Jack later introduced his wife to Lisi's husband, and the two couples became great friends.

Jackie Robinson was a Gracious Actor

After three years of thrilling big-league baseball fans, thirty-one-year-old Jackie Robinson was once again a rookie when he played himself in *The Jackie Robinson Story* in 1950. The Dodgers' second baseman was extremely nervous performing tender love scenes with beautiful Ruby Dee who played his wife. When the real-life Rachael Robinson showed up on the Los Angeles set to encourage him, Jackie began to calm down. After holding in his emotions during his first season, Robinson had developed into a fierce competitor on the diamond who taunted his opponents. The film crew saw only a gracious actor who did seemingly endless batting, fielding and running takes without complaint. The low-budget movie was criticized for exaggerating Robinson's real-life travails as the major league's first black player, did disappointing business in big cities but was a huge hit in small towns where baseball fans had yet to see Jackie play.

Welcome to Beverly Hills

Since the first movie stars moved into Beverly Hills, its citizens have always had an uneasy relationship with visitors. Drivers of oversized tour buses found it very difficult to navigate down the tiny street where Brad Pitt and Jennifer Aniston lived. The celebrity couple's neighbors angrily called the police to complain they were trapped in their driveways while waiting for the lumbering vehicles to turn around. City officials considered a complete ban in 2004, then decided that commercial sightseeing on residential streets would still be allowed in small vans. Regulated drive-bys were preferred over the alternative of people coming on their own with movie-star maps. A few years earlier, the single Brad Pitt had gotten a scare when an overzealous female fan had found his house, got past his security, climbed through his window, undressed herself and was waiting in his bed when he got home.

Extra: Founded in 1914, Beverly Hills is named after Beverly Farms in Massachusetts, which in turn is named after Beverly in Yorkshire. That English town was founded in the tenth century near a colony of beavers; the name Beverly was short for Beaver Lake.

Extra: In 1919, Douglas Fairbanks and Mary Pickford converted a fourteen-acre hunting lodge into the first Beverly Hills movie-star mansion, known as Pickfair. The famed couple kept shotguns in their cars, which they fired in the air to scare coyotes off their driveway. As other celebrities purchased lots near the "King and Queen of Hollywood," the little town became world famous. Yet it was still a sleepy place where the police chief locked up criminals in his own house. A constant nuisance in the peaceful community of Beverly Hills was local drunk John Barrymore. The great actor was frequently incarcerated for stealing scraps from his neighbors' trash cans in order to feed his pet buzzard.

Extra: In 1932, famed aviator Charles Lindbergh's (1902-1974) twenty-month-year-old baby was abducted from his crib, in the Lindbergh's New Jersey family home, and brutally murdered. The rich-and-famous residents of Beverly Hills reacted fearfully to the heinous kidnapping. Douglas Fairbanks proposed building a walled the city but was rebuffed by civic leaders who wanted tourism. Instead, a new police headquarters was erected to house a substantially upgraded force. The Beverly Hills cops became renowned for responding to crime calls faster than any other squad in the world.

Trendsetter

Katharine Hepburn was often a difficult traveling companion. In 1954, the forty-seven-year-old actress visited some friends at Claridges, one of London's most famous five-star hotels. As usual, she wore comfortable trousers, which scandalized the management and guests. Her pals, afraid that she would get them kicked out the hotel, offered to chip in and purchase her a dress, but the stubborn New Englander refused. Miss Hepburn began avoiding the lobby and using the service elevator rather than submit to what she considered an idiotic policy. There were no more complaints but Kate had not gone unnoticed as she thought. A few years later, her friends returned to Claridges and noticed that most of the women staying there were wearing pants very similar to the ones that had gotten the trend-setting actress in trouble; this time no one seemed to mind.

Extra: One time Katharine Hepburn was performing on Broadway and tried to exit backstage through a crowd of jostling autograph hounds. Bodyguards helped push Katharine to her limo. Once safely inside, the very private star rolled down the window and shouted, "Run 'em down! We'll clean up the blood later!" The crowd scattered as the limousine sped away, pausing long enough for Hepburn to roll down the window and give a wave accompanied by an evil laugh.

When she lived in Beverly Hills, the same seclusion-loving actress once felt entitled to sneak into a neighbor's beautiful home; she just had to see what it looked like inside. Kate was inspecting the bedrooms when the lady of the house came home and got frightened by the strange sounds coming from the second floor. Just as she was about to call the police, Hepburn yelled that there was nothing to fear and came downstairs to introduce herself. The owner quickly went from being frightened to flattered, and offered the famous intruder a tour.

Albert Einstein's Perplexing Journey

Albert Einstein, who believed that imagination was more important than knowledge, was left bewildered by his vacation to Hollywood in 1931. Film Star Mary Pickford thought the fifty-two-year-old German scientist was actually a Russian movie director. Upon learning the truth, she expressed regret they would not be working together. Charlie Chaplin invited the professor to attend the first screening of his new movie *City Lights*. The theory of relativity was easier for Einstein to grasp then twenty-five hundred fans showing up to a film premiere. Einstein's favorite part of the trip was his visit to Warner Bros. He enjoyed watching Jack Warner's fascinated expression when he described various stars. For the first time in this strange land, the physicist felt he was in his element. After he left, the studio head told a staff member, "Sign this Polaris guy to a contract. Einstein thinks he has potential."

The Fresh Prince of Hollywood

Romanoff's Restaurant was the place to see and be seen in Beverly Hills in the late 1940s. Prince Michael Romanoff was really a con man from Chicago named Harry Gerguson. Michael charmed a few movie-star friends into lending him some money to start his legitimate establishment, and then surprised them when it became a huge success. A staunch conservative Republican, the Prince's place became a regular hangout for many of Hollywood's most liberal actors who enjoyed listening to his claims of royal lineage. Status meant nothing at Romanoff's; pretentious society types would be kept waiting for a table while unemployed war veterans would get fine dinners on the house. One night FBI head J. Edgar Hoover was dining there when he was approached by an actual jewel thief named Swifty Morgan. "Like to buy these gold cuff links?"

Amused, Hoover offered two hundred dollars. "Oh come on, John, the reward is worth more than that!"

Be All You Can Be!

Legendary animator Chuck Jones identified more with his less-than-perfect characters. Bugs Bunny was such an invincible force that he had to be minding his own business before he was provoked. Only then could the rabbit be justified in raining down complete destruction on his enemies. Chuck Jones felt more kinship with the perennial loser Daffy Duck. Likewise, the ever-hungry Coyote was made more sympathetic than the invulnerable Roadrunner. The helpless carnivore, that was responsible for his own destruction, represented Jones' personal ineptness with tools. How could someone with such an inferiority complex be a success in his own career? Chuck often told the story how when he was a kid in art school, he wanted to quit because the other students were so much more talented than he was. He changed his mind when the teacher advised him, "Just be the best Chuck Jones you can be."

Dead Shot Shirley

Ten-year-old Shirley Temple felt compelled to dispense justice when she attended a barbecue at Eleanor Roosevelt's Hyde Park estate in 1938. The child star had recently made the first lady an official member of the Shirley Temple Police Force; Eleanor had asked for two extra badges for her granddaughters. Shirley graciously complied after explaining that this was a serious organization with strict rules. Participants had to wear their emblems in public at all times, otherwise Shirley was authorized to collect fines, which were then given out to charities. And now at the party, the Roosevelt granddaughters were breaching protocol and refused to fork over the required cash. Clearly, Eleanor had failed to deputize them properly. While Mrs. Roosevelt was busy bending over the grill, the little actress subtly pulled out a slingshot from her purse and nailed her hostess in the rear with a pebble. The target straightened right up while her young punisher quickly hid the weapon before the secret service men noticed. Eleanor never mentioned the incident. Shirley remained proud of her action, even after she was walloped later that night by her mother who witnessed the whole thing.

Extra: Later that year, Shirley met Massachusetts Governor Charles Hurley (1893-1946). The Democrat politician accidentally slammed a car door on Temple's hand and chased kids away from his limo. The ten-year-old star didn't like the way Hurley treated others and decided that she would be a Republican.

Extra: Shirley Temple was proud of her sling-shot collection and claimed she could knock over a coke bottle from twenty feet away. The screenwriters of the 1935 Civil War drama *The Littlest Rebel* found out about the actress's skill and created a scene where Temple had to use her weapon against a nasty soldier. Without rehearsals or a double, the seven-year-old star hit her target perfectly when the camera rolled.

Dear Zsa Zsa

Once, when I was leading a tour through Beverly Hills, my group had a pleasant experience meeting the nine-times-married Zsa Zsa Gabor. It was a few years after the notorious incident when she slapped a policeman. We met her inside Fred Hayman, a now shut-down boutique on Rodeo Drive. The former Miss Hungary of 1936, who was always willing to sacrifice her time to go overseas with Bob Hope to entertain American troops, graciously took pictures and shared a cappuccino with us. Zsa Zsa also gave beauty advice to my friend Laura, the store's gorgeous bartender, who looked like supermodel Cindy Crawford. It reminded me of the time a few years back when Gabor was questioned by a girl who was about to break off her engagement. The wealthy fiancé had presented her with a Rolls Royce, diamonds, a fur coat and a stove. What should she do? "Give back the stove," said Zsa Zsa.

Extra: When Zsa Zsa approached the bar, she stated that Laura had beautiful skin. She emphatically advised the younger girl to stay away from booze to maintain her looks. Then Zsa Zsa said, "By the way, darling, put a little extra brandy in the cappuccino today," and laughed good-naturedly.

Extra: Sometimes when they were entertaining US troops, Bob Hope would ask Zsa Zsa Gabor if she had any domestic skills at all. "Of course, Robert darling, I'm a great housekeeper. Every time I get divorced, I keep the house."

Extra: Zsa Zsa Gabor was born in 1917 and as a young woman, became famous for her acting. The name Zsa Zsa is Hungarian for Susan.

Disconnected Lifestyles

The lifestyles of Hollywood's citizens have often disconnected them from their audience. In the 1930s, many conservative groups complained about the lack of moral content in the movies, which led to a declining box office and studio self-censorship. One time famed Chicago writer Ben Hecht, who was often sought out for his story advice, received a middle-of-the-night phone call from an MGM executive. The studio was having a problem with a screenplay. A young couple meets and falls in love at the beginning of the story. Why would they not wish to take their relationship to the next level? How could their restraint be logically explained for two hours on screen? With some amusement, Hecht suggested there were many people who waited till they were married before they were intimate. There was a pause on the other line and then the executive exclaimed, "You know, that's such a novel idea it just might work!"

Celebrity Chateau

From the privacy-seeking Greta Garbo to the wild-partying Lindsay Lohan, many movie stars have stayed at the Chateau Marmont Hotel. Shortly after it opened in 1929, the castle-like inn on Sunset Boulevard was recommended by studio heads to actors as the perfect hideaway for indiscreet behavior. Desi Arnaz, John Wayne and Marilyn Monroe all made the Chateau their home in between marriages. In the late 1960s, Doors' lead singer Jim Morrison claimed he used up eight of his nine lives when the rocker jumped off the Chateau roof and landed in the bushes. After the tragic death of comedian John Belushi in 1982, due to a drug overdose, the venerable hotel was purchased by new ownership who gave it an upgrade, but still retained its classic, old-style Hollywood atmosphere. The establishment continued to be frequented by celebrities, despite its thin walls that told tales. Like the time a young Chateau guest named Kirk Douglas was awakened by a sleepy female voice asking for a glass of water. The tired actor got up to fulfill the request, returned to his bed and only then realized he was sleeping alone.

What's in a Name?

Movie people are often labeled with nicknames that range from flattering to derogatory. During the silent film era, little Mary Pickford was known to her fans as "America's Sweetheart." Behind the scenes her success at the box office was so respected she was dubbed "Bank of America's Sweetheart." Likewise, the big-eared Clark Gable surprised his bosses with his dynamic screen sex appeal and earned the title "The King." On the less respectful side, Robert De Niro became notorious for giving small tips; Los Angeles limo drivers called him "No Dinero." When Demi Moore got a reputation for making extravagant on-set demands, the actress was blasted with the moniker "Gimme Moore." And some very petty remarks were aimed at director Cecil B. DeMille. Critics became so bitter that their harsh reviews failed to keep the public away from his Biblical spectacles and they started slamming his pictures as being "Run of DeMille."

Extra: Movies can also get unflattering nicknames. Director William Wyler's 1963 drama *The Children's Hour*, about two schoolteachers who contemplate and are scandalized by a potential same-sex relationship, got horrible reviews. One critic said it should have been called "The Less Being Said the Better." Likewise, Jim Carrey's 1996 bomb *The Cable Guy* became known as "The Straight to Cable Guy."

Coogan's Bluff

Eight-year-old Jackie Coogan was unable to cry when he played the title role in *Oliver Twist* in 1922. The scene called for Jackie as the grieving orphan to say, "My mother's dead," and burst into tears. Very patiently, the director suggested perhaps he could imagine that his real mother had died. Coogan eyed the woman in question who was standing some thirty feet away on the set. Jackie did not know that in eleven years she would refuse to give him the money that he was now earning as America's premier child star. He had no idea that the California legislature would set up trusts for kid actors in 1939, too late to keep his fortune from being squandered. There was no way Coogan could guess that forty-two years from now, while playing Uncle Fester on TV's *The Addams Family*, he would warn the producers not to mess with him, as he once sued his own mother.

The boy hesitated then said, "Sir, can I imagine my dog died instead?"

Mutiny at MGM

In the 1930s, film extras found creative ways to hustle some extra bucks. One common trick for actors working in massive costume dramas was to find a loose board in the fence of a studio such as MGM or Paramount. Four or five people would sneak out unnoticed during filming and, using a similar method, would infiltrate another movie set. With the help of friends punching out time clocks, they could collect two checks for one day's work. Another scam involved players showing up when they were not needed. An example was the 1935 MGM classic *Mutiny on the Bounty*. After careful viewing, producer Irving Thalberg angrily realized that he would have to order reshoots. Thalberg had been impressed by one of the rebels, a powerful physical specimen who helped first officer Fletcher Christian set the crew adrift. The problem was that in later scenes, the same cagey extra was also present on the raft with the deposed Captain Bligh.

Extra: Movie extras were not always happy if one of their own rose through the ranks. Some non-speaking actors were not above pressuring their pals who hit it big to intentionally blow lines so the background people could get paid overtime. Professional behavior and concern for their employer's bottom line sometimes cost new movie stars old friendships.

Thankful Hattie

Forty-five-year-old Hattie McDaniel had a lot to be thankful for as she prepared to celebrate Thanksgiving at her South Central Los Angeles home in 1938. Due to hard work, talent and a positive attitude, Hattie had gone from being a maid to pretending to be one in movies for far greater money. Now McDaniel was famous and could afford to give a little so some children wouldn't have to experience Christmas without presents, as she had growing up poor in Wichita, Kansas. And she was going to do a test for the role of Mammy in *Gone with the Wind.* If she got the part, Hattie was going to play her with some fire; she would never present a subservient image onscreen. Today she had been planning just a small get-together but the doorbell kept ringing. Several of her fans had found out where she lived; McDaniel was still listed in the phone book just like everyone else. Well, that was just fine; she'd cooked a twenty-pound turkey.

Extra: In 1946, Walt Disney hired Oscar Winner Hattie McDaniel to be Aunt Tempy in *Song of the South*. McDaniel, who had convinced producer David O. Selznick not to use the n-word in *Gone with the Wind* (1939), often suffered through long bouts of unemployment and depression. Black activists complained to her prospective employers that her maid-mammy portrayals reinforced negative stereotypes. Walt Disney appealed to Walter White (1893-1955), the head of the National Association of Colored People, to read an early

Song of the South script and voice any objections to the story he might have. Walt was not a racist; he simply wanted to present Joel Chandler Harris' (1845-1908) old American folk stories in the most tasteful way possible. White refused to meet with Disney, waited till the movie came out then blasted him without seeing the film for showing happy slaves on screen. Ironically, the story took place after the Civil War and the black characters were free laborers.

Every Day is Halloween on Hollywood Boulevard

After the Kodak Theater, the new home of the Oscars, was built in 2001, Hollywood Boulevard became awash in a sea of characters. Mostly out-of-work actors who dressed up as anyone from Supergirl to Catwoman, they posed for pictures with tourists hoping to be paid off with tips. Turf wars would erupt when two of them would have similar costumes; one time a couple of Batmen got into a shoving match. Some crossed the line of proper behavior; The Incredible Hulk was arrested for grabbing a girl on the rear, leaving green paint on her white pants. Elmo and Mr. Incredible were busted in a sting operation when they became too intimidating in their demands for money. But most behaved like friendly ambassadors for the city and kept their dreams of stardom alive. It was encouraging for the wannabes to know that superstar Brad Pitt's first Hollywood job was standing in front of a fast food joint trying to lure customers inside, while dressed in a chicken suit.

The Honorary Hyper

Sixty-eight-year-old Johnny Grant became the honorary mayor of Hollywood in 1992. The five-foot tall former radio DJ, who entertained more US troops overseas than Bob Hope, was determined to bring back Tinseltown's glamour. Some of the local merchants would roll their eyes when Johnny would tell tales about his encounters with past legends like Sinatra. Did not the old guy realize those days were gone? His honor surprised them by being forward looking; he convinced young stars like Tom Cruise to come out to the rundown district for public events. Who cared if Grant had never seen the newer actor's movies? Tourists visiting the Chinese Theater and the Walk of Fame were often personally greeted by the beaming little man. The movie capital once again became an attractive destination and in 2002, hosted the Oscars for the first time in forty-two years. Till his death in 2008, Grant never stopped hyping his town; he laughed when a neighborhood diner named a ham sandwich after him.

Hollywood Tattoos

Movie stars often sport tattoos for a variety of reasons. The nine cast members who took the title roles in the 2001 fantasy *The Lord of the Rings: The Fellowship of the Ring*, achieved solidarity by having the elfish symbol representing the number nine added to their skins. Other times famous personalities can use cosmetic additions to help an already dangerous image, such as actress Angelina Jolie who added a dragon and a tiger to her backside. Then there are the stars who graft on affectionate messages to loved ones; in Hollywood where relationships are often short-lived, this can be risky. In the 1990s, Johnny Depp announced his relationship with then girlfriend Winona Ryder by cosmetically adding the words "Winona Forever" to his arm. When they broke up, he could only remove it partially; afterward, Depp's tattoo read "Wino Forever."

Same War, Different Outcome

Gone with the Wind novelist Margaret Mitchell was awestruck seeing her work turned into a film. Born in 1900, when Mitchell was a young girl in Atlanta, various relatives took her on tours of Confederate battle sites. They described the conflicts so vividly that Margaret imagined that she had participated in them. It took Mitchell ten years to write the text for her Civil War romance tale. To her amazement, the book became a bestseller in 1936 and three years later a massive production beyond her wildest dreams. Mitchell showed up in Hollywood to watch the scene where Scarlett O'Hara, played by Vivian Leigh, nursed wounded soldiers at the Atlanta railway station. Producer David O. Selznick, who spared no expense on his numerous extras and their authentic costumes, proudly asked what she thought of the whole spectacle. The novelist hesitated then said, "My dear Mr. O. Selznick, if we would have had this many soldiers we would have won the war."

Extra: Margaret Mitchell (1900-1949) didn't want anyone besides her husband to know that she was writing a novel. The Atlanta newspaperwoman, who used the byline Peggy Mitchell, hid the pages behind towels, cabinets and under her bed. In 1935, Mitchell became acquainted with editor Harold Latham of Macmillan Publishers. Totally charmed by her Southern hospitality, he asked if Margaret had ever written a book. Mitchell said she hadn't. *Gone with the Wind* may have stayed a crumpled bunch of papers until one of the clandestine author's friends remarked, "Imagine someone as silly as Peggy writing a book."

Against her better judgment, Margaret sent her incomplete manuscript to Latham. Soon she changed her mind and wanted her work back, but by that time, the editor had read it and was rightly convinced he had discovered a blockbuster. Macmillan sent her a check and Mitchell reluctantly agreed to complete her Civil War classic.

Extra: Journalist Margaret Mitchell shunned the press attention she received when her famed novel was made into a film. One of her few public comments regarding the screen version of *Gone with the Wind* involved the casting. A huge Marx Brothers fan, Margaret expressed her hope that wise-cracking comedian Groucho Marx would be cast as the story's dashing hero, Rhett Butler.

Hollywood Rumors

Lana Turner being discovered at Schwab's Pharmacy is one of many lingering Hollywood legends. A gossip columnist who frequented the famous Sunset Strip hangout started the rumor; in real life, the teenage blonde bombshell had first been spotted wearing a tight sweater while crossing the street from Hollywood High School to a malt shop. Another myth involved Walt Disney being frozen after his death in 1966; a quiet funeral plus the mogul's interest in cryogenics overshadowed the fact that he was cremated. Moviegoers added to the falsehoods. Viewers of the 1959 ancient Roman epic *Ben-Hur* swore that they saw a sports car chasing a chariot and star Charlton Heston wearing a wristwatch, despite the actor's denials. Nobody hanged themselves in the 1939 classic *The Wizard of Oz*; it just looked that way onscreen when a bird spread its wings. And 1930s child star Shirley Temple had to grow up to disprove the nasty charge of jealous parents that she was actually a midget.

Extra: Born in 1928, Shirley Temple's career as child actress was guided largely by her mother Gertrude (1893-1977) who would grab her by the shoulders before each scene and say," Sparkle Shirley, sparkle."

20th Century Fox head Darryl Zanuck frustrated Mrs. Temple by not allowing Shirley to play more varied parts (not realizing she was a child, playwright George Bernard Shaw [1856-1950] offered her the lead in his stage version of *Caesar and Cleopatra*). Zanuck felt Shirley's spunky movie character had to be repeated for her to stay popular. Gertrude also demanded that the studio cut any scene where another child looked better than her daughter, which often infuriated the parents of Shirley's young co-stars.

Extra: In the 1930s, Shirley Temple's grit and determination represented the American spirit to the world. A false report of her death in Emperor Hirohito's Japan (still at war with the United States) in 1943 set off a wild celebration in the streets.

Extra: In the early 1990s, the gossip newspapers printed all sorts of wild tales about pop star Michael Jackson (1958-2009). The tabloids stated that the gloved one was sleeping in an oxygen chamber so he would live to age 150; that he was planning to buy the remains of the Elephant Man; and chronicled Jackson's "anger" at his one-year-older rival singer Prince for using ESP to destroy the mind of Jackson's pet chimp Bubbles. (When Michael's friend, fifty-nine-year-old Elizabeth Taylor, got married for the eighth time at Jackson's Neverland Ranch in 1991, some media sources falsely reported that Bubbles was the ring bearer.) It was later revealed that the rumors were coming from Jackson himself in order to perpetuate his image as a colorful, Peter Pan-like eccentric.

George Raft's Pals

Actor George Raft, who specialized in playing gangsters, enjoyed a good and sometimes dangerous friendship with real-life mobster Benjamin Siegel. Growing up in Hell's Kitchen in New York at the turn of the twentieth century, Raft knew and admired street thugs. Why shouldn't he hang out with Ben, who lived a lavish lifestyle and had a generous nature? In the 1930s, George often copied the handsome Siegel's mannerisms when he played hoods on screen. But sometimes, Ben, who would be gunned down in an apparent gangland hit in 1947, would display his darker side. He would punch anyone who dared to call him by his nickname Bugsy and once in a fit of anger pulled a gun on Raft before laughing and putting it away. One day Ben visited George on a movie set with some very tough-looking associates that made the star uneasy. The wise guy put an arm around Raft and tried to reassure him. "Hey, George, don't worry. We only kill each other."

Hooray for the Hollywood Sign

Erected in 1923 to advertise a real estate development, the Hollywood Sign became the most famous sight in Los Angeles. In 1932, twenty-four-year-old struggling actress Peg Entwistle climbed fifty feet to the top of the letter H and jumped. Later several hikers in the vicinity claimed to have encountered her restless ghost. Another time a man crashed his car into the letter H, knocking it down the mountain. Various pranks involving the famed structure have included blocking the H in honor of Oliver North, losing an L when the Pope came to town and marijuana activists covering the last two Os with Es. By 1978, the landmark was so damaged by weather, termites and vandalism that many locals wanted it taken down. A group of sentimental celebrities and other donors paid big bucks to replace it. Emotional feelings about the sign were never anticipated by the businessmen who built it; they originally planned to tear it down after two years.

There's No Place like Home

One way for some Los Angeles homeowners to offset their high mortgage payments is to rent their properties to moviemakers. The hassles of trailers parked in driveways, furniture being moved and too many people with too few bathrooms pale against the thousands of dollars residents can make. Most shooting takes place in the daytime with owners able to return at night without a hitch. Large insurance policies are taken out by studios to pay for the rare times they commit permanent property damage, but some mishaps can't be anticipated. The plot of the 1929 Laurel and Hardy short comedy *Big Business* had Stan and Ollie playing Christmas tree salesmen who destroy a potential customer's house. They rented a beautiful mansion in the plush neighborhood of Cheviot Hills; the owners were well paid and were sent off on vacation with the promise their house would be restored when they got back. Unfortunately, the comics made a mistake and used the home next door!

Extra: The 2004 TV show *Entourage* about fictional Hollywood movie star Vincent Chase and his childhood friends from Queens, New York, was filmed in real locations throughout Los Angeles. The show quickly became must-see viewing for people who worked in the Hollywood industry. Fans of the program were able to see the insides of hot spots where sometimes-civilians (people outside the movie business) were not always welcome. Vincent and his posse lived in actual mansions in ritzy spots like Beverly Hills and Malibu but often had to move after a few weeks because local residents (perhaps a little jealous of the fees their neighbors got paid) complained to the filmmakers about the loud noise and inconvenience.

John Wayne Went For the Green

In 1968, John Wayne decided to counter Vietnam War protests by turning *The Green Berets,* a collection of short stories by author Robin Moore about the superhero-like exploits of the US Army Special Forces, into a movie. Eight years before, the cowboy star had taken a financial bath while producing *The Alamo;* he considered *The Green Berets* an appropriate freedom-fighting sequel. Wayne, who never served in the military, hated being called a hero by the press while the young soldiers he visited in Vietnam were accused of being murderers. *The Green Berets* production problems ranged from a lack of cooperation from the Pentagon (the military brass initially rejected a plot line that had the Green Berets kidnapping a North Vietnamese general; in real life, the covert special forces would have never been sent on such an aggressive assignment; the quietly operating elite force performed training and scouting missions in Saigon) to battle scenes repeatedly being ruined when twirling helicopter blades blew the sixty-one-year-old Wayne's toupee off. It took all of the Duke's persuasive abilities to get Jack Warner to distribute the film. Upon its release, many critics who opposed the war called *The Green Berets* vile and boring, but to their great distress, it was a huge box-office success. Wayne publicly thanked the East Coast reviewers who hated the movie for bringing it more attention, and laughed all the way to the bank.

Extra: No project meant more to fifty-three-year-old John Wayne than *The Alamo* (1960). which he both starred in and directed. For over twenty years, the Duke had dreamed of putting the true story of Davy Crockett (1786-1836) and his fellow doomed freedom fighters on the screen. As a young man attending the University of Southern California, John had flirted with socialism as a philosophy. Time, high taxes and the influence of his right-wing friends had changed him. The big-screen hero would have preferred not to have been involved with politics, but liberals were so determined to destroy traditional American values that he felt compelled to engage them. To Wayne, the ideals of the men willing to make their last stand against overwhelming odds in the legendary San Antonio fort was symbolic of the battle the cowboy star had taken up against Hollywood's Communists and other subversive elements trying to destroy America from within. The financially struggling actor had chosen to put up his own meager funds to partially finance *The Alamo.* Wayne, often feeling weak and dizzy from dehydration, gamely lead his film troops through months of blistering Texas heat, budget shortfalls, scorpions and rattlesnakes in order to recreate the epic 1836 conflict. The finished three-hour product failed to make a profit at the box office. Wayne hoped that he could raise *The Alamo's* profile with an Oscar victory and put out trade paper ads suggesting that it would be unpatriotic to vote against him; in some quarters, the Duke's campaign efforts were met with derision. Was it treason to call *The Alamo* a boring piece of cinema? *The Apartment* won Best Picture and *The Alamo* left the disappointed and somewhat humiliated Wayne heavily in debt, but he still had a large loyal fan base, many of whom shared his beliefs. Soon his subsequent movies allowed the high-in-demand actor to replenish his bank account.

Coast to Coast

Some New York actors who moved to Hollywood felt that the potential pay raise was not worth the drop off in lifestyle. For years, transplants from the Big Apple complained that LA lacked culture and style. Broadway performers who were used to walking, riding subways or taking cabs had a hard time adjusting to being stuck on freeways. From the museums to the sports arenas, they felt everything in LA was too spread out. Former Gothamites fretted that they couldn't get a decent slice of pizza and a few oddballs were even homesick for a good mugging. Still, not everyone hated being on the West Coast. Once, the late actor Edward G. Robinson was having lunch in Beverly Hills with an old pal from Brooklyn. "God, look at this weather, it never changes," said the friend. "You know, Eddy, I really miss the springs back home."

"Yeah, I remember them well," replied the star. "Especially the ones that came up through my mattress."

Girl plus Midget

The real Gidget had to laugh when she saw the film about her life in 1959. As a teenager, Kathy Kohner started hanging with the Malibu surfing crowd and had fallen in love with the sport herself. Her nickname came from the colorful characters she met on the beach who said Kathy was both a girl and a midget. Her father Fred, a professional screenwriter, was fascinated by her stories and turned them into a bestselling book, which became the source material for the *Gidget* movie. Kathy had sneaked down to Malibu to watch the cast shoot the picture a couple of times. Sandra Dee, the actress who was supposed to be playing her, looked silly on her board and some of those other kid actors couldn't even swim. God, those shots on the ocean looked so fake; they had to have been done at the studio. Well, it was kind of fun to watch. Kathy never imagined that the success of this goofy picture would help to turn an activity enjoyed by a small subculture of wave riders into a billion-dollar industry.

Extra: In 1956, fifteen-year-old Brentwood resident Kathy Kohner was ordered by her mother to go to the beach and get some sunshine. The teenager became intrigued by the young boys she saw surfing in Malibu, with nicknames like "Moondoggie" and "The Big Kahuna." Unlike most of the bikini-clad girls who sat on the beach and watched, the five-foot-two Kohner chose to participate in the sport. She earned the respect of the sometimes hard-to-get-to-know wave riders, after buying a board for thirty dollars and teaching herself how to "hang 10" (walking up to the front of the board and dangling all your toes over the edge). She later allowed her father Frederick to listen in secretly on her phone conversations so he could learn her new friends' lingo, words like "stoked," "jazzed" and "bitching." After the *Gidget* movie came out in 1959, many of Kathy's pals blamed her for ruining their favorite pastime; in their opinion, the Southern California beaches became too darn crowded.

Extra: In preparation for playing the title role in *Gidget,* Sandra Dee (1942-2005) tried to surf one time off camera and almost drowned. The moviemakers filmed close-ups of her standing on a board with the ocean projected behind her.

The Keeper of the Secrets

In the 1930s, when MGM was the Tiffany of the movie studios, publicist Howard Strickland was the keeper of the secrets. A high school dropout, Strickland had informants in every newspaper office and police station in Los Angeles. He squelched embarrassing stories before they became public knowledge. Howard assigned security guards dressed as paramedics to protect the hard-drinking Spencer Tracy. They would follow the actor into bars, strap him into a stretcher, and whisk him away before he could be recognized. For the well-liked PR man, the toughest job was playing peacemaker. If head mogul Louis B. Mayer told Howard to make a star follow his orders, the message diffused into *L.B. would be obliged if you would do him this favor.* Likewise, if Strickland said to Mayer that a Metro contract player needed a day to mull it over, it meant that *the employee wanted to tell his boss where to shove it.*

Elementary, My Dear Conan Doyle

Once, in the 1920s, Sherlock Holmes creator Sir Arthur Conan Doyle was surprised when a taxi driver in Marseilles recognized him. The very logical author who believed in fairies and dabbled in mysticism wondered how the cabbie knew who he was. "Deductive reasoning," the man said. "Your tan indicates that you are on vacation, your clothes are of British origin and the ink spot on your index finger shows that you are a writer."

The scribe, who had no idea at that time his famed fictional detective would go on to be the most portrayed character in movie history, was impressed. This was more astonishing than anything he'd ever witnessed at a séance. "Sir, I am merely an amateur sleuth, but you are the real life counterpart to my Sherlock Holmes."

The Frenchman smiled and nodded as he finished loading his client's luggage in the trunk. "Of course my best clue was that your name was on your suitcase."

Rocky's Funeral

In Chester, Illinois, some ninety miles southeast of Saint Louis, a second funeral was held for Frank "Rocky" Fiegel in 1976. A beloved local character, he died fifty years earlier, too poor to afford a marked grave. His feats of strength were legendary around the small town. Rocky could lift a bale of hay by himself, a job usually reserved for two men. For a time he worked in a saloon and was often challenged to fights; he once knocked three bullies unconscious. The neighborhood kids, now grown up with grandchildren, fondly told stories about the toothless little man that bought them candy. Did Rocky ever have a romance with the tall dowdy woman who ran the general store and wore her black hair in a bun? On that day, a new tombstone was placed at Fiegel's resting place, complete with an etching of the hero he inspired. Those who remembered him were proud to pay homage to the real-life Popeye the Sailor.

The Natural Rascals

Between 1922 and 1944, forty-one youngsters starred in 221 *Little Rascals* comedies. Created by producer Hal Roach, the series also known as *Our Gang*, showed working-class urchins outwitting both adults and rich rivals. Prominent members included Spanky who got his nickname when his mother threatened to punish him; his lovesick buddy Alfalfa, a sometimes nasty prankster who put dead frogs in his co-stars' sandwiches; Butch, actually a nice guy whose bullying ways onscreen led non-movie kids to challenge him to fights, and the much parodied Buckwheat who staunchly defended the films against charges that they were racist. Roach never wanted pampered child actors; visitors to the *Our Gang* set found unpretentious and innocent little people who seemed unaffected by their fame. One time Spanky was asked how many years he'd been in pictures. "Seven."

And how old was he? "Six."

It's a Wonderful World

Seven years before he was perfectly cast in *It's a Wonderful Life*, Jimmy Stewart felt out of place starring in the 1939 comedy *It's a Wonderful World*, directed by the fast-working W. S. Van Dyke. The movie's ridiculous plot had Jim's private-detective character jumping from a train to avoid being incarcerated in Sing Sing Correctional Facility, capturing a Boy Scout leader and stealing his clothes, and punching co-star Claudette Colbert on the jaw. It was a role far better suited to a star like Clark Gable, and the typically nice guy Stewart had great difficulty with dialogue like, "I never met a dame that wasn't a nitwit." Director Van Dyke's pace was thrown off by the star's mistakes and the filmmaker remarked that the other leading man he worked with did not blow his lines. Jimmy was hurt until he realized that the director was referring to Johnny Weissmuller who rarely had to say more than, "Me, Tarzan!"

Extra: *Tarzan of the Apes* was written in 1912 by a pencil-sharpener salesman named Edgar Rice Burroughs (1875-1950). Under the loincloth, the fictional jungle hero was a sophisticated British Lord named John Clayton. After his parents were killed, he was raised in a simian culture and given the name Tarzan (the ape word for White-skin). When Burroughs' novel became a huge success, the writer set out to promote his character in other media. Tarzan appeared in comics, movies and inspired the name of Burroughs' hometown, Tarzana, California. The author enjoyed meeting leading man Johnny Weissmuller (1904-1984), but he hated the unsophisticated version of *Tarzan* presented onscreen by director W. S. Van Dyke (1889-1943) in the 1930s. Some Hollywood wags joked that when Weissmuller was first offered the role, his reply was, "Me? Tarzan?"

Tarzan's Triangle

Twenty-seven-year-old Johnny Weissmuller was told not to show fear when he met Cheetah, his co-star in the 1932 movie *Tarzan the Ape-man*. Dressed in his loincloth, the five-time Olympic gold medal winner for swimming approached the chimp who bared his teeth at him. Johnny pulled out his hunting knife, held it under the animal's nose and hit him on the head with it. Cheetah glared, then jumped into Weissmuller's arms and hugged him. From then on they were great buddies and were often seen holding hands and walking around the movie set together. Cheetah loved beer and cigars, lived for over seventy years and always protected his leading-man buddy. One time the lovely Maureen O'Sullivan, who played Tarzan's mate Jane in six movies, was asked if she ever had an interest in the virile Weissmuller. "Oh, of course I found Johnny very attractive and was interested. But Cheetah would never let me get near him."

Extra: The six-times-married Johnny Weissmuller was a wild womanizer who was known to go to the hotels of his latest potential conquests, stand on the sidewalk below their windows, beat his chest and make the Tarzan yell.

Extra: In *Tarzan Triumphs* (1943), Tarzan and Cheetah teamed up to help win World War II on the screen. After the Ape Man dispatched some very dangerous Nazis in the jungle, his furry pal got on the radio and broadcasted a message to Berlin. The soldiers on the receiving end mistook the chimp's chattering for Hitler and saluted their imagined Fuhrer while goose-stepping.

Stars' Homes

Whether they go in their own cars or ride on sightseeing vans, many people want to see the celebrity mansions of Beverly Hills. The endeavor can be hazardous; pop-icon Prince was known for throwing rocks at buses that went by his residence. Likewise, rocker Ozzy Osbourne would threaten to get his dogs to chase off lookie loos. Visitors can get frustrated when the estates are hidden; singer Britney Spears almost fell and hurt herself when she stood on her car and tried to look over the hedges at Brad Pitt and Jennifer Anniston's house.

Often the best homes to see belonged to luminaries who are no longer with us. Many of them were proud to display beautifully manicured lawns, expensive cars in their driveways and seemed to have a good sense of humor. During the silent film days, actors Charlie Chaplin and Douglas Fairbanks would sometimes pull up alongside tourists reading star maps and ask them for directions.

Extra: Sometimes the famous put out the welcome mat to strangers. Before he became an ultra-recluse, Elvis Presley (1935-1977) loved taking his Memphis relatives on tours of the star's homes. The singer once shocked his date Natalie Wood (1938-1981) by taking time to chat with fans that blocked his driveway, after they agreed to move out of the way so he could park. Jack Benny and George Burns, who like Ozzy Osbourne gave out their addresses on their TV shows, used to instruct their maids to give out autographed pictures to fans who knocked. If Benny or Burns answered the door, complete strangers were sometimes invited in for lemonade. Sitting in his swimming pool, Oliver Hardy would welcome fans who climbed over his fence. "Hey, how about a dip?"

And in the 1990s television producer Aaron Spelling (1923-2006) would come out of his 56,500-square-foot mansion to pitch show ideas to tourists.

Extra: A frightening situation happened in 1960 when a burglar found John Wayne's address. The Duke was watching TV when the brazen criminal came into his house. "What the hell?"

Reacting quickly, Wayne ran down to the basement and grabbed a shotgun. He chased the fiend into the backyard and said, "Hold it. I got you covered."

He yelled to his wife Pilar to call the police, which she already had. After the robber was cuffed, he asked to speak to the cowboy star. "Mr. Wayne?"

"What do you want, punk?"

"Well, I came here in a cab. The taxi driver is still outside. The meter's running. He didn't know I came to rob you. Could you take care of him, Mr. Wayne?"

The Duke swore under his breath, but after the police hauled the bad guy away, John went outside and paid the driver.

Extra: One day in 1935, passengers on a tour bus in Brentwood were greeted by the biggest star in the world, standing on the sidewalk in front of her house. Seven-year-old Shirley Temple had talked some stonemasons working on her property into giving her some wet mortar, which the little girl formed into small pies that she was now selling to sightseers. Business was brisk, especially when Shirley put her handprints in the cement souvenirs. The moppet needed the extra cash; she was surviving on an allowance of four dollars a week; the rest of her vast wealth had been placed in a trust fund. Unfortunately for the young entrepreneur, one of the household staff tattled, resulting in her mother, always fearful of the famous child being kidnapped, came out to haul Shirley back inside.

Call of the Wild Hare

Cartoonist Tex Avery added the final ingredient to Bugs Bunny's winning personality when he made the animated short *The Wild Hare* in 1940. The clever cartoon animal had been onscreen for three years, and was just now developing into an individual. He was a trickster influenced by American folklore figures, such as Br'er Rabbit, who used his wits to thwart his enemies. He was a wiseacre like Groucho Marx; voice artist Mel Blanc had given the bunny a streetwise accent that mixed Brooklyn and the Bronx. Then there was the carrot eating, inspired by Clark Gable chewing down on the vegetable in the 1934 movie *It Happened One Night*. But what could Bugs say that would make him appear cool in the face of danger? Avery recalled a common greeting people used in Texas. To Tex's surprise, audiences went crazy when Bugs, confronted by the speech-impeded hunter Elmer Fudd, asked him, "What's up, Doc?" And with those words, the wascally wabbit became an instant superstar.

Extra: *It Happened One Night* (1934) starring Clark Gable and Claudette Colbert (1903-1996) was one of the most unlikely successes in Hollywood history. Louis B. Mayer, the head of MGM, decided to punish contract player Gable for complaining too much about gangster roles. The big-eared actor got drunk when he found out he was being sent to lowly Columbia Pictures to play a roughneck reporter who tangles with a spoiled heiress. Metro, at least, was a classy place to work, not like that little outhouse on Gower Street run by Harry Cohn. Likewise, the temperamental Colbert hated the romantic comedy script and only agreed to do it at double her normal salary. Director Frank Capra (1897-1991) did not think highly of the story either but tried to make it fun. At one point, the filmmaker had his actors, playing bus passengers, sing an old ditty called "The Daring Young Man on the Flying Trapeze" (1867). Colbert complained it was ridiculous that a bunch of people would know the lyrics to a nineteenth-century song. She changed her mind watching the delighted look on her maid's face while the scene was performed. *It Happened One Night* overcame initial bad reviews to become one of the most popular and profitable films in history, with Gable, Capra, Colbert and the picture itself all winning Oscars.

The Greatest Costume Designer

With no prior experience, twenty-six-year-old Edith Head was hired as a costume designer by Paramount Studios in 1923. The bespectacled, hard-working Head quickly made a name for herself by letting scripts dictate how the characters should look on film. Whether a movie required glamour or authenticity, she became an expert in supplying casts with the appropriate clothes. Edith was nominated for an incredible thirty-four Academy Awards, won eight and showed the statues to stars who argued with her about wardrobe choices. She enjoyed using diplomacy to get her way. Ingrid Bergman's character in the 1943 movie *For Whom the Bell Tolls* required working clothes; Head picked out an extra's old shirt and trousers. The furious director Sam Wood demanded she create something new. No problem. Edith cheerfully copied the old outfit, and then bleached it till it looked as worn out as the original.

Communication Breakdown

People from all around the world come to Los Angeles to take sightseeing tours. Each group that rides on the bus has a unique makeup. Various attractions hold different levels of interest; some visitors love the colorful bohemian atmosphere of Venice Beach full of rollerbladers, artists and weight lifters. Others are excited to have a chance to see a celebrity shopping at the posh boutiques on Rodeo Drive. Movie buffs are thrilled to look at the handprints of stars at Grauman's Chinese Theater, while the cultured prefer to spend time at the fabulous Getty museum. With the wide variety of guests and interests, it's important that tour guides constantly upgrade their communication skills. One time one of the managers at the hospitality company I work for emphasized that when you talk to clients it is crucial always to use the right connotation. One colleague of mine, who was a very witty guy, replied," You mean like a letter from a prisoner?"

Extra: On one of my tours of Rodeo Drive, the guests were returning to the bus after their visit when former Los Angeles Dodgers' first baseman Steve Garvey came walking by. A lifelong Dodger fan, I said," Hi Steve. Everyone, this is Steve Garvey!" Very pleasantly, the smiling ex-baseball star came over to meet the people on the bus. Unfortunately, the entire group was from England and Germany and not a single person knew who he was.

The Wildest Guest

Longtime staff at the old Ambassador Hotel in Los Angeles had many candidates for the most outrageously behaved celebrity guest. There were the hammy Barrymore brothers who always tried to outdo one another; after the drunken John earned many stares for bringing his pet monkey in the hotel's famed Moroccan-style club, the Cocoanut Grove, Lionel arrived there with seven chimps. Chaos erupted when the well-dressed guests chased the animals as they swung through the paper Mache trees. Then there was famed movie theater owner Sid Grauman who told Charlie Chaplin that he found a dead body in his hotel bed. The tramp fled in terror when Sid pulled back the blankets, not realizing he was looking at a wax dummy covered in ketchup. But it was hard to top the antics of actress Tallulah Bankhead who once called for room service, answered the door in the buff and told the bell boy no tip; she had nothing on her.

Improbable Movie Events

In the movies, slow-moving monsters can catch screaming girls running at top speed, strutting street gang members can burst into song and lots of time and effort is spent making things appear authentic. Technical advisors are on hand to get audiences to believe that actors are skilled swordsmen, competent in police procedure, world-class athletes or a convincing band of well-trained soldiers, but sometimes reality is a lesser priority. In the 2000 science fiction film *Mission to Mars*, director Brian De Palma listened to a representative from NASA to make sure the outer space scenes were correct. The highly paid expert's counsel was ignored when he strongly objected to a sequence where a female astronaut cried, which they are trained not to do. De Palma felt that most cinemagoers would be so caught up in the story they would not care that in zero gravity the tears would rise up and burn her eyes.

David Niven's Yarns

British actor and raconteur David Niven never let the facts get in the way of a good yarn. In his wonderful 1975 book about Hollywood, *Bring on the Empty Horses*, Niven described Christmas in 1947 when he convinced his neighbor Tyrone Power to dress up as Santa Claus at a party for Niven's children. At the last moment, Power came down with a bad bout of stage fright and tried to back out of his promise; only after downing a great deal of Scotch did he stumble into the backyard as St. Nick. Like most actors, once Tyrone got into character, he began to enjoy himself. At one point, the inebriated matinee idol put Gary Cooper's daughter Maria on his knee. "Ho, Ho, Ho, little girl. You tell your old man Santa enjoyed watching him in *High Noon*. And ask him to get that pretty Grace Kelly's phone number for me while you're at it. Ho, Ho, Ho."

High Noon was released in 1952, five years after Tyrone supposedly put on the white whiskers.

Another Dinner at Chasen's

Opened in 1937, Chasen's Restaurant in West Hollywood provided a lighthearted atmosphere for celebrities. Drunken actors Humphrey Bogart and Peter Lorre were forgiven for the time when they stole the eateries' safe and carried it out onto busy Beverly Boulevard. Another night Jimmy Stewart was given a bachelor party complete with diaper-clad midgets popping out of cakes. Chasen's management was happy to arrange for Elizabeth Taylor to have their trademark chili delivered to her all over the world, and proud to create a non-alcoholic cocktail for child-star Shirley Temple. Not all guests got royal treatment. Once, W. C. Fields received some sullen glances when he showed up at Chasen's with a strange woman. None of the staff objected when his longtime girl friend Carlotta Monti called up nearby Cedar Sinai hospital, told them that the comedian was having a heart attack and arranged for paramedics to fetch him during dinner.

David's Gift

Ten-year-old David Niven found that his mischief making could bring happiness to others. In 1920, while attending a prestigious boy's school, the future Oscar-winning actor once sent what looked like a box of chocolates to an extremely ill classmate. Before the bedridden youth could examine the present, it was snatched up by his heavyset nurse. She unwrapped it to find a smaller, similarly decorated package. The hungry battle-axe repeated the same act until she ripped open the last tiny parcel, which revealed a smelly souvenir left by a dog. Niven, who years later entertained millions with his funny memoirs, immediately got expelled and hauled off to a reformatory. After the bad seed served his sentence, he sought out his friend to apologize. The sickly kid turned out to be grateful; the sight of his shrieking caretaker accidentally flinging David's gift into the medicine cabinet made him laugh and feel better.

LEADING MEN AND
LEADING LADIES LORE

"They don't pay me to watch them."
— Actor Robert Mitchum explaining why he didn't see his own movies.

"I'm sort of the boy next door; if that boy has a good scriptwriter."
— Michael Caine

Ten Percent of Jimmy Stewart

In 1941, thirty-one-year-old Jimmy Stewart won the Best Actor Oscar for *The Philadelphia Story*. He was in a position to make big money and was dating some of the most beautiful women in Hollywood. Yet he chose to sacrifice the good life to enter military service. Jim would eventually transfer to the Air Corps and lead a thousand men into battle in the European theater, but the humble star began his new career as a buck private peeling potatoes. Stewart's salary was reduced from fifteen hundred to twenty-one dollars a month. Upon receiving his first paycheck, the star immediately sent a check for two dollars and ten cents to his agent.

Extra: James Stewart resisted strong pressure from MGM Studio executives when he chose to join the army. Many people during World War II, including General Dwight Eisenhower, felt that the best thing the Hollywood leading men could do for the often bored, waiting around servicemen was to entertain them by continuing to make movies. Another obstacle to Stewart's enlistment was that at 148 pounds, he was rejected for being too skinny. But the determined actor convinced the army recruiting offer to give him another weight test, which he somehow passed. He eventually became a brigadier general in the Air Force Reserves. In 1966, he flew as a non-duty observer on a bombing mission in Vietnam. Still a big star, Stewart insisted his action receive no publicity.

Extra: When I first became a tour guide, Jimmy Stewart was always one of the friendliest stars to see. He drove around in a green Volvo and always had a smile and wave for the guests on my bus. I was surprised to read stories of him ignoring people who said hello to him in light of his obvious good nature. It turned out that, like his famed George Bailey character in *It's a Wonderful Life* (1946), Stewart had partially lost his hearing, mostly due to flying very loud B-24 bomber planes in the service of his country.

The Reformed Cagney

James Cagney was a street kid from the tough part of Manhattan whose mother Carey raised to be decent and nice. As he became rich and famous playing gangsters, it was difficult for the churchgoing Irish actor to explain why he was often untrustworthy onscreen. A pleasant change came when Jim was cast as a crusading lawyer avenging the death of a friend, in the Warner Bros. 1935 crime drama 'G'Men. Cagney ignored suggestions from the producers to make his well-bred character into a mug that came out of the gutter. Jim welcomed co-star Barton MacLane, who played 'G'Men's heavy, delighted that the newcomer would be taking over the bad-guy roles at the studio. 'G'Men featured plenty of gun violence to satisfy audiences, and, as millions of dollars poured into the box office, a gleeful James Cagney called Carey and exclaimed, "Honest at last, Mom!"

Extra: James Cagney (1899-1986) based many of his gangster characters on the street hoods he knew growing up in the Hell's Kitchen neighborhood of New York City. Cagney had an outstanding memory, which he loved to show off. One time, while walking on Fifth Avenue with his wife Frances, the actor excitedly pointed at a man across the street. "Oh my God, it's my old school chum Nathan Skildalsky." He described the man's background in detail to his skeptical spouse. "Oh come on, you've never met that man in your life."

"Oh yeah? Go ask him."

Frances crossed the street, engaged the stranger in a quick conversation and came back smiling. "Well?"

"You were right, that's Nathan Skildalsky. But he has no idea who James Cagney is."

The All-Nighter

Cary Grant and Fred MacMurray were both millionaires many times over, raised lots of money for charitable causes and were known for being two of the biggest cheapskates in Hollywood. One possibly apocryphal tale involved the two film legends meeting for an expensive dinner at a popular Beverly Hills restaurant. Both men seemed to enjoy each other's company greatly and the conversation went well. When the last course was finished, the check was placed between them, but neither Cary nor Fred made any effort to pick it up. As they slowly ate their desserts, the trendy eatery began to clear out. The oblivious stars drank coffee and smoked cigarettes, while their small talk continued. Their waiter stayed on well after all his colleagues went home. After a time, he approached the two actors and politely inquired if they wished to see the breakfast menu.

Extra: Frederick Martin MacMurray (1908-1991) was the first person to admit that he was frugal. When director Billy Wilder (1906-2002) offered him the part of Jack Lemmon's rotten, womanizing boss in the 1960 drama *The Apartment*, the actor had objections. Wilder reminded MacMurray that sixteen years prior, he'd cast him as a heel in the very successful *Double Indemnity*. Fred, who at that time was playing fathers in Disney movies, wasn't worried about ruining his nice-guy image. What bothered MacMurray about *The Apartment* script was the scene where Fred tipped a shoeshine boy fifty cents. There was no way in real life he would give him more than a dime.

Extra: For many years, Fred MacMurray and John Wayne had the same business manager. In 1959, after a hundred or so movies, the Duke had made millions. Always a trusting soul, the lackadaisical cowboy star felt his fortune was in good hands. Then shockingly, Wayne found out he was getting bad management and had gone completely broke. Meanwhile, his fellow conservative Republican MacMurray aggressively called the financial advisor every week. Sensing trouble, the actor broke off the relationship with the moneyman and took charge of his own investments, buying up real estate in Southern California. When MacMurray died in 1991, his estimated fortune was five hundred million dollars.

The Male Stars of World War II

When prominent leading men like Clark Gable and Jimmy Stewart left Hollywood for the military in World War II, they were replaced by actors better suited to fight in the movies. Those left behind included former pre-med student Gregory Peck, who achieved stardom after injuring his back in a college play. John Wayne, still suffering from an old shoulder injury, became a noble soldier on the screen. Frank Sinatra's punctured ear drum kept him singing stateside. The dashing Errol Flynn was tight lipped about his heart condition as he parachuted into occupied Burma on a film set. Then there was Van Johnson, who was loved by teenage girls following a bad car accident, which left him with a metal plate in his head. One day while the war was still raging, an agent had a meeting with a mogul about a potential new discovery. "You'll love him! He's handsome, he's talented and best of all he has a double hernia."

Extra: The Hollywood film industry grew tremendously in the United States during World War II. Motion pictures were one of the few products that (unlike sugar, gasoline, meat, etc.) were not rationed. Lonely women on the home front flocked to the cinemas. With hotels in major cities booked, servicemen would often buy movie tickets just to have a place to sleep.

Extra: For Los Angeles, home to aerospace companies such as Hughes, Lockheed, Northrop and MacDonald Douglas, World War II was an economic boon. After World War I ended in 1918, the size of the United States armed forces was greatly reduced. By 1932 the country was left with the sixteenth-biggest military in the world, trailing behind Romania. America counted on the British Navy plus being surrounded by two oceans to provide for its defense. The fallout from Japan's attack on Pearl Harbor in 1941 led to a massive buildup of the armed forces with an emphasis on air power; during the war, LA became the number-two manufacturing city in the USA after Detroit.

Extra: Shortly after Japan attacked Hawaii, many Southern Californians thought they would be the next target. In Burbank, Jack Warner fretted about his studio being down the street from Lockheed. Aircraft companies and motion picture lots looked similar from above; what if Warner Bros. was bombed by mistake? The mogul ordered a giant sign painted on one of his sound stages, complete with a twenty-foot arrow that stated, "THIS WAY TO LOCKHEED!"

Extra: Actresses helped the war effort as well. Ginger Rogers (1911-1995) told of a letter she received from an American soldier who had been incarcerated in a Japanese POW camp. His guards had screened Rogers' romantic comedy *Tom, Dick and Harry* (1941) and were so enthralled by it that he was able to escape.

Extra: The happiest time in Clark Gable's life was when he married Carole Lombard in 1939. They got along famously despite her being a liberal Democrat and he a conservative Republican. Clark loved his third wife's antics, like the time she threw a party and served all the meals in bedpans. Carole joined Clark on hunting and fishing trips, and kept up with him in the boozing and swearing departments. Strangely, at times she seemed more threatened by Gable's male friends than the rumors of his philandering. But it bothered Carole to be in Fort Wayne, Indiana, selling War Bonds, while her husband was back home working with the well-endowed, twenty-one-year-old Lana Turner (1921-1995) in the romantic drama *Somewhere I'll Find You* (1942). (Turner had a reputation for being a buccaneer when it came to male conquests.) Not wanting to spend three days on the train trip back to LA, Lombard and her mother hitched a ride on a military transport plane. Gable was just leaving the studio with a borrowed nude wax dummy sporting a blonde wig; he couldn't wait for Carole to get home and see his new "girlfriend" lying next to him in their bed. Right as the actor got into the car, he was informed by a studio policeman that something had gone wrong with his Lombard's flight. A few hours later, the tragic news was confirmed; Carole's plane had crashed in the Table Rock Mountains near Las Vegas; there were no survivors. The grief-stricken Gable took care of the funeral, went off on a three-week bender, finished the movie, and then enlisted in the army despite a phone conversation with President Roosevelt who begged him to stay home and keep making pictures. Captain Clark Gable flew in five missions as an air gunner over Germany before being discharged in 1944. The movie star's greatest fear during combat had been that Hitler would capture him, put him in a zoo and charge admission.

Ronald Reagan's Talent

In the 1930s, liberal Democrat Ronald Reagan resisted friends' suggestions that he give up his movie career to run for office. Gosh, couldn't a guy just be interested in issues without going into politics? Didn't people think he had talent? As the years passed, his Hollywood opportunities slowed down, public service became more appealing and he became less defensive. In 1981, the seventy-year-old conservative was able to laugh about a meeting with a congressional Democrat. "We are going to cut taxes!" Reagan told him. "And do you know why? Because back when I was at Warner Bros. in the forties, I suddenly found myself in a ninety percent tax bracket. Ninety percent! Now nobody in this country should pay ninety percent. Well? What do you have to say about that?"

The congressman whistled. "Ninety Percent...My God, Mr. President...I never thought you were that good of an actor."

Extra: In 1937, twenty-six-year-old Chicago Cubs radio announcer Ronald Reagan (1911-2004) found his acting bug biting again. The former Dixon, Ill., native performed on stage in high school and college, but during the Great Depression, he had drifted into the sports world. In those days, the Cubs trained in California, and Reagan traveled with them to get away from the Iowa cold and pursue his movie-star dream. A friend arranged a screen test for him at

Warner Bros.; however, studio executives had mixed reactions. The kid was no matinee idol, but he did have more of an all-American look than some of the stars that toiled in the Warners' factory, such as James Cagney and Humphrey Bogart. The glasses and crew cut had to go. When questioned about his acting experience, Reagan told several lies to pad his resume. The casting director asked him to stick around an extra day for more tests. "No dice," he said feigning indifference when he was really desperate. "I'm on the train with the Cubs."

Ron left the studio thinking he had blown any chance to be signed by them. He was amazed that same day when Warners made an offer to put him under contract at two hundred dollars a week, and hastily agreed before they changed their minds.

Extra: In typical Hollywood fashion, the former radio announcer was cast as a radio announcer. It seemed like in every film he appeared in Ron's big line involved him grabbing a phone and shouting, "Get me the city desk! I have a story that will break this town wide open!"

Reagan, a former lifeguard who kept a written record of all the people he saved, preferred playing B movie heroes over less likable characters, such as the drunken socialite he portrayed alongside Bette Davis in *Dark Victory* (1939), even if it meant he made less money.

Extra: In the late 1930s, Ronald Reagan drove many in the mostly conservative community of Hollywood to distraction with his praise of President Franklin Roosevelt. One time he was yammering on about the necessity of New Deal policies when a friend suggested to Ronnie that he run for president. "You don't like my acting either?" Reagan wailed.

Extra: Young Ronnie quickly learned that Hollywood could be a cutthroat town. Reagan dated some of his leading ladies who fell out of love with him after their movie work was over. And there were tough directors like the Hungarian-born Michael Curtiz, with whom Ron made *Santa Fe Trail* (1940). During one scene, the novice actor watched in amazement as Curtiz kept telling an extra, playing a minister, to keep moving backwards until he fell of a scaffold, severely injuring his leg. The people on the set froze in shock until the angry director shouted, "Get me another minister!"

Extra: In order to better his career, the sports-loving Reagan suggested to his bosses that they buy the story of the legendary Notre Dame football coach

Knute Rockne (1888-1931). Ron wanted the role of the tragic halfback George Gipp (1895-1920). The executives at Warner Bros. only liked the first idea. "You're too small to play George Gipp!"

Reagan produced an old college photograph of himself in his football uniform and pads; he was actually bigger than Gipp, and he edged out John Wayne and William Holden for the part. But *Knute Rockne All American* (1940) was not all fun and games. One day Ronald showed up to shoot the scene where Gipp made a spectacular long run for a touchdown. He was told he was not needed. They would film something else instead. Ron proceeded to eat a huge, unhealthy breakfast. Then the actor was hastily informed they were going to film the run after all. After the third eighty-yard take, Reagan dashed far past the goal line where he privately lost his meal.

Extra: Ronald Reagan's star rose with his performance in the dramatic *King's Row* (1942) in which his character's legs were amputated, and he screamed out, "Where's the rest of me?"

The success of *King's Row* provided Reagan with the leverage to negotiate a solid movie-star salary. But his career momentum slowed when later in World War II, he became an army captain in the Officers' Reserve Corps of the Cavalry. His terrible vision kept him from seeing combat; Ronald was told that if he were sent overseas he would accidentally shoot an American general and probably miss him. Reagan appeared in propaganda films like the Irving Berlin musical *This is the Army* (1943) where he received only his military pay. Ronald overheard young girls who worked at his army base swooning over newer, younger stars, and when the war ended, Reagan felt insecure and past his prime.

Extra: Reagan met his first wife Jane Wyman (1917-2007) on the set of *Brother Rat* (1938). She wondered if his niceness was just the act of another Hollywood phony. Then Jane saw that Ron treated waiters with the same kindness and respect as he did studio big shots. The harmony in their relationship disappeared as her career eclipsed his. Ron once stated that the movie *Johnny Belinda* (1948), for which Wyman won an Academy Award for her portrayal of a deaf mute, should be a co-defendant in their divorce. There was gossip about Jane having a love affair with her *Belinda* co-star Lew Ayres (1908-1996). And her husband's constant harping about politics drove Wyman crazy; the couple's friends would note her yawning away in public when he got on his soapbox. Still Reagan was shocked in 1948 when the eight-year union came to an end; broken marriages were for other people. The stressed-out Midwesterner came down with a severe case of pneumonia that nearly killed him.

Extra: In *The Hagen Girl* (1947), forty-year-old Ronald Reagan reluctantly became the first man on screen to kiss twenty-year-old Shirley Temple. He argued that he should end up with Shirley's schoolteacher, but the director was Ron's age, had a teenage girlfriend and wanted to make a point. At the premiere, the audience shouted, "Oh no!" when Reagan and the former child star got into a clinch.

Ronald, who was in attendance, slunk down in his seat and sneaked out of the theater before the screening ended and he had to face the press.

Extra: As Reagan's acting career spiraled downward, his political activism increased. He became president of the Screen Actors Guild in 1947. As his personal philosophy drifted rightward, Ron was threatened by the Communists in Hollywood. There were rumors that his enemies might throw acid in his face or bomb his house. He began carrying a gun for protection. Studio bosses saw the fading star more as a labor negotiator than a viable commodity at the box office. Things went from bad to worse when Reagan broke his leg at a charity baseball game, which cost him two movie roles and a sizable amount of money. The frustrated union leader publicly stated he could do a better job at choosing his parts than Jack Warner; the movie boss responded by firing Reagan after fourteen years without a handshake.

Extra: Freelancing for Universal Studios, Ronald enjoyed making the comedy *Bedtime for Bonzo* (1951). He found his role as a professor who tries to teach human morals to a simian quite interesting. But the struggling leading man knew his amazing chimp co-star was stealing the show when the director started giving personal instructions to Bonzo instead of his trainer. Reagan's money problems became so severe in the early 1950s that he tried to eke out extra cash by selling autographed pictures by mail to his dwindling fan base.

Extra: In 1949, a not-very-ambitious twenty-eight-year-old actress named Nancy Davis sought out the SAG president. She told him she was having trouble finding work after being falsely accused of being part of a Communist organization. Reagan investigated her background, found nothing incriminating and helped clear her name. The grateful Davis agreed to go out with him. The now more-cautious divorcee Reagan took it slow with Nancy and played the field with several Hollywood starlets. When Ron woke up one morning with a girl whose name he couldn't remember, he decided it was time to marry again. Ronald and Nancy co-starred in the disappointing, big-budget *Hellcats of the*

Navy (1957) but the new Mrs. Reagan placed much more value on her marriage than her career.

Extra: Ronald Reagan became a rich man by moving into television. Thanks to the advice of his longtime agent and manager Lew Wasserman, he became the host of the popular anthology series *General Electric Theater* (1953-1962). But small-screen success did not translate into high demand at movie houses. In 1964, he made his final film, *The Killers*, in which Ronnie played a villain for the first time. Audiences were shocked and dismayed when the nice guy they thought they knew smacked his beautiful thirty-three-year-old co-star Angie Dickinson in the face. Faced with a future of playing heavies, the now financially secure Reagan chose to trade Hollywood for a political career.

Extra: Ronald Reagan denied that he was a great communicator. He felt that the content of his words was more important than his style. But he never forgot his movie roots. "Win one for the Gipper!" "May the force be with you!" "Go ahead! Make my day!" They all became his political catch phrases. And sometimes he could use film references as a source for witticisms. In 1966, the new California Governor Reagan colorfully described an encounter with a hippie: "He looked like Tarzan, acted like Jane, and smelled like Cheetah!"

Dinner at the Hepburns'

Katharine Hepburn always laughed whenever Spencer Tracy told the story of his visit to her family home in Connecticut. One night at dinner, the outspoken actress got into a lively argument with her father Doc Hepburn about how to best help the less fortunate. Tired of their moralizing, Tracy went out to the porch for a smoke. After a couple of puffs, he looked up to see a very lost, very timid-looking Mexican fisherman who had somehow stumbled onto the property. Tracy yelled inside, "Hey, better get another plate ready in there, the poor are here to collect."

Old man Hepburn came out on the porch. "Hey you, get the hell out of here! I'll sic the dogs on you."

After the frightened trespasser ran away, Thomas Hepburn told the startled Tracy, "Got to get the alarms fixed." Then the men went back inside, and the family resumed their discussion on aiding society's downtrodden.

Extra: In 1932, twenty-five-year-old Katharine Hepburn arrived in Los Angeles with a theater person's snobbish attitude toward Hollywood. In person, she impressed no one with her looks and style, and executive David O. Selznick worried about her "horse face." Hepburn finished her first film, *Bill of Divorcement* with John Barrymore and told him, "Thank God we're finished. I never want to act with you again."

The Great Man replied, "My dear girl, I wasn't aware that you had."

Extra: Many of Miss Hepburn's co-stars couldn't stand her. *Stage Door* (1936) called for Kate to make a speech, which would cause Ginger Rogers to cry. The director Gregory La Cava (1892-1952) knew that the conservative Rogers hated liberal Hepburn, so he called Ginger to the set alone. "Babe I got terrible news. Your mother called, your new house burned down." After filming Ginger's tearful reaction, La Cava confessed that he lied, the relieved actress was excused, and Hepburn was called to the set to recite her dialogue.

Extra: Hepburn struggled with the role of an heiress who chases after a stuffy paleontologist, played by Cary Grant, in the light-hearted comedy *Bringing Up Baby* (1938). Like many new movie actresses, she didn't at first understand the concept of playing comedy straight, letting the script dictate the humor. Her meddling and constant suggestions drove director Howard Hawks to distraction. "Katie, will you please shut up!"

Hepburn replied calmly," Howard, you shouldn't talk that way to me. I have many friends on the set. They might arrange for an accident to happen to you."

Hawks looked up into the rafters at one of the film techs manning a huge spotlight. "Hey Joey, who would rather drop that light on, me or Miss Hepburn?"

"Get out of the way, Mr. Hawks."

Extra: Because of a downturn in her career in the late 1930s, Hepburn was willing to play Scarlett O'Hara in *Gone with the Wind* for free. Producer David O. Selznick was mindful of what the reaction from the South would be to a New Englander taking the role. He cruelly rejected Kate by saying," I can't imagine Rhett Butler chasing after you for 10 years."

Extra: Hepburn turned her career around by playing a social-climbing heiress much like herself in the 1940 high-society comedy *The Philadelphia Story*. A year later, she met one of her idols, forty-one-year-old Spencer Tracy. She observed that she was to too tall for him; a director promised that the five-foot-ten Tracy would cut the three-inches-shorter Hepburn down to size. The two actors went on to co-star in nine pictures together; his everyman personality meshed perfectly onscreen with her sophisticated style. They started a relationship off camera, in spite of the Roman Catholic Tracy's marriage. Hepburn, who was often fiery and combative, became putty in her new lover's hands. She so admired his down-to-earth humor, talent and masculinity; the fact that he was guilt ridden and drank just made him more irresistible. When Tracy came home some nights in an inebriated stupor, Kate blamed it on the bad influence of his mostly Irish pals. In person, Spencer would sometimes verbally demean her in front of others, making statements like, "she's a bag of bones," "she's not hamming it up right now," "she talks like she has a broom up her #&*#".

When asked why he always got top billing over Hepburn, the Milwaukee-born actor explained it was a movie not a lifeboat. Kate, who stayed loyally attached to Spencer even after he once struck her in a drunken rage, later admitted that her love for Tracy was unrequited, rather than a star-crossed romance.

Extra: The four-time Oscar winner Hepburn was a fearless and generous performer. She contacted a permanent eye infection after falling backwards into the garbage-filled Venice canals five times to please her *Summertime* (1950) director David Lean. During the making of the 1949 legal comedy, *Adam's Rib*, Kate gave up close-up shots to her co-star Judy Holiday, which helped advance the latter actress' career. Katharine agreed to swim in a river inhabited with crocodiles while filming *The African Queen* in 1951. Then thirty years later, the seventy-four-year-old Kate dove in the freezing cold of Squam Lake in Laconia, New Hampshire, without a wet suit, when she appeared in the sentimental drama *On Golden Pond*. Hepburn was admired by women for her strong, independent stances, but her first marriage ended in divorce, and her long-time lover, Spencer Tracy, never divorced his wife Louise. After Tracy died in 1967, Kate disappointed feminists by saying she did not believe a woman could have it all, meaning both a successful career and a relationship.

Extra: Hepburn got along famously with her philosophical opposite John Wayne when they teamed up to take on a bunch of killers in the 1975 western *Rooster Cogburn*. Like many liberals, Hepburn, who had been accused of being a Joseph Stalin lover in the 1940s, saw the Duke as a right-wing reactionary who stood against everything she believed in. But he treated Kate in such a respectful, charming way, never feeling the need to put her down like Spencer Tracy had. She was shocked and thrilled when, in front of the press, Wayne grabbed her around the waist and kissed her on the lips. He called Hepburn, "a hell of a woman" and Kate stated that making the movie with the conservative icon was a wonderful experience.

Marlon Brando, Identify Yourself

In 1951, twenty-seven-year-old Marlon Brando had to grin when the checkout girl at Schwab's Pharmacy in Hollywood recognized him and started screaming in excitement. Just three years earlier, Brando had lived among the beggars scrounging for food on Paris's left bank. His magnetic performance as the brutal Stanley Kowalski in *A Streetcar Named Desire* had made him a star. Marlon wasn't going to let any studio trot him out like a show dog at one of those phony Hollywood premieres, but if wearing a torn t-shirt meant he could make a few mill, buy an island someplace and retire in a few years that was cool. This girl seemed like a nice kid. Brando admitted he was who she thought he was and enjoyed watching her face light up as he signed an autograph. Then the actor put his items on the counter for her to ring up.

"Can I write a check?" Marlon asked.

"Sure. Do you have an ID?"

Extra: In Marlon Brando's first movie, *The Men* (1950), he played a paralyzed soldier. The actor stayed at a veterans' hospital for several weeks while confining himself to a wheelchair and became very good friends with some real paraplegics. One day the new buddies went out for a beer. As the men sat in their wheelchairs drinking and conversing, they were approached by a nun. "Gentlemen, I just want you to keep the power of positive faith. If you pray and believe you can walk, some day you will get out of those chairs."

Brando said, "OK, I'll try it."

He shut his eyes. "I believe, I pray...OH MY GOD, IT'S A MIRACLE! I'M CURED!"

He got up and ran off. The poor nun fainted but the men had a very therapeutic laugh.

Joan Crawford's True Love

Joan Crawford's love affair with her fans superseded any of her personal relationships. Unlike most stars, Crawford preferred to answer all of her mail. In her later years, she would personally fix breakfast for admiring correspondents who were invited to stay over at her house. Once, in the thirties at the height of her fame, Joan was staying in New York when she received a

"Dear Jane" letter from Clark Gable. Broken-hearted, she wandered through the streets followed at a discreet distance by her entourage. Crawford shocked them by wandering into Grand Central Station. Someone shouted her name, which turned the depot into a mob scene. It took her beleaguered staff an hour to get their boss out of harm's way and back to her hotel suite. The scratched and bruised actress leaned back against the door in her torn dress, huffing and puffing. "Oh...oh my...let's do that again!"

Public Grapefruit Eater

A violent act in the classic 1931 gangster film *The Public Enemy* became James Cagney's signature onscreen moment. One scene called for him to get rough with co-star Mae Clark. She pulled him aside right before the take and said loud enough for other people on the set to hear, "Go easy on me, Jimmy. I have a cold."

Director William Wellman heard the conversation and called him over. "Listen, Jimmy, this scene could make or break you. The audience has to believe you mean it."

When the cameras rolled, Cagney shocked the crew by picking up a grapefruit and shoving it hard into Mae's face, knocking her off her chair. Clark's worried request had been a joke contrived by the two leads who both laughed hard after Wellman yelled, "Cut!"

To the actors' surprise, the shot remained in the film. Despite women's groups throughout the USA protesting the brutal treatment of Clark onscreen, James Cagney became a big star and for many months could not go to a restaurant without the other patrons sending him a complimentary grapefruit.

Call Me Al

Thirty-two-year-old Al Pacino found it difficult to adjust to fame after his Oscar-nominated performance as rising mafia leader Michael Corleone, in the 1972 classic *The Godfather*. How odd to be in this position after months of staying up till five in the morning to brood about the role. The five-foot-seven actor had inspired no confidence on the Paramount lot by refusing to make eye contact in meetings. Al had isolated himself, choosing not to join his fun-loving castmates when they rolled down their limousine windows and mooned each other while being driven to locations. The same executives who had wanted to fire Pacino now were wooing him to be in the sequel. So what do you do when you're a superstar? Al bought a BMW, which he felt awkward driving, and began using disguises out in public. When the car was stolen and his false beard fell off at a baseball game, Pacino laughed about his new status and decided to just be Al.

Extra: Al Pacino could have taken a lesson in balancing fame and privacy from a past icon. One time in New York, an unnoticed Marilyn Monroe was walking down Madison Avenue accompanied by Eli Wallach. "My God, don't these people know who you are?" Wallach asked her.

Marilyn, whose application of make-up took nearly as long as Boris Karloff's Frankenstein Monster, grinned at him. "I'm only recognized when I want to be. Watch this."

Monroe began to swing her hips as she walked in a way that was familiar to moviegoers and was eventually mobbed by adoring fans.

Extra: Just because you're recognized once doesn't mean you will continue to be. After losing his driving privileges because of drunkenness, actor Sean Penn was forced to ride the city bus. One day another passenger came up to him. "Hey, you look like Sean Penn. But I know he wouldn't be riding a bus."

Penn replied, "How do you know? Do you know Sean Penn?"

"Yeah, I worked on a film he starred in."

"Oh yeah? Well, what do you think of him?"

"Oh God, he was a total $%#%!"

Our Spencer Tracy

MGM headman Louis B. Mayer was reluctant to add the heavy-drinking Spencer Tracy to their roster of stars in 1935. It took several well-placed bribes for the studio publicists to keep the Milwaukee-born actor's antics out of the papers. Several times while fulfilling his contract, Spencer was involved in barroom brawls, destroyed hotel rooms and movie sets, and was taken away in straitjackets. Some of Tracy's co-stars looked forward to working with him because they knew he would go off on a binge and they would have a few weeks off with pay. All the bad behavior was overshadowed by his wonderful performances in films like *Fury*, *Captains Courageous*, *Boy's Town*, *Adam's Rib* and many others. Joan Crawford, who played Tracy's love interest in the 1937 romantic drama *Mannequin*, once went to Mayer and complained that Spencer was a no-good blankety-blank. Mayer swelled with pride and said, "Yes, but he is *our* no good blankety-blank."

Gable's Potential

Clueless about thirty-year-old Clark Gable's potential, MGM Studios tested him as Tarzan. The former oil rigger had walked across the lot in a loincloth, turning red with humiliation when secretaries heckled him with whistles and catcalls. Shortly after his ape-man debacle, Gable got a small role as Norma Shearer's gangster boyfriend in the 1931 crime drama *A Free Soul,* also starring Lionel Barrymore. Norma's husband, studio vice president Irving Thalberg, saw the completed film and fumed. That no good Barrymore had stolen the picture from his wife! The producer decided to get Norma more sympathy by adding an extra sequence where the brutish Gable slapped her around. MGM received an unexpected avalanche of fan mail for Clark; women loved him and men wanted to be like him. His instant rise to superstardom amazed Hollywood executives who thought Gable was a big bat-eared galoot.

Extra: With limited media scrutiny, it was easier for studio publicity people to create mysterious and alluring images for their stars. During the Golden Age of Hollywood (approximately 1930-1945), contract players were required to pose for beautiful, touched-up still photos when they weren't making motion pictures. At MGM it was decided that Clark Gable should be presented dressed in hunting and fishing clothes. Not really much of an outdoorsman prior to his working in films, Gable found he liked being a sportsman in real life. Eventually, the actor's make-believe personality became indistinguishable from his real one.

The Stuff Dreams Are Made Of

Humphrey Bogart's ability to make light of his problems helped him deal with threats both on and off the screen. The forty-one-year-old actor had tired of gangster roles; he was always getting shot at the end of movies. Bogart jumped at the chance to play hard-boiled private eye Sam Spade in the 1941 crime drama *The Maltese Falcon.* Humphrey's sudden opportunity for success angered his jealous third wife Mayo; at home one night, the unemployed actress tried to stab him in the back with a knife. Bogie laughed off questions about his marriage, claiming that both he and his spouse loved a good fight. He brought the same attitude to his performance as Sam Spade. Whether facing killer thugs, ill-tempered policemen or a dangerous lover trying to frame someone else for her crimes, the onscreen tough guy met each hazard with sardonic humor. Audiences responded favorably; Humphrey Bogart emerged from the completed *Falcon* a major star.

Gable Versus Tracy

Even though he received top billing and always got the girl, Clark Gable was uneasy working with his friend and rival Spencer Tracy. Insiders who observed them together thought Tracy secretly wanted to be more of a he-man, while Gable desired the great respect that Spencer got for his acting. In their 1938 buddy movie *Test Pilot*, Gable's love interest was Tracy's real life ex Myrna Loy. In one scene where Clark was trying to sweet talk her in a convertible, Tracy drew the audience's attention by chewing gum in the back seat. "The King of Hollywood", who was used to having his way with his leading ladies, was further humiliated when he tried to kiss Loy off camera and she shoved Clark into some rose bushes. The last straw was when Tracy had his big death sequence near the end of the film. Spencer stretched it out till Gable came out of character, shook his co-star and said, "Damn you, Spence, die already!"

The Date

For a celebrity, the desire for privacy is always in conflict with the need they have for attention. One night in Paris in 1958, twenty-four-year-old Sophia Loren wanted to go out for a romantic dinner with Cary Grant. The jaded Briton, who was thirty years her senior, fussed and complained about being recognized and insisted on leaving the hotel with an elaborate disguise that made him look like the Invisible Man. As they walked the sidewalks of Paris, Sophia was asked for autographs, which she joyfully signed. As she posed for pictures, hugged children and amiably chatted with fans, the ignored Grant started to become jealous; he began subtly removing his heavy articles of clothing. Down came his hat, off came his dark glasses, his coat was lowered and his scarf removed, and soon Cary was standing under neon lights to get noticed.

Extra: Cary Grant fell in love with his leading lady Sophia Loren while making *The Pride and the Passion* (1957); their co-star Frank Sinatra got extremely jealous. Trying to make friends, Loren explained to Sinatra in Italian that she was worried about her English-speaking skills for upcoming publicity interviews in the States. The mischievous singer advised her to use foul language in every sentence, which according to Frank was a way of showing endearment to Americans. When Sophia conducted her first obscenity-filled press conference, the shocked reporters asked her where she learned to speak like that. After the actress revealed the culprit, there were a few good belly laughs, and Loren was advised to make Cary Grant her new language teacher.

King Yul

Forty-one-year-old Yul Brynner seemed a perfect fit to portray the ruler of Siam in the 1956 movie *The King and I*. The five-foot-nine bald actor threw his weight around on the set and became a new symbol of screen virility. Teenage boys were suspended from high schools for imitating Brynner's hairless look. The heavy-smoking Yul, who had to suck oxygen after his dance scenes, claimed he was one of the very few real men left in Hollywood. Not everyone appreciated his efforts; the real-life ruler Brynner played had lived a humble, hand-to-mouth existence as a monk for twenty-seven years and instituted a great many reforms for his people. In Thailand, the musical was considered disrespectful and was permanently banned. Undaunted, Brynner won the Best Actor Oscar for *King* and continued to act like a monarch. The producer of Yul's next film was required to pay for a huge, full-length mirror, which was placed directly over the demanding star's hotel room bed.

Extra: When a movie star like Yul Brynner gets a big salary, they often do not see it directly; it goes to their business manager to play around with. The actors and their agents sometimes demand perks (privileges that keep leading men and ladies feeling like royalty). The producers often wrongly figure that the extra gifts may stop prima donna-like behavior on the set. On the other hand, the talent, sometimes bitter about years of being rejected at auditions, can get revenge by having their agents ask for eye-popping extra benefits in addition to their multi-million-dollar contracts. One example was when thirty-three-year-old Jim Carrey got the makers of the 1995 comedy *Ace Ventura: When Nature Calls* to pay a personal chef to prepare meals for the funny man's pet iguana (Carrey ponied up half the food costs). Then there was thirty-nine-year-old Geena Davis who, on the set of the 1995 adventure *Cutthroat Island,* was provided with four masseuses at her beck and call (one body expert was on hand just to rub the leading lady's throat). Davis may have been topped two years later by the star of the military drama *G.I. Jane*. In addition to her ten-million-dollar salary, thirty-five-year-old Demi Moore got free use of two private planes, one for herself and her entourage, the other for their luggage.

Extra: Winnebago trailers were introduced to the movie business as a way to move actors to and from different locations. Agents realized they could make their clients happy by asking for bigger vehicles with more amenities. Some of the "Winnies" included features such as built-in gyms and Jacuzzis. A few stars were caught on film sets using tape measures outside their trailers. They needed to make sure that their temporary mobile homes were at least as long as those of their castmates.

The Untalented Inventor

In 1940, twenty-six-year-old screen siren Hedy Lamarr was sitting at a piano when she had an idea to give the Allied forces an edge during World War II. The very anti-Nazi Viennese beauty noted that radio signals were usually sent over one frequency and thus easy to intercept. What if like different piano keys adding up to make music you could send messages over different wavelengths continuously? Hedy patented the idea but did not have the technological aptitude to pursue it; the concept never paid off for her. Meanwhile, Lamarr slogged along in poorly reviewed movies including the successful but campy *Sampson and Delilah* in 1949. After her acting career ended, Hedy received welfare checks and was twice accused of shoplifting. When she died in 2000, it was generally agreed that Lamarr lacked talent. Hedy was just another pretty face who once came up with a notion that made it possible for the rest of us to use cell phones.

The Redheaded Bombshell

One night in 1932, twenty-one-year-old Jean Harlow wore a red wig and stood unnoticed outside a movie house. That evening she wanted to escape from her blonde-bombshell image. Jean had recently lost her husband, producer Paul Bern. It had been ruled a suicide but there were ugly rumors that a jealous woman from his past had killed him. The scandal had not hurt Jean's popularity; peroxide sales had increased throughout the country as American women tried to imitate her platinum look. Would not they be surprised to know she would have traded the movie-star limelight to be a wife and mother? That night there would be no reminders of Harlow's so-called glamorous life; she would hook up with somebody normal. When the show ended, the disguised actress approached a handsome patron who came out of the theater. Hours later in his apartment, he suggested that she get a job doubling for Jean Harlow.

Marilyn's Longing

Marilyn Monroe longed for the coming of X-rated films. The blonde actress, who passed on in 1962, five years before Hollywood began labeling their adult content with letters, pointed out that more flesh was needed in pictures to lure people away from their television sets. In Monroe's time, every feature was required to get a purity seal from the Production Code Office before it was released in the theaters. Marilyn's first actual meeting with a censor was on the set of the 1960 comedy *Let's Make Love*. The content controller was concerned about a scene that involved her wriggling and rolling on her bed. Very pleasantly, the thirty-four-year-old icon asked what the problem was. The watchdog explained that when Monroe moved around in a horizontal position, it suggested she was about to have sex. Marilyn look surprised, then smiled. "Oh, is that all. But I can do the same in a vertical position."

She won the argument and the scene remained in the movie.

If I Were a Rich Man

Thirty-eight-year-old Burt Reynolds ignored warnings and socialized with convicts when he made the 1974 football drama *The Longest Yard*. Officials at the Georgia State Penitentiary, where filming took place, worried that the prisoners could decide to kidnap the actor and demand their releases, or worse. But Reynolds was determined to do accurate research for the movie about cons playing against their guards. Besides, maybe he could be a good influence. Burt posed for pictures, chatted amiably with the inmates and had no problems. The only unsettling incident was when one of the criminals told the well-meaning star that meeting him was inspirational. "That's great to hear," said Burt.

The thief said he needed Burt's address. Why was that? Well, he was serving time for robbing poor people. The celebrity encounter made him realize how much better his life would be if he could steal from a rich man.

Rising Lake

Rising star Veronica Lake continued her pattern of infuriating co-workers at Paramount Studios on the set of the 1941 film *Sullivan's Travels*. The blonde actress, famed for her "peekaboo" hairstyle that covered her face, was constantly late and did not bother to learn her lines. Her resentful leading man Joel McCrea was forced to do tons of retakes in their scenes together. The twenty-two-year-old also lied to writer/director Preston Sturges about not being pregnant; he had to restrain himself from hitting Veronica when she confessed the truth. A tramp's outfit and careful camera angles hid her growing belly. The completed movie about a filmmaker who lives like a hobo was a challenge for the Paramount marketing people; they decided to make Lake the main selling point. Unaware of her antics, cinemagoers were once again drawn to Veronica's sexy screen presence and she was praised for her fine performance.

Extra: During World War II, Veronica Lake's (1922-1973) immense popularity was partly due to her blonde hair covering her right eye. Her "peekaboo" style was imitated by women throughout the country. Government officials became concerned about the Veronica Lake look-alikes who worked in the munitions factories. What if their long locks got stuck in the machinery? The bureaucrats convinced the patriotic leading lady to cut her hair in front of newsreel cameras in 1943. Lake's new look plus some very weak roles led to a career decline. Veronica had developed a reputation for being unkind to her co-workers in Hollywood, many of whom were not sad when the no-longer-in-demand actress left town and disappeared from public view for several years. In 1960, at a New York hotel bar, a reporter ordered a drink and was shocked when he recognized his ex-movie-star server.

Beverly Hills Honeymooners

Michael Caine had a hard time convincing his beautiful Indian love Shakira he was not the lazy roustabout he played in the 1966 movie *Alfie*. After several months of courtship, Shakira found out she was pregnant; Michael assured her that, unlike his screen character, he definitely wanted to get married. With a film to make in Los Angeles, the Caines' honeymoon was spent at the Beverly Wilshire, the hotel that would later become world famous when it was used in the 1990 comedy *Pretty Woman*. In the couple's honor, the Wilshire's employees made up their own version of an Indian honeymoon suite. It came complete with a bed that was suspended from the ceiling with bells underneath so the neighbors could hear the joy of the happy newlyweds, even though there was nothing like it in India. The staff's efforts were wasted when the jet-lagged Caine ordered four hamburgers and stuffed the buns in the bells so he and his new bride could get some sleep.

Mature Was not Yellow

Those who got to know movie hunk Victor Mature realized he was a total phony. The Kentucky-born leading man, who once claimed his real profession was being a golfer, took acting far more seriously than he let on. Victor refused to do simple stunts in his films and would agree with anybody who would call him yellow. In 1942, the twenty-nine-year-old Mature had traded stardom for a fourteen-month stint in the Coast Guard. He had risked his life to spot enemy ships in the North Atlantic until he was honorably discharged. Mature spread rumors on movie sets that he was a selfish heel; his co-workers thought he was great and would angrily wonder who was saying bad things about him. And Victor was moved to tears when people sent him money after he publicly stated his three divorces left him broke. He sent it all back and informed his fans that in the late 1940s, he had bought a TV shop that sold over a million units.

The Unusual Pirate

Johnny Depp knew his bosses would be upset with his interpretation of Captain Jack Sparrow in the 2003 family film *Pirates of the Caribbean*. Prior to the start of production, Depp asked his startled dentist for four gold caps; the fictitious sea thief explained he only wanted two and needed something to bargain with. The forty-year-old actor, who had never been a huge draw at the box office, based his eccentric swashbuckler on rocker Keith Richards and cartoon skunk Pepe Le Pew. The Disney executives were aghast; who ever heard of a limp-wristed buccaneer that wore mascara? They demanded Johnny get rid of half of his metallic teeth and briefly considered replacing him. Depp calmly stood his ground and the completed *Pirates* was a smash hit with Johnny being nominated for an Oscar. Two years later, Depp took on another beloved children's character: the candy maker Willy Wonka in *Charlie and the Chocolate Factory*. Johnny wore oversized dentures, spoke with a deliberately creepy voice and once again expected admonishments from the men who hired him. Still not used to being a bankable movie star, Depp was a little unsettled when the suits at Warner Bros. smiled and approved.

Extra: The traditional definition of a pirate is anyone who plunders on the high seas. There were different types of pirates in the Caribbean. Privateers such as Henry Morgan (1635-1688) terrorized the Spanish Main with the blessings of England. The privateers were not paid by their bosses; instead, they took a percentage of the spoils off the ships that they captured. Then there were the buccaneers, mainly former French sailors who jumped ship, settled in the Caribbean and barbecued boar and oxen. The Spanish Crown saw the buccaneers as vagrants and started killing them. Many on-the-run buccaneers became privateers. Another type of ocean thief was the marooners, or low-paid deserters of the brutally run Spanish Navy. Leaving shipmates on small islands became known as marooning, which was the fate of Alexander Selkirk (1676-

1721) who became the inspiration for the English writer Daniel Defoe's (1659-1731) novel *Robinson Crusoe* (1719).

Extra: In 1994, thirty-one-year-old Johnny Depp was arrested for tearing up his expensive suite at the Mark Hotel in New York. He was moved to three different precincts due to policewomen mobbing him at each location. Depp made light of the incident claiming a big rat had been in his room, the actor chased it around with a baseball bat and it had jumped out the window (in other versions the intruder was a dachshund or an armadillo). The most amazing thing about the story was that the man who called the cops on Johnny that night was fifty-year-old Roger Daltrey, the lead singer of the legendary rock and roll band The Who. A famous hotel room wrecker in his own right, Roger's biggest complaint was that Depp's wave of destruction took "too bloody long." "The Who could have done the job in one minute flat."

Natalie Wood Lampooned

In 1966, Natalie Wood stunned the editors of the *Harvard Lampoon* by showing up on campus and accepting their award for the worst actress of the year. Did the twenty-eight-year-old Russian beauty realize she was being insulted? The undergraduates saw no sign of the sad and lonely woman who desperately wanted to be loved. Clearly having fun, Wood batted her eyelashes and said it would be impolite to turn down an award. The year before she had been completely miserable making the slapstick comedy *The Great Race*, receiving an honor like this was much more in line with her sense of humor. Charmed by her good sportsmanship, the undergraduates burst into applause. Nominated three times, Natalie would never take home an Oscar. But on that day she was a winner in Cambridge; several male students hoisted her up on their shoulders and paraded her around the University in triumph.

Errol's Surprise

One night in the late 1930s, Errol Flynn was introduced to a very attractive forty-something woman and her beautiful nineteen-year-old daughter. Mom left Flynn's residence to run an errand and the lecherous star quickly maneuvered the teenager onto the couch. She giggled and slapped his hand as he tried to undress her. Slowly, Errol's seductive words took effect and the college-age girl started to breathe heavily. Flynn had just dropped his trousers when the mother returned. "Mr. Flynn, what are you doing?"

Errol turned red, lost his balance and fell to the floor. Mother angrily told her kid to go outside and wait in the car. Alone with the handsome actor, she demanded his explanation. "I lost my head," he mumbled.

Her glare turned into a sly smile. "I sent her away because I want you for myself!"

It turned out both women were ladies of the evening that Errol's roommate actor David Niven had hired as a practical joke.

Verbal Shoot Out at Harvard Square

At high noon on a cold November day in 1974, sixty-seven-year-old John Wayne faced off with the staff of the *Harvard Lampoon* on the famous campus in Cambridge, Massachusetts. The students had issued their challenge by calling the beloved American icon a fraud. Wayne, who had his new movie *McQ* to promote, responded by saying he would be happy to show his film in the pseudo-intellectual swamps of Harvard Square. After the screening, without writers, the former USC footballer delivered a classic performance. When one smart young man asked where he got his phony toupee, Wayne insisted the hair was real. It was not his, but it was real. The appreciative underclassmen loved him and after the Q and A session, they all sat down to dinner. Later Wayne, who was suffering greatly from both gout and the after effects of lung cancer (sadly the Duke only had five years to live), said that day at Harvard was the best time he ever had.

Mickey, Come Hither

Fifteen-year-old Mickey Rooney beat out several actors and actresses to win the role of Puck the fairy in the 1935 version of Shakespeare's *A Midsummer Night's Dream*. Performing with very little clothing on in a lush forest-like set, Rooney amused his co-stars during rehearsals. One time the scantily clad sprite was supposed to leap out of a tree prompted by the cue "My gentle Puck, come hither." The line was repeated three times before Mickey responded that he couldn't come hither because his jock strap was stuck on a branch. It was less funny when the irresponsible teenager broke his femur bone while snow tobogganing, causing his boss Jack Warner to say, "First I'll kill you, and then I'll break your other leg."

Eventually, Mickey finished the picture, his enthusiastic performance was highly praised and his personal stock rose in Hollywood. Later, Rooney claimed he never understood any of the Shakespeare dialogue that he had to recite.

Bad News Burt

Actor Burt Lancaster sometimes revealed a more lovable side underneath his curmudgeonly exterior. Starting with his movie debut at age thirty-three in the 1946 drama *The Killers*, the former circus acrobat from Harlem was not shy about expressing his opinions. "The kid made one movie and thought he knew it all," a producer said about him.

Lancaster's co-workers, who sometimes were intimidated by the physically imposing, muscular leading man, often wondered why he had to question everything: "To get to the truth of the character," he replied.

Burt pointed out that when he started pictures, his complaints would drive people crazy, but by the time the show finished, the crew would be fond of him. Lancaster demonstrated similar traits around his son Bill, who inherited none of his father's athleticism and was sadly diagnosed with polio at age nine. Twenty years later, the younger Lancaster related his youthful experiences with his father in a screenplay, transferring their relationship onto a Little League baseball diamond. It became the 1976 comedy hit *The Bad News Bears*, about a team of misfit kids coached by a manager modeled after Bill's grumpy dad.

The Reluctant Matinee Idol

Thirty-two-year-old Laurence Olivier thought that director William Wyler was being a bully on the set of the 1939 drama *Wuthering Heights*. The great stage actor felt that all movie work was beneath him. How could anyone expect him to be convincing when his romantic interest was Merle Oberon. She was an untalented amateur; how dare she complain that he spat on her during love scenes. And now this fool of a director wanted another take. "Listen, Willie, I played it smiling, I played it with a smirk, you had me facing the camera, I scratched my head, I hopped up and down, what do you want?"

"I want you to stop hamming it up and do it better."

Olivier sniffed, "I suppose this little medium can't take great acting."

The finished picture got great reviews and the surprised Olivier became a matinee idol. Years later, he admitted he behaved like a pompous fool and that Wyler helped him to learn to love the cinema.

Extra: During the long, arduous filming of *Gone with the Wind* in 1939, Vivien Leigh rarely got to see her soon-to-be husband Laurence Olivier (1907-1989). It was partly because the movie's producer, David O. Selznick, felt that gossip about the unhitched couple would hurt the Civil War drama at the box office. One night during production, O. Selznick relented and allowed Olivier, who was performing on Broadway, to come visit his lover in Los Angeles for twenty-four hours. In between their embraces, Vivien poured her heart out. She hated Hollywood. The isolated fools who lived there had no idea what Hitler was planning in Europe and didn't care. And movie work was so beneath stage actors like themselves. But Olivier surprised her, telling Vivian after being in *Wuthering Heights,* Laurence now felt that the hammy antics he'd used while performing in the theater seemed phony and artificial to him compared to cinema acting.

Gosling's Prescription

After taking on three heavy roles, twenty-three-year-old actor Ryan Gosling felt sick. A former member of TV's *The All New Mickey Mouse Club* alongside singers Britney Spears, Christina Aguilera and Justin Timberlake, Gosling had earned respect playing a Jewish-born Neo-Nazi in the 2001 drama *The Believer.* He had followed up the next year as a crazed killer tormenting Sandra Bullock in *Murder by Numbers.* Off camera, he and Bullock dated; the homicide scenes made him vomit. Ryan then stabbed an autistic boy and ended up in juvenile prison in 2003's *The United States of Leland.*

Shortly after completing the last film, Gosling went to see his physician. The budding star, who was uncertain if being in movies could be considered a real job, shared his recent professional experiences. The doctor listened patiently for a few minutes, then pulled out his prescription pad and wrote down, "You should try acting in a light comedy."

The Frugal Wealthy Life

Cary Grant never let his immense wealth get in the way of his frugal lifestyle. The thirty-three-year-old Grant had become a major star in 1937 with the comedy hits *Topper* and *The Awful Truth.* Not under contract to any studio, the free-agent performer was able to charge high fees plus healthy percentages for his film work. Despite his four divorces, the money kept pouring in; late in his career, Cary was rumored to be richer than NATO. But he never forgot his poor upbringing in Bristol, England, and was determined to protect his earnings at all costs. Tongues wagged in Hollywood when in the late 1930s, Cary moved into a house with his good friend, western star Randolph Scott. Why did two rich and famous young men need to live together? Big savings, said Grant. Their friend, actress Carole Lombard, summed it up: Randy writes out the checks for the bills and if Cary can cheat somebody out of a stamp, he sends them.

Extra: One time Cary Grant was having breakfast at the Beverly Hilton Hotel when he noticed that his bread dish had three half muffins. The very rich but frugal actor called his server over for an explanation. He had ordered muffins and wondered why he had only been served a muffin and a half. When neither the waiter nor the manager provided a sufficient answer, Cary had a phone brought to his table and made several calls until he tracked down the hotel's owner, Conrad Hilton (1887-1979). The top man, who was vacationing in Istanbul, explained that most customers left the fourth half uneaten so the hotel stopped serving them. When the British star accused Hilton of false advertising, the Baron ordered that beginning with Grant, the fourth half would be served from then on. The now satisfied star finished his meal and paid his bill, complete with one hundred dollars in phone charges.

Joan Crawford's Last Day

Tough-as-nails Joan Crawford wanted no pity in 1977, the last year of her life. In her heyday, Joan saw other actresses as competitors; there had been so many feuds with people like Betty Davis and Marilyn Monroe; now she enjoyed the company of other women including her housekeeper and a longtime fan who shared her New York apartment.

Why not? Her four husbands spent her money and left her broke! Crawford made no apologies for the controversial way she had disciplined her children; she gave a job to a troubled teenage son of a friend and he took it to heart when Joan told him to stop feeling sorry for himself. Why did young people these days feel the need to see an analyst all the time instead of talking to a good friend? After suffering in quiet pain due to pancreatic cancer, the former big-screen beauty succumbed at the age of seventy-two; but not until she fixed breakfast for and cleaned up after her roommates.

Robert Mitchum Needed a Little Push

In 1936, Julie Mitchum saw hidden talent beneath the crusty demeanor of her nineteen-year-old younger brother Robert. Bob had sneered at her idea that he should become an actor; she had dragged him to the local theater guild. Before he came to live with her in California, he'd been a hobo, riding railway cars and working on a chain gang. His relaxed attitude, combined with his life experiences and good looks, made her sure he'd be a natural. He would always be a vagabond; even after he became a rich and famous movie star, Robert would prefer to stay in flea bag motels and dress like a tramp. But right now he needed a push to get going. Julie was sitting behind him when a casting director asked for a volunteer to play a part. Her brother yelled out, "Ah," stood up, went onto the stage and started the career that would make Robert Mitchum a Hollywood icon.

Who could say how his life would have turned out if his sister had not goosed him?

The Great Swashbuckler?

Director Michael Curtiz worried that Errol Flynn was not giving it his all during the climactic sword fight in the 1935 adventure film *Captain Blood*. The Hungarian filmmaker suspected that the first-time leading man Flynn was sympathetic to the extras and was deliberately blowing his lines so they could get paid overtime. Or perhaps he was tentative because his dueling partner Basil Rathbone had accidentally gashed Errol's face. Right before they re-shot, Curtiz whispered new instructions to Rathbone. With a sneer, the famed movie villain announced in front of the company that he was getting paid way more money than the twenty-six-year-old Flynn. The angry Tasmanian responded with ferocity and out-fenced his enemy on camera. When the scene finished, the smiling Flynn received applause from the coworkers that he had just hit in the pocketbook, and was on his way to becoming the screen's greatest swashbuckler.

Extra: Swashbuckler was a sixteenth-century term that referred to a fighting style where men used a side sword teamed with a buckler, or small shield, to protect the sword hand. The sword made a great swash or noise on the buckler. Over time, swashbuckler came to mean a clever, boastful, honorable and usually fictitious swordsman.

Mr. Laker

Beginning in 1969, Jack Nicholson became known as the Los Angeles Lakers' most famous fan. For the New Jersey-born actor, watching basketball evolved into a passion equal to romance and making movies. Unlike many front-running celebrities, Jack loyally showed up to cheer even when LA had a losing record. The renowned spectator occasionally let his emotions get the best of him. Once, Jack was thrown out of the arena for running out on the floor to argue with an official. During a highly contested championship game in Boston, the outnumbered Nicholson mooned the home crowd. But mostly Jack got along fine with everyone in the vicinity of his courtside seats. Laker opponents found it could hurt their cause to chat with the star season-ticket holder. A skilled mimic, the Oscar winner sometimes tricked referees into believing that obscenities were being hurled at them from the enemy team's bench.

Extra: For many years, visitors to Jack Nicholson's mansion on Mulholland Drive in Los Angeles noticed an oddity: a vase near his front door that contained ripped up one-hundred-dollar bills. Jack, who reportedly made a record-breaking sixty million dollars when he played the Joker in *Batman* (1989), explained it was a reminder that fame and riches were fleeting and could all be lost.

Cary's Health and Fitness Guide

Cary Grant's emphasis on health and fitness helped to keep him viable as a leading man. Cinemagoers flocked to see the British-born actor paired up romantically with beauties such as Grace Kelly, Sophia Loren and Audrey Hepburn, all more than twenty years his junior. In the 1959 thriller *North by Northwest*, actress Jessie Royce Landis played the fifty-five-year-old Grant's mother; it was hardly noticed that she was barely older than he was. While many in his profession abused alcohol, Cary sometimes annoyed ex-wives and friends by insisting they follow his regimen of swimming, wheat germ and carrot juice. Feeling that his fans would start to resent his onscreen dalliances with younger women, he retired from film work in 1966, with his movie-star vanity intact. Once, a curious reporter who was doing a profile on him sent a telegram asking: HOW OLD CARY GRANT? The reply? OLD CARY GRANT FINE, HOW ARE YOU?

Pitchman

Before his breakthrough role in the 1967 comedy *The Graduate*, actor Dustin Hoffman excelled at being a salesman. The twenty-something future superstar once held a job in a mental institution but felt that Macy's before Christmas was a far crazier work environment. Once Hoffman was visited at the famed department store by actor Gene Hackman and Gene's tired young son Christopher. Observing the sea of sweating humanity struggling to find potential presents, Gene wondered how Hoffman could stand being there all day. The boastful employee said that he enjoyed what he did and bet he could get someone to buy Christopher. Grinning, the unemployed Hackman said, "Go ahead, I could use the money."

To Hackman's astonishment, Dustin held the sleepy boy up like a doll and a crowd gathered to hear his pitch. One lady was willing to pay $16.95 but only if she got to take home a newer model.

Extra: Thirty-one-year-old Robert Redford was the first choice to play the barely out-of-college young man who has an affair with an older friend of his family, in the 1967 drama *The Graduate*. Director Mike Nichols felt that the good-looking blonde was not right for the job. "Why not?" asked Redford.

"Let me put it this way, Bobby; have you ever had your heart broken by a girl?"

"What does that mean, ever had my heart broken by a girl?" Redford's bewildered tone when he gave his answer helped to lose him the job; Nichols, instead, went with the shy, less traditionally handsome Dustin Hoffman, which at the time was considered a revolutionary casting choice. (Hoffman admitted later that the main reason he became an actor was to do better with women.)

The Unusual Audition

Lana Turner felt odd when she tried out for the role of Scarlett O'Hara in the 1939 classic *Gone with the Wind*. Since being discovered two years earlier, Lana was best known for portraying cute girls who wore tight sweaters; how could anyone think she was up to the challenge of playing a continuously marrying schemer? There were tons of more qualified actresses who wanted it. The well-endowed eighteen-year-old felt she was nothing like Scarlett; she wanted one husband and seven children. At that time, Lana would have been shocked to know that the numbers would turn out opposite. But at the moment, she was not in a position to refuse the requests of powerful Hollywood executives. The blonde gave it her best shot, didn't get the part, but Turner's steamy screen test opened the door to other opportunities. Lana later wondered if she was the only candidate who had been asked to audition for the Civil War drama in a revealing bathing suit.

Spencer Tracy, Ultimate Villain

Those who worked with Spencer Tracy were willing to put up with his cantankerous nature. Whether he was complaining about an uncomfortable wig, a boring script, working outdoors or an overbearing director, the great actor was not shy about expressing his feelings. Spencer was often short with interviewers and could be rude to friends. Nevertheless, as he aged, he gained more respect, was loved by many of his co-stars and often showed great kindness. On the set of the 1951 comedy *Father of the Bride*, the fifty-year-old Tracy comforted his big screen daughter, Elizabeth Taylor, who was worried about her first marriage; the nineteen-year-old beauty felt that he was like a second dad to her. But not everyone could deal with the Grand Old Man. The creators of the 1966 TV show *Batman* thought Tracy would be perfect as the villainous Penguin. Negotiations were broken off when Spencer insisted that he only wanted the role if he got to kill Batman.

Extra: One night in the early 1960s, some ABC executives were at a party at the Chicago Playboy Mansion. Late in the evening, the 1943 *Batman Serials* were shown to the guests. The Caped Crusader's first screen outing depicted him as an FBI man going up against Japanese agents in World War II. Each episode had the Dark Knight and his partner, Robin the Boy Wonder, placed in a seemingly inescapable trap; the masked heroes would somehow emerge unharmed the next week. (In one episode, Batman crawled out of the wreckage of a plane crash, a little dazed but otherwise OK.)

Despite the shoddy production values, the inebriated audience loved it. They loudly cheered the heroes, and booed and hissed at the dastardly villains. Hoping that sober adults might have a similar response in the privacy of their own homes, the television suits created the pop art campy *Batman* series in 1966. The program lasted three years and became the in-thing for Hollywood stars to appear in. Luminaries like Cary Grant and Frank Sinatra contacted the producers and begged to appear on the show (they were both turned down). The resulting publicity kept the twenty-seven-year-old, low-selling *Batman* comic books from being cancelled.

The Legend of John Wayne

To many Americans, John Wayne was more than just a movie star. Sometimes criticized for never having been in the military, the Duke was told by General Douglas MacArthur that his onscreen portrayals were great representations of the American serviceman. Though he wasn't really a cowboy and was generally cautious about riding horses, Wayne's opinions were sometimes sought out about the plight of the American Indian. He would cynically point out that he never shot them nor placed them on reservations. People who met the six-foot-four actor were often in awe of his cinematic accomplishments. Once, Wayne joined a buddy on a private plane for a journey that required two licensed pilots. The friend told an FAA investigator that the western hero had flying experience; hadn't the agent seen *The High and the Mighty*? The government man nodded, "Yes, I remember that picture!" and cleared them for takeoff.

ACKNOWLEDGEMENTS

Special thanks to my book coach Bill Gordon, author of *The Ultimate Hollywood Tour Book*, for his exacting but very necessary advice, and to Adam McDaniel for going beyond the call of duty in designing the look of this book.

Also thanks to Judy Paparelli for listening to every one of these stories and offering great feedback! And big thanks to Anne Roesch for her advice and input! And thanks to Tye Millaud, Jim Monroe, Mike Farr, Ken and Darlene Tipton, Len Morganti, Sharon Goldinger, my brother Michael, Sandy Skeeter, the Zahavi family, the drivers, staff and management at VIP tours and especially my parents.

And thanks to everyone else who encouraged me to do this project.

ABOUT THE AUTHOR

Stephen Schochet is a tour guide in Hollywood who, years ago, began researching and telling colorful anecdotes about Tinseltown to his customers.

Stephen is the host of a syndicated one minute radio feature called *Hollywood Stories*, and is the author and narrator of two audio books, *Tales of Hollywood* and *Fascinating Walt Disney*.

He is available for private tours and speaking engagements.

For more information, please visit
www.hollywoodstories.com.

Alexander, David. *Star Trek Creator The Authorized Biography of Gene Roddenberry.* New York: Roc, 1994.

Amende, Coral. *Hollywood Confidential* New York: Plume, 1997.

Astin, Sean, and Joe Layden. *There and Back Again An Actor's Tale.* Boston: St. Martin's Griffin, 2005.

Bacon, James. *Hollywood is a Four Letter Town.* Chicago: Regnery, 1976.

Bacon, James, *How Sweet It Is The Jackie Gleason Story.* New York: St. Martin's Press: 1985.

Bacon, James. *Made In Hollywood.* New York: Warner Books 1977.

Bart, Peter. *Shoot Out: Surviving Fame and (mis)Fortune in Hollywood.* New York: G.P. Putnam's Sons, 2002.

Bathroom Readers Historical Society. *Uncle John's Bathroom Reader Plunges into Hollywood.* San Diego, CA: Portable Press, 2005.

Benny, Jack, and Joan Benny. *Sunday Nights at Seven The Jack Benny Story.* New York: Warner Books, 1991.

Berg, A. Scott. *Goldwyn.* New York: Riverhead Books, 1998.

Bergman, Ingrid. *Ingrid Bergman My Story.* London: Warner, 1993

Biskind, Peter, *Easy Riders Raging Bulls.* New York, Simon & Schuster, 1998

Biskind, Peter. *Down and Dirty Pictures Miramax, Sundance, and the Rise of Independent Film.* New York, N.Y.: Simon & Schuster Paperbacks, 2005.

Biskind, Peter. *Gods and Monsters.* New York: Nation Books, 2004.

Blanc, Mel and Bashe, Phillip. *That's Not All Folks.* New York: Warner Books. 1989.

Bogdanovich, Peter. *Peter Bogdanovich's Movie of the Week: 52 Classic Films for One Full Year.* New York: Ballantine Books, 1999.

Bogdanovich, Peter. *Who the Devil Made It: Conversations With Robert Aldrich, George Cukor, Allan Dwan, Howard Hawks, Alfred Hitchcock, Chuck Jones, Fritz Lang, Joseph H. Lewis, Sidney Lumet, Leo McCarey, Otto Preminger, Don Siegel, Josef von Sternberg, Frank Tashlin,* Raoul Walsh. New York: Alfred A. Knopf, 1997.

Bogdanovich, Peter. *Who the Hell's in It: Conversations with Hollywood's Legendary Actors.* New York: Ballantine Books, 2005.

Boller, Paul F. *Hollywood Anecdotes.* New York: Morrow, 1987.

Boller, Paul F. *Presidential Campaigns.* New York: Oxford UP, 1985.

Bragg, Melvyn. *Richard Burton: A Life.* Boston: Little, Brown, 1988.

Brett, David. *Errol Flynn: Satan's Angel.* New York: Robson Books, Limited, 2005.

Brownlow, Kevin. *David Lean.* London: Faber and Faber, 1997.

Brownlow, Kevin. *The Parades Gone By...* Berkeley: University of California.

Brownstein, Ronald. *The Power and the Glitter: The Hollywood-Washington Connection.* New York: Vintage Books, 1992.

Burk, Margaret Tante. *Are the Stars Out Tonight?: The Story of the Famous Ambassador Hotel.* Los Angeles, Calif: Round Table West, 1980.

Burns, George. *All My Best Friends.* New York: Putnam, 1989.

Burns, George. *Gracie a Love Story.* New York, N.Y., U.S.A: Penguin Books, 1989.

Burns, George. *Living It Up.* NY: G.P. Putnam's Sons 1976.

Caine, Michael. *What's it all About?* New York: Turtle Bay Books, 1992.

Callan, Michael Feeney. *Richard Harris: Sex, Death and the Movies.* New York: Robson Books, Limited, 2005.

Carr, Charmian. *Forever Lies I: A Memoir of The Sound of Music.* New York: Penguin (Non-Classics), 2001.

Chandler, Charlotte. *The Girl Who Walked Home Alone: Bette Davis, a Personal Biography.* New York: Simon & Schuster, 2006.

Collier, Peter. *The Fondas: A Hollywood Dynasty.* New York: Putnam, 1991.

Cordova, Frederick De. *Johnny Came Lately: An Autobiography.* New York: Simon and Schuster, 1988.

Cotter, Bill. *Wonderful World of Disney Television.* Chicago: World Publications, 2000.

Custen, George F. *Twentieth Century's Fox.* New York: Basic Books, 1998.

David, Jay. *The Life and Humor of Robin Williams: A Biography.* New York: Quill, 1999.

Davis, Ronald L. *The Glamour Factory: Inside Hollywood's Big Studio System.* Dallas: Southern Methodist University Press, 1993.

Douglas, Kirk. *The Ragman's Son.* New York: Pocket Books, 1999.

Edmonds, Andy. *Frame-Up! The Shocking Scandal That Destroyed Hollywood's Biggest Comedy Star Roscoe "Fatty" Arbuckle.* New York: Avon Books, 1992.

Eisner, Michael. *Work in Progress.* New York: Random House, 1998.

Emery, Robert J. *Directors In Their Own Words.* New York: TV Books, 1999.

Emery, Robert J. *Directors Take Two.* New York: Allworth, 2002.

Emery, Robert J. *Directors Take Three.* New York: Allworth P, 2003.

Emery, Robert J. *Directors Take Four.* New York: Allworth, 2003.

Erickson, Hal. *Baseball in the Movies a Comprehensive Reference, 1915-1991.* Jefferson, N.C: McFarland, 1992.

Evans, Robert. *The Kid Stays in the Picture.* London: Aurum, 1994.

Fein, Irving. *Jack Benny.* New York: Pocket, 1977.

Finstad, Suzanne. *Natasha: The Biography of Natalie Wood.* New York: Three Rivers, 2002.

Finstad, Suzanne. *Warren Beatty: A Private Man.* New York: Harmony Books, 2005.

Fishgall, Gary. *Against Type: The Biography of Burt Lancaster.* New York: Scribner, 1995.

Fishgall, Gary. *Pieces of Time: The Life of James Stewart.* New York: Scribner, 1997.

Fraser-Cavassoni, Natasha. *Sam Spiegel.* New York: Simon & Schuster, 2003.

Friedrich, Otto. *City of Nets: A Portrait of Hollywood in the 1940's.* Berkeley: University of California Press, 1997.

Gabler, Neal. *An Empire of Their Own.* New York: Crown 1988.

Gabler, Neal. *Walt Disney: The Triumph of the American Imagination.* New York: Knopf, 2006.

Givens, Bill. *Film Flubs: Memorable Movie Mistakes.* New York, NY: Carol Pub. Group, 1990.

Gomery, Douglas. *Movie History: A Survey.* Belmont, Calif: Wadsworth Pub. Co., 1991.

Goodwin, Cliff. *Evil Spirits: The Life of Oliver Reed.* New York: Virgin Books, 2002.

Gordon, William A. *The Ultimate Hollywood Tour Book.* Laguna Hills, CA: North Ridghe Books, 1992.

Graham, Sheilah. *Hollywood Revisited: A Fiftieth Anniversary Celebration.* New York: St. Martin's, 1985.

Griffin, Nancy. *Hit and Run.* New York: Simon & Schuster, 1997.

Gronowicz, Antoni. *Garbo.* New York: Simon and Schuster, 1990.

Harris, Warren G. *Sophia Loren a Biography.* New York: Simon & Schuster, 1998.

Haver, Ronald. *A Star is Born The Making of the 1954 Movie and its 1983 Restoration.* New York: Applause Theatre & Cinema, Distribution, North America, Hal Leonard Corporation, 2002.

Hay, Peter. *Broadway anecdotes.* New York: Oxford UP, 1990

Hay, Peter. *Canned laughter the best stories from radio and television.* New York: Oxford UP, 1992

Hay, Peter. *Movie Anecdotes*. Oxford, England: Oxford University Press, 1990.

Hepburn, Katharine. *The Making of The African Queen, or, How I went to Africa with Bogart, Bacall, and Huston and Almost Lost My Mind*. New York: Knopf, Distributed by Random House, 1987.

Helfer, Ralph. *The Beauty of the Beasts Tales of Hollywood's Wild Animal Stars*. New York: Harper Paperbacks, 2007

Herman, Jan. *Talent For Trouble The Life of Hollywood's Most Acclaimed Director, William Wyler*. New York: Da Capo, 1997.

Heston, Charlton. *In the Arena: An Autobiography*. New York: Berkley Trade, 1997.

Hickman, Dwayne. *Forever Dobie: The many lives of Dwayne Hickman*. Secaucus, NJ: Carol Publishing Group, 1994.

Higham, Charles. *Cecil B. DeMille*. New York, N.Y: Da Capo, 1980.

Hill, Doug and Weingrad, Doug, *Saturday Night*. New York: Vintage Books, 1987.

Higham, Charles. *Howard Hughes: the Secret Life*. New York: St. Martin's Griffin, 2004.

Higham, Charles. *Louis B. Mayer M.G.M., and the Secret Hollywood*. London: Sidgwick and Jackson: 1993

Holden, Anthony. *Laurence Olivier*. New York: Atheneum, 1988.

Hope, B., and M. Shavelson. *Don't Shoot, It's Only Me*. New York: Jove, 1991.

Howard-Maurer, Joan, Jeff Lenburg, and Greg Lenburg. *The Three Stooges Scrapbook*. New York: Citadel, 2000.

Hunter, Jack. *Johnny Depp: Movie Top Ten*. New York: Creation Books, 2000.

Huston, John. *John Huston Interviews*. Jackson: University of Mississippi, 2001.

Huston, John. *Open Book*. New York: Knopf: distributed by Random House, 1980.

Hyams, Joe. *Bogie: The Definitive Biography of Humphrey Bogart*. New York: New American Library, 1966.

Kanin, Garson. *Hollywood*. New York: Viking, 1974.

Kanin, Garson. *Tracy and Hepburn an Intimate Memoir*. New York: Primus, 1988.

Koenig, David, *Mouse Tales: A Behind the Ears Look at Disneyland*. Irvine, CA: Bonaventure Press, 1994.

Jackson, Carlton. *Hattie The Life of Hattie McDaniel*. New York: Madison Books, 1993.

Javna, John. *Cult TV: A Viewer's Guide to the Shows America Can't Live without*. New York: St. Martin's, 1985.

Jones, Chuck. *Chuck Amuck The Life and Times of an Animated Cartoonist*. New York: Farrar, Straus and Giroux, 1999.

Kelly, Kitty, *Elizabeth Taylor: The Last Star.* New York: Simon & Schuster, 1981.

Kinn, Gail. *The Academy Awards The Complete History of Oscar.* New York: Black Dog & Leventhal, Distributed by Workman Pub. Co., 2002.

Knelman, Martin. *Jim Carrey: The Joker is Wild The Trials and Triumphs of Jim Carrey.* New York: Firefly Books, 2000.

Kramer, Stanley. *Mad, Mad, Mad, Mad World: A Life in Hollywood.* New York: Harcourt Brace, 1997.

Kurson, Robert. *The Official Three Stooges Encyclopedia The Ultimate Knucklehead's Guide to Stoogedom.* New York: McGraw-Hill, 1999.

Leaming, Barbara. *Orson Welles: A Biography.* New York, NY: Penguin Books, 1986.

Lenburg, Jeff. *Dustin Hoffman: Hollywood's Anti-hero.* New York: St. Martin's, 1983.

Lord, Rosemary. *Hollywood Then & Now.* San Diego, Calif: Thunder Bay, 2003

Louvish, Simon. *Monkey Business The Lives and Legends of The Marx Brothers.* Boston: St. Martin's Griffin, 2001.

Louvish, Simon. *Stan and Ollie.* New York: Thomas Dunne Books 2001.

Manchester, William Raymond. *The Glory and the Dream.* New York: Bantam Books, 1990.

Maltin, Leonard. *Disney Films.* New York: Disney Editions, 2000

Maltin, Leonard. *Little Rascals The Life and Times of Our Gang.* New York: Crown, 1992

Maltin, Leonard. *Movie Comedy Teams.* New York: New American Library, 1985.

Marshall, Garry, and Lori Marshall. *Wake Me When It's Funny How to Break into Show Business and Stay There.* New York: Newmarket, 1997.

Marx, Samuel. *Deadly Illusions Jean Harlow and the Murder of Paul Bern.* New York: Random House, 1990.

Marx, Groucho. *Marx Brothers Scrapbook.* New York: Perennial Library, 1989.

Mayersberg, Paul. *Hollywood: The Haunted House.* New York: Stein and Day, 1968.

McCabe, Bob. *Sean Connery: A Biography.* New York: Thunder's Mouth, 200.

McGilligan, Patrick. Jack's Life, New York: W.W. Norton & Co., 1994.

McGilligan, Patrick. *Alfred Hitchcock A Life in Darkness and Light.* New York: Harper Perennial, 2004.

Medavoy, Mike, and Josh Young. *You're Only as Good as Your Next One: 100 Great Films, 100 Good Films, and 100 for Which I Should Be Shot.* NEW YORK: Atria, 2002.

Medved, Harry. *The Fifty Worst Films of All Time.* New York: Warner Books, 1984.

Messing, Bill. *A Day in the Life of Hollywood.* San Francisco: Collins, 1992.

Mirisch, Walter. *I Thought We Were Making Movies, Not History*. Madison, Wis: University of Wisconsin, 2008.

Morley, Sheridan. *The Other Side of the Moon: The Life of David Niven*. New York: Harper & Row, 1985.

Moser, Margaret. *Movie Stars Do the Dumbest Things*. Los Angeles: Renaissance Books, 1999.

Nichols, Nichelle. *Beyond Uhura: Star Trek and Other Memories*. New York: G.P. Putnam's, 1994.

Niven, David. *Bring on The Empty Horses*. London: Hamish Hamilton Limited, 1975.

Niven, David. *The Moon's a Balloon*. New York: Penguin Books Ltd, 1994.

O'Brien, Pat. *The Wind at My Back*. New York: Doubleday, 1964.

O'Hara and John Nicoletti. *Tis Herself: a Memoir*. New York: Simon and Schuster, 2004.

Oller, John. *Jean Arthur The Actress Nobody Knew*. New York: Limelight Editions, 1999.

Quirk, Lawrence J. *Bob Hope: The Road Well-Traveled*. New York: Applause Books, 1998.

Quirk, Lawrence J. *Paul Newman*. Dallas: Taylor Publishing Company.

Parish, James Robert. *The Hollywood Book of Extravagance: The Totally Infamous, Mostly Disastrous, and Always Compelling Excesses of America's Film and TV Idols*. New York: Wiley, 2007.

Parrish, Robert. *Growing up in Hollywood*. New York: Harcourt Brace Jovanovich, 1976.

Parrish, Robert. *Hollywood Doesn't Live Here Anymore*. Boston: Little, Brown, 1988.

Payne, J. Julian. *Celebrity Anecdotes: Funny Stories About the stars*. New York: Anecdotage Press, 2005.

Pollock, Dale. *Skywalking the Life and Films of George Lucas*. New York: Harmony Books, 1983.

Randall, Stephen. *The Playboy Interviews Larger Than Life*. New York: M, 2006.

Reagan, Ronald. *Where's the Rest of Me? The Autobiography of Ronald Reagan*. New York: Dell Pub Co, 1981.

Reynolds, Burt. *My Life*. New York: Hyperion, 1994.

Reynolds, Debbie. *Debbie--My life*. New York: Morrow, 1988.

Rivers, Joan. *Bouncing Back*. New York: HarperCollins, 1997.

Rivers, Joan. *Still Talking*. New York: Turtle Bay Books/Random House, 1991.

Roberts, Randy. *John Wayne American*. Lincoln: University of Nebraska Press, 1997.

Sanders, Coyne S., and Tom Gilbert. *Desilu The Story of Lucille Ball and Desi Arnaz*. New York: Harper Paperbacks, 1994.

Sanello, Frank. *Spielberg the Man, the Movies, the Mythology*. Lanham, MD: Taylor Trade Publications, 2002.

Sanford, Christopher. *McQueen*. New York: Taylor Trade Publishing, 2001.

Schessler, Kenneth. *This is Hollywood: An Unusual Movieland Guide*. Redland, CA: K. Schessler Publishers, 2002.

Schochet, Stephen. *Fascinating Walt Disney*. New York: Hollywood Stories, 1998

Schochet, Stephen. *Tales of Hollywood*. New York: Hollywood Stories, 2000.

Schwartz, Sherwood. *Inside Gilligan's Island*. New York: St. Martin's, 1994.

Scott, Ridley. *Ridley Scott Interviews*. Jackson: University of Mississippi, 2005.

Shapiro, Marc. *James Cameron: an Unauthorized Biography*. Los Angeles: Renaissance Books, 2000

Shatner, William. *Star Trek Movie Memories*. New York, NY: HarperCollins, 1994.

Shorris, Sylvia and Abbott, Marion. *Talking Pictures with the People Who Made Them*. New York: W.W. Norton, 1994.

Shulman, Irving. *Harlow: an Intimate Biography*. Lincoln: IUniverse, 2000.

Sklar, Robert. *Movie-made America*. New York: Vintage Books, 1994.

Skretvedt, Randy. *Laurel and Hardy: The Magic behind the Movies*. Beverly Hills, CA: Past Times Publishing Co., 1994.

Spitz, Bob. *The Beatles: The Biography*. New York: Back Bay Books, 2006.

Spoto, Donald. *Enchantment: The Life of Audrey Hepburn*. New York: Three Rivers P, 2007.

Story, David. *America on the Rerun*. New York: Citadel Publishing Group. 1993.

Strait, Raymond. *Bob Hope: A Tribute*. New York: Kensington, Press 2003.

Swindell, Larry. *The Last Hero: A Biography of Gary Cooper*. New York: Robson Books Ltd, 1998.

Talking Pictures with the People Who Made Them. New York: W.W. Norton, 1994.

Taylor, John Russel. *Hitch: The Life & Times of Alfred Hitchcock*. New York: Berkley, 1980.

Taylor, Robert Lewis. *W. C. Fields his Follies and Fortunes*. New York: St. Martin's P, 1989.

Thomas, Bob. *Astaire? The Man, The Dancer*. New York: St. Martin's, 1984

Thomas, Bob. *Bud & Lou the Abbott & Costello Story*. Philadelphia: Lippincott, 1977

Thomas, Bob. *Building a Company Roy O. Disney and the Creation of an Entertainment Empire*. New York: Hyperion, 1998.

Thomas, Bob. *Clown Prince of Hollywood: The Antic Life and Times of Jack L. Warner*. New York: McGraw-Hill, 1990.

Thomas, Bob. *King Cohn*. Beverly Hills: New Millennium Press, 2000.

Thomas, Bob. Joan Crawford: A Biography. London: Weidenfeld and Nicolson, 1979.

Thomas, Bob. *Marlon, Portrait of the Rebel as an Artist*. New York: Random House, 1973.

Thomas, Bob. *One and Only Bing*. New York: Grosset & Dunlap, 1977.

Thomas, Bob. *Selznick*. New York: Pocket Books, 1970.

Thomas, Bob. *Thalberg*. Beverly Hills, Calif: New Millennium, 2000.

Thomas, Bob. *Walt Disney: An American Original*. New York, N.Y: Hyperion, 1994.

Thompson, Dave. *Travolta*. Dallas, Tex: Taylor Pub., 1996.

Tosches, Nick. *Dino*. New York: Dell, 1993.

Ulmer, James. *James Ulmer's Hollywood Hot List: The Complete Guide to Star Ranking*. Boston: St. Martin's Griffin, 2000.

Walker, Alexander. *Vivien: The Life of Vivien Leigh*. New York: Grove P, 1994.

Wallace, David. *Dream Palaces of Hollywood's Golden Age*. New York: Harry N. Abrams, 2006.

Walls, Jeannette. *Dish: How Gossip Became the News and the News Became Just Another Show*. New York: Harper Paperbacks, 2001.

Weddle, David. *If They Move...Kill 'Em! The Life and Times of Sam Peckinpah*. New York: Grove Press, 2001.

Weeney, Don. *Backstage at the Tonight Show From Johnny Carson to Jay Leno*. Lanham, MD: Taylor Trade Publishers, 2006.

Widener, Don. *Lemmon a Biography*. New York: Macmillan, 1975.

Wilk, Max. *The Wit and Wisdom of Hollywood*. New York: Warner Books, 1973.

Whitfield, Eileen. *Pickford: The Woman who Made Hollywood*. Lexington, KY: University of Kentucky, 1997.

Wiley, Mason. *Inside Oscar*. New York: Ballantine Books, 1996.

Zollo Paul. *Hollywood Remembered: an Oral History of its Golden Age*. New York: Cooper Square Press. 2002.

Websites
www.imdb.com
www.wikipedia.com
www.salon.com
www.anecdotage.com
www.eonline.com
www.billcotter.com/zorro
www.highbeam.com
www.seeing-stars.com
www.titanichistoricalsociety.org
www.townhall.com

Magazines
Venice
Entertainment Weekly
US Weekly
Hollywood Reporter
Variety
People
Premiere
Details
Interview

Newspapers
Los Angeles Times
Los Angeles Daily News
Chicago Tribune
New York Daily News
New York Times
Daily Telegraph
Washington Post
USA Today
New York Daily News

THE ULTIMATE
HOLLYWOOD TOUR BOOK

written by William Gordon

The Ultimate Hollywood Tour Book is the first and only book to reveal where today's Hollywood lives, works and plays.

The book features the following:

- Over three hundred celebrity homes.
- The hot-spot restaurants and nightclubs where tourists are most likely to see the stars.
- Sites where dozens of classic and popular motion pictures and television shows were filmed.
- Sites of Hollywood's most notorious murders, scandals and suicides.
- The major motion-picture studios.
- Celebrated Hollywood landmarks.
- Tinseltown's many hidden attractions, including castles in the Hollywood Hills, and sites that inspired songs.

Available in all Barnes & Nobles and
most gift shops in Los Angeles, Amazon.com,
or www.nrbooks.com.

Visit **www.thisishollywood.com**
for the best selection online for
Hollywood Gifts and Memorabilia.

Made in the USA
Middletown, DE
07 March 2016